AGING LIFE PROCESSES

Publication Number 729

AMERICAN LECTURE SERIES®

A Monograph in

The BANNERSTONE DIVISION *of*
AMERICAN LECTURES IN LIVING CHEMISTRY

Edited by

I. NEWTON KUGELMASS, M.D., Ph.D., Sc.D.
Consultant to the Department of Health and Hospitals
New York, New York

AGING LIFE PROCESSES

Compiled and Edited by

SEYMOUR BAKERMAN, MD., Ph.D.

Department of Pathology
Division of Clinical Pathology
Medical College of Virginia
Richmond, Virginia

With Contributions by

M. EARL BALIS   JOHAN BJORKSTEN
DAVID A. HALL   PERCY J. RUSSELL
ANITA ZORZOLI

CHARLES C THOMAS · PUBLISHER
Springfield · Illinois · U.S.A.

Published and Distributed Throughout the World by

CHARLES C THOMAS • PUBLISHER

BANNERSTONE HOUSE

301-327 East Lawrence Avenue, Springfield, Illinois, U.S.A.

NATCHEZ PLANTATION HOUSE

735 North Atlantic Boulevard, Fort Lauderdale, Florida, U.S.A.

© *1969, by* CHARLES C THOMAS • PUBLISHER

Library of Congress Catalog Card Number: 68-20779

With THOMAS BOOKS *careful attention is given to all details of manufacturing and design. It is the Publisher's desire to present books that are satisfactory as to their physical qualities and artistic possibilities and appropriate for their particular use.* THOMAS BOOKS *will be true to those laws of quality that assure a good name and good will.*

Printed in the United States of America

I-1

CONTRIBUTORS

M. EARL BALIS, Ph.D.
Sloan-Kettering Institute for Cancer Research
Sloan-Kettering Division of
Cornell University Medical College, New York

JOHAN BJORKSTEN, PH.D.
Bjorksten Research Foundation
Madison, Wisconsin

DAVID A. HALL, PH.D.
Department of Medicine
University of Leeds
Leeds, England

PERCY J. RUSSELL, PH.D.
Department of Biochemistry
University of Kansas Medical Center
Kansas City, Kansas

ANITA ZORZOLI, PH.D.
Department of Biology
Vassar College
Poughkeepsie, New York

This book is dedicated to Winona, John, Paul, Beth, to others, and to the personal choices of the coauthors.

FOREWORD

Our LIVING CHEMISTRY SERIES was conceived by Editor and Publisher to advance the newer knowledge of chemical medicine in the cause of clinical practice. The interdependence of chemistry and medicine is so great that physicians are turning to chemistry, and chemists to medicine in order to understand the underlying basis of life processes in health and disease. Once chemical truths, proofs, and convictions become sound foundations for clinical phenomena, key hybrid investigators clarify the bewildering panorama of biochemical progress for application in everyday practice, stimulation of experimental research, and extension of postgraduate instruction. Each of our monographs thus unravels the chemical mechanisms and clinical management of many diseases that have remained relatively static in the minds of medical men for three thousand years. Our new Series is charged with the *nisus élan* of chemical wisdom, supreme in choice of international authors, optimal in standards of chemical scholarship, provocative in imagination for experimental research, comprehensive in discussions of scientific medicine, and authoritative in chemical perspective of human disorders.

Dr. Bakerman of Richmond, Virginia, four collaborators from this country, and one from England view aging processes in terms of biochemical changes. It is a well-integrated longitudinal study of human biology rather than a critical analysis of disease entities reflected in aging. It does not consider life an aging disease wherein the difference between one man and another is the stage of aging. It is an extraordinary interpretation of vital factors where everything has to do with everything in life processes without setting artificial boundaries in deteriorative disorders. Aging begins in the first stages of egg division, but each component of the body proceeds at its own rate of deterioration. He that begins to live begins to die. Every human being is an arena of conflict between his primitive organs of different functional ages—the innate heterochronism that shortens life. The highly integrated individual with 10^{28} cells, organized and controlled from within, can be examined completely, but the inner regulating force is not amenable to such close scrutiny. It is the biological force that triggers mechanisms involved in the aging processes and controls and integrates the chemical reactions of cellular metabolism.

The biological alterations in aging are evaluated in terms of heredity with special emphasis on proteins, enzymes, collagens, lipids, and pigments correlated by theories on aging and cross-linking that prolong life and maintain vitality. The psychodynamics of aging reflects the change in the vector of psychic and somatic processes with the giving, goal-seeking, expressive attitudes of maturity gradually displaced by retentive, self-centered, purposeless tendencies that result in introversion of psychic energy. The power of self-adjustment and self-maintenance thus declines with the passage of time and the probability of disease and death increases so steeply that the limit of life is approached rapidly. Man has a fixed life-span under genetic control. The only nonaging animal, the sea anemone, is more of a culture than an organism replacing all its cells continually. The unit of life in all is the cell, bearing basic equipment for the maintenance of continuity of life. When a cell is damaged, reparative processes are invoked to restore its original form and function. When essential constituents are destroyed beyond repair, it is only a matter of time before its activities will cease and its working parts disintegrate. To survive, a cell must have a minimal organization of membranes to control the chemical economy and contain key catalysts, a mechanism for reproducing exact copies of the cell and replicating key parts, and an apparatus for powering all activities through coupled oxidations. To extend cell lifespan is another problem. To maintain the optimal vigor of age twelve indefinitely would require seven hundred years for half the population to die and another seven hundred for the survivors to be reduced by half again.

How can man control age deterioration? One organ may be more affected than another, but there is increased vulnerability of the whole being. Scientific physicians can postpone death without increasing vigor or preventing decline. But experimental biologists are attempting to alter the timing mechanism of human aging as a whole. The processes of aging are studied in terms of three alternative hypotheses. The first involves loss or deterioration of irreplacable cells such as brain or muscle cells. The second involves deteriorative changes in successive generations of renewable cells that divide clonally via faulty copying, such as blood or liver cells. The third involves colloid changes in structural macromolecules such as collagen and elastin. Gerontology offers no effective regime for prolonging life. Hormone changes occur with age, but the timing is not a function of the declining activity of any one endocrine gland. Timekeeping mechanisms must be discovered to alter their rates. The lifespan can be extended in experimental animals by restricting the diet. Drugs can protect fixed cells against deterioration. Deteriorated organs and tissues can be replaced as palliative measures. Application of medical, social, and industrial techniques are extending survival to the natural lifespan in the East as in the West with no effect on the rate of aging. Man's relationship to the earth he inhabits is now completely reversed. He was once its child, keeping a precarious foothold on its surface. Today he is its master and may well become master of his own life and lifespan. As yet medical wisdom enables more to be done to protect the spring in life's clock and prolong its vitality than to rewind it for longevity. *Dum vivimus, vivamus.*

Enlarge my life with multitude of days,
In health, in sickness, thus the suppliant prays;
Hides from himself his state, and shuns to know
That life protracted is protracted woe.
—*Samuel Johnson*

I. NEWTON KUGELMASS, M.D., PH.D., SC.D., *Editor*

CONTENTS

AGING LIFE PROCESSES

Chapter 1

BIOLOGY

SEYMOUR BAKERMAN

Biology of Aging

All the world's a stage
And all the men and women merely players.
They have their exits and their entrances;
And one man in his time plays many parts,
His acts being seven ages. At first the infant,
Mewling and puking in the nurse's arms.
And then the whining school-boy, with his satchel
And shining morning face, creeping like snail
Unwillingly to school. And then the lover,
Sighing like a furnace, with a woeful ballad
Made to his mistress' eyebrow. Then a soldier,
Full of strange oaths, and bearded like the pard;
Jealous in honor, sudden and quick in quarrel,
Seeking the bubble reputation
Even in the cannon's mouth. And then the justice,
In fair round belly with good capon lined,
With eyes severe and beard of formal cut,
Full of wise saws and modern instances;
And so he plays his part. The sixth age shifts
Into the lean and slipper'd pantaloon,
With spectacles on nose and pouch on side;
His youthful hose, well saved, a world too wide
For his shrunk shank; and his big manly voice,
Turning again toward childish treble, pipes
And whistles in his sound. Last scene of all,
That ends this strange eventful history,
Is second childishness, and mere oblivion,
Sans teeth, sans eyes, sans taste, sans everything.

—AS YOU LIKE IT, Act II, Scene 7

INTRODUCTION

THE MAIN OBJECTIVE in the study of aging is to obtain information that can be applied to humans for the prolongation of lifespan and, at the same time, for the maintenance of vitality. There are different ways in which this objective may be obtained.

Through greater understanding of biological processes, lifespan may be prolonged. This may be accomplished through research in classical biology on the supramolecular level or through chemistry on the molecular level. In the former, biologists have described anatomical, physiological, and pathological alterations with age occurring in organs, tissues, and cells. These descriptions are important in that they reflect changes that occur on the molecular level. It is becoming apparent that basic mechanisms necessary to describe aging will be elucidated through chemical studies which are the subject of the other chapters in this text. With such knowledge, it is hoped that it will be possible to manipulate the chemical interactions occurring in the body, and thus add additional years to human lifespan while maintaining vitality.

The purpose of this introductory chapter is to survey the biological alterations with aging which reflect the changes that occur on a molecular level. Biological alterations with aging are observed from the level of the total body to the tissues and organs and finally to the cellular milieu, cells, and cellular organelles. Changes in gross body composition; physiological parameters; tissue, organ, and cellular pathology; and tissue, organ, and cellular anatomy are observed. Although changes are noted throughout the lifespan, the emphasis in this monograph will be on those alterations occurring after adulthood has been reached or when generalized deterioration takes place.

GENETICS

Human aging starts at the time of fertilization of the egg and, in the beginning, is a function of the chemical properties

4

of genetic material. Life is programmed for cell division and differentiation with growth, inhibition of these processes with maturation, and finally, generalized deterioration with its inevitable sequelae. Genetic factors in aging have been reviewed and evaluated critically by Clark (1964). The important evidence for genetic transference of aging rate is that each animal species has its own characteristic lifespan (see Ciba Symposium on *Lifespan of Animals*, Vol. V; and Comfort, 1965) which is programmed by the information inherited in its genes. In man, evidence for genetic control of aging is derived from studies on comparisons between longevity of identical and fraternal twins and on the comparisons between longevity of parents and their offspring. Kallmann (1965) studied twin partners dying over age sixty of natural causes and found that the differences in the lifespans of senescent identical twins were significantly less than the differences in lifespan of senescent nonidentical twins. In other studies (Kallmann, 1957) it was found that there was a direct relationship between the lifespans of parents and their offspring.

At least some of the effects of heredity on lifespan are mediated through the transmission of susceptibility or resistance to disease. There are a very large number of known or suspected hereditary diseases (some of these are described by McKusick, 1965). Some diseases are clearly genetic in origin (autosomal dominant inheritance) and relatively easy to recognize since the affected person usually has a clinically affected parent and grandparent, e.g. hereditary spherocytosis. There are diseases that are more difficult to recognize because the parents are usually normal clinically, but the siblings may be affected (autosomal recessive inheritance), e.g. sickle cell anemia. In others, the carriers, the affected males, do not transmit the disease to their offspring (sex-linked recessive inheritance), e.g. hemophilia. Some common diseases in which hereditary susceptibility may be programmed are coronary atherosclerosis, hypertension, rheumatoid arthritis, diabetes mellitus, gout, tuberculosis, and cancer.

The outcome of practically all genetic diseases can be modified or markedly altered by treatment and environment. In hereditary spherocytosis, which is genetically transmitted, the symptoms and signs are alleviated by removing the spleen. The influence of environment on hereditary disease is amply illustrated in a patient with sickle cell trait where disability may be induced by exposure to situations involving some degree of hypoxia such as high-altitude airplane flights or trips to high altitude regions. Elevated serum-lipid levels, which have a suggested relationship to atherosclerosis of the coronary arteries, is affected by dietary fat intake. A further example is that of individual immunity to tuberculosis which appears to be largely genetic in origin, but preventive measures and improved treatment have resulted in marked reduction in the incidence of and mortality from this disease. In these illustrations, the genetic disease may become evident (a) regardless of environmental influences on the one hand, or (b) because the environment plays an important role in exposing the genetic tendency on the other.

The genetic information for lifespan can also be modified by environment both in the experimental animal and in humans. In experimental animals, manipulations of diet have resulted not only in the prolongation of the life of the animals, but have resulted in the delay of the onset of major diseases. Simms and Berg (1962), using restricted food intake, delayed the onset of all major diseases of their rats; the life expectancy of the males showed a 25 per cent increase, and the females showed a 39 per cent increase. Ross (1964), using different diets in rats, measured the effect of different diets on lifespan and on the onset and prevalence of degenerative diseases. In his studies, the level of hepatic enzyme activity was correlated with age. In humans, mortality is modified by geography, socioeconomic and occupational variations, and personal habits (Spiegelman, 1960).

Alterations

Individuals of the *same* chronological age may show wide variation in physiological performance indicating differences in biological age. A clear distinction should be made between chronological and biological age. The chronological age is age in exact time, while biological age is age with reference to one or more biological parameters, e.g. cardiovascular, respiratory, or kidney function. Alterations in biological age may be reflected in alteration of the total organism or of specific organs.

Physiological Processes

Changes in some physiological processes that reflect the status of the cardiovascular, respiratory, urinary, nervous, integumental, and multicomponent systems are given in Table I.

TABLE I

FUNCTIONAL CHANGES WITH AGE

Organ System	Function	%Function at Age 80 (age 30 = 100)
Multi-component systems		
	Basil metabolic rate[1]	85
	Standard cell water[1]	80
	Blood pressure[2]	
	Systolic	115
	Diastolic	104
Cardiovascular		
	Cardiac output[1]	65
	Total peripheral resistance[3]	150
	Velocity of pulse wave (aorta)[4]	200
Respiratory		
	Vital capacity[1]	60
	Maximum breathing rate[1]	40
Urinary		
	Renal plasma flow[1]	45
	Glomerular filtration rate[1]	60
Nervous		
	Nervous conduction velocity[1]	90
Muscle		
	Hand grip strength[5]	65
	Creatinine excretion, mg./24 hrs.[6]	65

[1]Shock, N. W.: In *The Biology of Aging*. Strehler, B. L., Ed. Baltimore, Waverly, 1960, p. 23.
[2]Lasser, R. P., and Master, A. M.: *Geriatrics, 14*:345, 1959.
[3]Landowne, M., and Stanley, J.: In *Aging—Some Social and Biological Aspects*. Baltimore, Hara-Shafer, 1960, p. 159.
[4]Landowne, M.: *J. Appl. Physiol., 12*:91, 1958.
[5]Norris, A. W., and Shock, N.: In *Science and Medicine of Exercise and Sports*. Johnson, W. L., Ed. New York, Harper, 1960, p. 466.
[6]Norris, A. H.; Lundy, T., and Shock, N. W.: *Ann. N.Y. Acad. Sci., 110*:623, 1963.

In this table, the per cent performance of specific functions in an average eighty-year-old person is compared to that of a thirty-year-old person. The data, however, cannot be used to describe the functional status of a specific individual because of individual variation; performance in an eighty-year-old may actually approach that of a much younger individual and vice versa. In studies of liver function tests in the aged (Haberman, 1962), 74 per cent of the patients had one or more abnormalities. Since no pathological correlations were available in these cases, it is impossible to know the significance of these data. It is thought that the decline in function reflects (a) the loss of cells, or (b) an alteration of these cells, or (c) a combination of both. Loss of and changes in cells do occur (see section on cellular changes with aging).

Body Composition

In Table II, the relative gross chemical composition in terms of fat, water, cell solids, bone mineral, and specific gravity, of a twenty-five-year-old "reference" man (Brozek, 1954) is compared to that of a seventy-year-old "reference" man. The relative quantities of each of the constituents in the table may vary with the nutritional and pathological state, the sex, and the exercise habits of the subject. Fat content has been observed to vary from as low as 3 per cent to as high as 45 per cent of body weight (Siri, 1962). High fat content may have a deleterious effect in that fat is supplied by a significant fraction of the total cardiac output which must then increase with increasing deposition of fat (Lesser, 1962).

TABLE II

COMPARISON OF A TENTATIVE "REFERENCE MAN"

AGED 70 WITH ONE AGED 25

	*Age 25**	*Age 70+*
Fat (%)	14	30
Water (%)	61	53
Cell Solids (%)	19	12
Bone Mineral (%)	6	5
Specific Gravity	1.068	1.035

*Brozek, J., Washington, D. C., Department of the Army, Office of the Quartermaster General, 1954.
+Fryer, J. H.: In *Biological Aspects of Aging.* Shock, N. W., Ed. New York, 1962, p. 59.

Today body water content decreases with age. A value of 75 per cent of the total body weight in newborns drops precipitously during the first year of life to 65 per cent (Edelman, 1962).

The average proportion of water in the fat-free body or the lean body mass appears relatively constant with aging, although variations from an average of 74 per cent are relatively large, ranging from 67 per cent to 80 per cent (Siri, 1962). The decrease in specific gravity with age reflects, in part, the increase in fat content and the loss of lean body mass.

The most significant values in Table II are the comparisons of cell solids which decrease from a value of 19 per cent in the younger to 12 per cent in the older reference man. Cell solids consist mainly of protein. The greatest change in protein with age occurs in muscle whose total mass is reflected directly by the excretion in the urine of one of its breakdown products, creatinine. Creatinine excretion shows a significant decrease with increasing age from a value of 2040 mg./24 hrs. in young men of average age 22.5 to a value of 1419 mg./24 hrs. for older men (Fryer, 1962). Since muscle represents at least 16 per cent of body protein, the change in its mass can explain partially the change in percentage of cell solids. Another indication of loss of cell solids with age, probably reflecting loss of cells, is given by total exchangeable potassium. The total exchangeable potassium, which is the principle cation of cells, declines so that its value at age sixty is about four fifths of that at age twenty (Edelman, 1962.) Change of other electrolytes with age, e.g. chloride and sodium, which reflect the size of the extracellular space do not show a clear trend. It is concluded from measurements of (a) creatinine, and (b) total exchangeable potassium, that there is a decrease in cell solids and number of cells with age.

Some studies indicate no change in certain important body constituents. The serum protein, total protein, total globulin, albumin, euglobulin, pseudoglobulins, and antibody formation are unaltered in aged adult individuals without disease (Parfentjev, 1960).

Cellular Changes

Cells can be classified in order of increasing relative life-span and decreasing regenerative capacity as labile, stable, and permanent. The labile cells, characteristic of lining mucosal cells and hematopoietic tissue, show marked mitotic activity and are replaced continually; while the permanent cells, character-istic of more specialized tissue such as nerve cells, myocardium, and sensory organs, are unable to divide. The stable cells, char-acteristic of the liver, kidney, endocrine, and exocrine glands, have a turnover intermediate between the labile and permanent cells.

Age changes are more apparent in the permanent cells and are degenerative in nature. Degenerative changes, although well classified and described, have been poorly understood. These changes, described in Table III, have been viewed with either the light or electron microscope and essentially involve an altera-tion in size and shape of cellular components.

TABLE III

SUMMARY OF CELLULAR ALTERATIONS IN AGING

Component	Alteration
Nucleus	Clumping, shrinkage, fragmentation and dissolution of chromatin
	Increased staining
	Intranuclear inclusions
	Nuclear enlargement
	Amitotic division
	Invagination of nuclear membrane
Nucleolus	Increased size and number
Cytoplasm	Accumulation of pigments
	Accumulation of fat
	Depletion of glycogen
	Hyaline droplets
	Formation of vacuoles
Mitochondria	Decrease in numbers and alteration in shape
Golgi apparatus	Fragmentation
Endoplasmic Reticulum	Loss of Nissl substance

The functional status of cells cannot be derived from the morphologic appearance as described in Table III. In fact, cells may show marked or total loss of functional activity without morphologic alterations. For example, cyanide poisons the res-piratory enzymes of the mitochondria and the cells cannot use the oxygen supplied to them. These cells die so rapidly that no structural changes are observed.

It is noteworthy that those cells which show the most pro-found changes during aging have the least capacity to replace themselves or regenerate. Furthermore, capacity to regenerate (a) decreases as age increases, (b) is affected by the state of nutrition, and (c) decreases with increased tissue specialization. Theories that have been proposed to explain the stimulus for regeneration include circulating humoral factors such as erythropoietin, decrease in functional capacity, and decreased blood supply. When destruction of tissue occurs and regeneration does not follow, repair is by connective tissue or, in the central nervous system by neuroglial cells. In spite of these observations, the significance of regeneration in the pathogenesis of aging remains unknown.

Tissue culture has been used to study the morphologic alterations in cells following many replications and to compare the characteristics of cells of different ages. It has been noted that artificial media apparently can support only a limited number of replications before the cells die or take on characteristics of malignancy (Hayflick, 1966). However, under conditions where special effort was made in preparation of the media (Puck, 1966), no visible chromosomal change was noted following nine hundred cell replications.

In other studies, Hayflick states that cultures of aged cells undergo *fewer* multiplications than cultures of embryonic cells. This would indicate that aging in cells is due to the inherent properties of the cells. Another interpretation is that older cells have different nutritional requirements than the embryonic cells.

Pathological Alterations

Disease may be associated with aging or superimposed upon the aging process. It cannot, however, be stated that aging necessarily causes disease, since people can die from no recognizable disease and, in some species of animals, disease is essentially unknown.

A recent book on the pathology of the aged (McKeown, 1965) has listed a number of the general features of age changes. The skin shows thinning, glossy appearance, wrinkling, decrease in elasticity, and increased pigmentation; hair is lost or graying with coarsening of texture; the eye develops cataracts of the lens, loss of muscle mass occurs through atrophy; the joints are decreased in flexibility with joint swelling (osteoarthritis). Bone changes are reflected by flexion of thoracic vertebrae with a decrease in stature and increased brittleness. On gross internal examination, there is generalized organ and tissue atrophy with decrease in size, serous atrophy of fat, and alterations in color and texture of organs occur with transitions to gray-brown.

In Table IV, organ weights are related to age. Not all organs change significantly in weight. The greatest change, occurring in the skeletal muscle mass, is consistent with the previously mentioned decreased urine creatinine excretion in the aged.

TABLE IV

COMPARISON OF AVERAGE RELATIVE HUMAN ORGAN WEIGHTS*

Organ	*Percentage Change* *21-30 and over 70*
Heart	+ 11.1
Lungs	+ 10.8
Brain	+ 4.5
Skeletal Muscle	−403
Spleen	− 28.0
Liver	− 20.1
Kidneys	− 8.9

*G/kg body weight for an over-70-year-old man compared with that of a man in the 21 to 30 year age group. (+) = increase; (−) decrease. Data taken from Korenchevsky, V.: *Physiological and Pathological Aging.* New York, Hafner, 1961, Table 16, p. 41.

Studies on tissue transplantation are useful in age studies; these studies also have clinical applications. Skin from animals of different ages was grafted to other animals of different ages (Mariani *et al.*, 1960). The relative ages of donor and recipient and the percentage takes were, in the case of young animals animals paired to young, 75 per cent; in the case of old animals paired with young, the takes were 65 per cent; in the case of young animals to old, takes were recorded as 47 per cent; and finally in the case of old animals paired to old, there were no takes. These data show that, with increasing age, the rejection of skin grafts increases. The results have been interpreted to mean that with increasing age, immunologic alterations develop which decrease the probability for a successful skin graft.

Krohn (1966), found that segments of skin of mice transplanted many times had exceeded twice the known maximum lifespan of any mouse. Again, using skin transplants, he showed that the decrease in metabolic activity is dependent on the tissue itself rather than the age of the host to which the skin had been transplanted.

The most important histologic changes in organs are partial cell replacement by the connective tissues composed of collagen, ground substance, and fat. Organ weights in the aged thus reflect not only the cell content but also the increased connective tissue.

Cell numbers may be obtained by direct counts of cells of tissues by light microscopy and by determination of DNA content per unit weight of tissue. The latter method is complicated by infiltrates of other cells including fibroblasts, lymphocytes, plasma cells, and macrophages. The number of cells for a few tissues are given in Table V.

TABLE V

CELL COUNT CHANGES WITH AGE

Brain		
	cerebral cortex	decreases in neurons[1]
	cerebellar cortex	25% decrease in Purkinje cells[2]
	thoracic spinal ganglia	30% decrease in ganglion cells[3]
Liver		
		no decrease[4]
Kidney		
	glomeruli	decrease[5]

[1]Brody, H.: *J. Comp. Neurol., 102*:511, 1955.
[2]Ellis, R. S.: *J. Comp. Neurol., 32*:1, 1920.
[3]Gardner, E.: *Anat. Rec. 77*:529, 1940
[4]Shock, N. W.: In *Age with a Future.* Hansen, P. F., Ed. Copenhagen, Munksgaard, 1964, p. 13.
[5]Arataki, M: *Amer. J. Anat. 36*:399, 1926.

Two processes have some of the characteristics seen in aging: (a) experimental total body chronic irradiation (Handler, 1961); (b) the disease of youth called progeria.

Experimentally irradiated animals show the following characteristics: (a) decreased lifespan as described by the Gompertz equation (see below), and (b) increased susceptibility to disease. The pathological alteration common to both radiation effects and aging is arteriocapillary fibrosis. The increased fibrous tissue in capillaries is the result of cells depositing collagen. Therefore, we conclude that new collagen is a secondary effect of the radiation; a result of cellular response to the stimulation or radiation.

Progeria means premature senility and is used to describe a rare condition occurring in children who cease growth, develop superficial characteristics that are suggestive of aging, and die prematurely. These patients resemble the aged in that they often have wrinkled skin and are weak and emaciated. Some of these patients have diseases commonly found in the aged, e.g. atherosclerosis, myocardial infarcts, cerebral vascular accidents, and arthritis. Although the appearance and diseases of these young patients bear similarity to those found in the aged, there is no evidence that the basic mechanisms for aging and progeria are related.

UNIQUE BODY CONSTITUENTS

Certain substances recently isolated from cells may be important in the aging process. These substances have been called retine, promine, and infertine (Szent-Györgyi *et al.*, 1963). Retine is a preparation which has a strong inhibitory action on malignant growth; promine has a strong promoting action on malignant growth; and infertine has sterilizing activity. Retine and promine are general tissue constituents while infertine has been identified in the thymus. More promine and less retine were isolated from aortas of old animals as compared to young animals. Extracellular constituents also may be important in maturation and its reversal. The juvenile hormone of insects apparently alters the amounts and types of proteins synthesized by specific cells and tissues and may be able to reverse the process of maturation in certain tissues (Schneiderman, 1964). The balance between these substances may be important in inhibiting growth and starting an individual into the phase of generalized deterioration.

DEATH RATE

Aging can be described mathematcially in terms of its endpoint. It was found more than one hundred years ago by Gompertz (1825) that the logarithm of the reduced death rate for a number of animal species is a linear function of age during the period of generalized deterioration. This is expressed by an equation, log D/D_0 = kA, which describes a first-order decay process where D is the death rate, D_0 is the death rate at zero time, k is a genetically inbuilt constant which varies with species, and A is the age in years. For humans, this equation approximates a straight line between the ages of thirty and ninety. This relationship which can be derived statistically, is characteristic of many naturally occurring phenomena including some chemical reactions, growth, diffusion processes, radioactive decay, etc. It appears more than coincidence that many other biological phenomena that change with chronological age may be described approximately by the same mathematical equation. A few examples include the amount of citrate extractable collagen (Bakerman, 1962), changes in the body weights, changes in liver weights, and the decrease in the number of liver cells engaged in duplication (Post and Hoffman, 1964).

Other biological systems that show this same time-dependent logarithmic change are red cell survival curves in health and disease (Prankerd, 1961), the rate of change of the volume of mitochondria with aging time of these subcellular organelles (McGaughey, 1962), and the breakdown of mitochondria (Sanadi and Fletcher, 1962). Additional biological processes can be described similarly. Some biochemical measurements which change in a regular fashion with age are hepatic enzyme activity (Ross, 1964), weight required to prevent contraction of tendon collagen (Verzár, 1963), creatinine excretion (Norris, *et al.*, 1963), total exchangeable potassium (Edelman, 1962), 17-ketosteroid excretion (Pincus, 1956), and the increase of viscosity against time of a protein gel being cross-linked (Bjorksten and Andrews, 1960). These parameters may vary not only with age but with the disease and nutritional state of the subject. Additional parameters require measurement in order to describe chronological aging in this objective manner.

Theoretical treatments of aging have been developed using this logarithmic equation. The Gompertz equation may actually reflect a composite of different changes, each of which may be described by other mathematical relationships or it may describe the characteristic of a single, limiting phenomenon. Further studies are necessary to determine its general application to aging.

MORTALITY STATISTICS

Aging increases susceptibility to disease. The ten leading causes of death in the United States in 1961 are given in Table VI. Heart disease, cancer, and cerebral vascular lesions account for two thirds of all the deaths. This is in marked contrast to the statistics at the turn of the century when four of the first ten causes of death were infectious diseases; pneumonia and influenza, tuberculosis, diarrhea and enteritis ranked first, second, and third respectively. The increase in incidence of diseases of the heart, cancer, and cerebral vasculature is related to the increasing age of the population with an increasing number of people in the age group most likely to suffer from these diseases. Presently there are approximately twenty million persons over the age of sixty-five. This is compared to about three million in 1900.

TABLE VI

THE 10 LEADING CAUSES OF DEATH IN THE
UNITED STATES IN 1961*

Cause of death	Death rate per 100,000 population	Percent of deaths from all causes
1. Diseases of the heart	363	39.1
2. Malignant neoplasms	150	16.1
3. Cerebral vascular lesions	106	11.3
4. Accidents	50	5.4
5. Certain diseases of early infancy	36	3.9
6. Pneumonia and influenza (except of the newborn)	30	3.2
7. General arteriosclerosis	19	2.1
8. Diabetes mellitus	17	1.8
9. Congenital malformations	12	1.3
10. Cirrhosis of liver	11	1.2

*U.S. Bureau of the Census: *"Statistical Abstract of the United States, 1963,"* 84th ed., Washington, D. C. No. 70, 1963, p. 65.

The primary causes of death in populations in different geographic areas may show marked variation when comparing similar age groups. However, when individuals of a population are relocated to an area in which the leading causes of death are different from their native environment, these individuals tend to die from diseases prevalent in the area of relocation. As an example, atherosclerosis, a leading cause of death in the United States, is significantly more common in this country than in Japan which has one of the lowest mortality rates ascribable to that disease. Japanese living in Hawaii and California develop an incidence of atherosclerosis approaching that of the population in these areas (Keys *et al.*, 1958). These geographic differences in incidence are seen in many other diseases such as carcinomas of the stomach, lung, liver, nodular hyperplasia of the prostate, collagen diseases, multiple sclerosis, etc. The environmental factors which may influence the incidence of disease include diet, climate, public health measures, mores of the society, and numerous other factors.

A discussion of the biological factors in human mortality are given by Spiegelman (1960) and are summarized below. Life expectancy is partially determined at the time of fertilization of the egg as shown by the tendency for the inheritance of longevity. Following a normal gestation period, the chance for live birth is greatest for a single birth of a second pregnancy of a mother in her early twenties, having no previous history of fetal death. In the perinatal period, the mortality rate has been markedly reduced in some economically underdeveloped countries through intensive public health efforts. With respect to sex, the death rate of the female is less than that of the male for all ages of life. In addition, persons with markedly excess weight have excess mortality and higher incidence of diseases. The marital status of the individuals affects longevity; married individuals have a lower death rate than single, widowed, or divorced persons. With respect to occupation, laborers, excepting farm workers, have the highest death rates. Geographically, adult residents of the West North Central part of the United States have a greater life expectancy than individuals living in other parts of the United States.

Life expectancy may be increased by increasing the standard of living, by improving the environment, and by offering public health services. In the United States, life expectancy at birth has increased from less than fifty years in 1900 to about seventy years in 1960, a difference of some twenty years. This increase has been due mostly to a decreased mortality in infancy, early childhood, and early adulthood. The decreased mortality in early childhood can be attributed partially to the better environmental control of communicable diseases; immunization, antibiotics, and control of the transmission of the pathogenic organisms have had a marked influence in this regard. This is reflected by the fact that life expectancy at age forty has increased from twenty-eight years in 1900 to thirty-three years in 1960, a difference of only five years; at age sixty, life expectancy in 1900 was only three years less than in 1960 despite the increased standard of living, improved environment, increased public health services, and manyfold increases in industrial output.

CONCLUSION

Many biological parameters have been used to describe aging. Despite these studies, we have accrued limited knowledge of the mechanisms of aging, and certainly no experiments have been done that can be directly applied to human populations that can achieve the objectives of prolonging human lifespan and at the same time maintain vitality.

Research on human aging is being done in many diversified fields in an attempt to define chemical mechanisms. These mechanisms cannot be obtained without basic data, some of which are presented in the following chapters. The subject matter covers the broad spectrum ranging from nucleic acids and proteins, through enzymes and connective tissues, to lipids. Each of these bodily constituents show distinctive changes during aging. It has yet to be shown which of these systems may be the most important in defining the basic mechanisms of aging.

In the next chapter, the central role of nucleic acid and proteins in carriers of information in biological systems is established. The carriers of hereditary information are the deoxyribonucleic acids (DNA). In different species, these molecules determine the differences in lifespan. The information in the gene is transmitted through ribonucleic acids (RNA) to the cytoplasm of the cell and serves to govern the synthesis of proteins. Alterations of DNA with aging may alter the quantity and quality of the proteins important in metabolism.

REFERENCES

BAKERMAN, S.: *Nature* (London), *196*:375, 1962.

BJORKSTEN, J., and ANDREWS, F,: *J. Amer. Geriat. Soc.*, 8:632, 1960.

BROZEK, L.: Washington, D. C., Department of the Army, Office of the Quatermaster General, 1954, p. 265.

CLARK, A. M.: Genetic factors associated with aging. In *Advances in Gerontological Research*. Strehler, B. L., Ed. New York, Academic, 1964, vol. 1, p. 207.

EDELMAN, I. S.: In *Biological Aspects of Aging*. Shock, N. W., Ed. New York, Columbia, 1962, p. 46.

FRYER, J. H.: In *Biological Aspects of Aging*. Shock, N. W., Ed. New York, Columbia, 1962, p. 59,

GOMPERTZ, B.: On the nature of the function expressive of the human mortality and on a new mode of determining life contingencies. *Phil. Trans. Roy. Soc. (London)*, *Ser. A.*, *115*:513, 1825.

HABERMAN, JOAN L,: Clinical tests and aging. *Northwest Med.*, Dec., 1962.

HANDLER, P., Ed.: *Radiation and aging - synopses of panel discussions*. *Fed. Proc.* 20(No. 2, Part II): 1, 1961.

HAYFLICK, L.: Aging Symposium. San Diego, California. Summarized by Krohn, P. L., in *Science*, *152*:391, 1966.

KALLMANN, F. J.: In *Aging and Levels of Biological Organization*. Brues, A. M., and Sacher, G. A., Eds., Chicago, U. of Chicago, 1965, p. 35.

KALLMANN, F. J.: In *Methodology of the Study of Ageing*. Ciba Foundation Colloquia on Aging. Wolstenholme, G. E. W., and O'Connor, C. M., Eds. Boston, Little, 1957, vol. 3, p. 131.

KEYS, A.; KUNURA, N.; KUSUKAWA, A.; BRONTE-STEWART, B.; LARSEN, N., and KEYS, M. H.: *Ann. Intern. Med.*, 48:83, 1958.

KROHN, P. L.: Aging Symposium. San Diego, California. *Science*, *152*:39, 1966.

LESSER, G. T.; PERL, W., and STEEL, J. M.: In *Biological Aspects of Aging*. Shock, N. W., Ed. New York, Columbia, 1962, p. 92.

MARIANI, T.; MARTINEZ, C.; SMITH, J. M., and GOOD, R. A.: *Ann. N.Y. Acad. Sci.*, 87:93, 1960.

McGAUGHEY, C.: *J. Appl. Physiol.*, 17:979, 1962.

McKEOWN, FLORENCE: *Pathology of the Aged*. London, Butterworths, 1965.

McKUSICK, V. A.: *Human Genetics*. Englewood Cliffs, New Jersey, Prentice-Hall, 1964.

NORRIS, A. H.; LUNDY, T., and SHOCK, N. W.: *Ann. N.Y. Acad. Sci.*, *110*:623, 1963.

PARFENTJEV, I. A.: In *The Biology of Aging*. Strehler, B. L., Ed. New York, Stechert, 1960, p. 236.

Pincus, G.: In *Hormones and the Aging Process.* Engle, E. T., and Pincus, G., Eds. New York, Academic, 1956, p. 1.

Post, J., and Hoffman, J.: *Exp. Cell Res., 36:*111, 1964.

Puck, T.: Aging Symposium. San Diego, California. Summarized by Krohn, P. L. in *Science, 152:*39, 1966.

Prankerd, T. A. M.: *The Red Cell.,* Oxford, England, Blackwell, 1961, p. 5.

Ross, M. H.: In *Diet and Bodily Constitution.* Wolstenholme, G. E. W., and O'Connor, M., Eds.: Boston, Little, 1964, p. 90.

Sanadi, D. R., and Fletcher, M.: In *Biological Aspects of Aging.* Shock, N. W., Ed. New York, Columbia, 1962, p. 298.

Schneiderman, H. A.: Insect hormones. In *McGraw-Hill Yearbook of Science and Technology.* 1964, p. 253.

Spiegelmann, M.: In *The Biology of Aging.* Strehler, B. L., Ed. New York, Stechert, 1960, p. 292.

Simms, H. S., and Berg, B. W.: *Geriatrics, 17:*235, 1962.

Siri, W.: In *Biological Aspects of Aging.* Shock, N. W., Ed. New York, Columbia, 1962, p. 58.

Szent, Györgyi, A.; Hegyeli, A., and McLaughlin, J. A.: *Proc. Nat. Acad. Sci. U.S.A., 49:*878, 1963.

Verzár, F.: *Lectures on Experimental Gerontology.* Springfield, Thomas, 1963.

Wolstenholme, G. E. W., and O'Connor, M., Eds.: *The Lifespan of Animals.* Ciba Foundation. Boston, Little, 1959, vol. 5.

SUPPLEMENTARY READINGS
Books and Symposia

Birren, J. E.; Butler, R. N.; Greenhouse, S. W.; Sokoloff, L.; Yarrow, M. R., Eds.: *Human Aging—A Biological and Behavioral Study.* U.S. Department of Health, Education, and Welfare, Public Health Service, National Institute of Health, Bethesda, Md., 1963.

Bourne, G. H., Ed.: *Structural Aspects of Ageing.* New York, Hafner, 1961.

Brues, A. M., and Sacher, G. A., Eds.: *Aging and Levels of Biological Organization.* Chicago, U. of Chicago, 1962.

Comfort, A.: *Ageing—The Biology of Senescence.* New York, Holt, 1964.

Curtis, H. J.: *Biological Mechanisms of Aging.* Springfield, Thomas, 1966.

Engle, E. T., and Pincus, G., Eds.: *Hormones and the Aging Process.* New York, Academic, 1956.

Korenchevsky, V.: *Physiological and Pathological Ageing.* Bourne, G. H., Ed. New York, Hafner, 1961.

Lansing, A. E., Ed.: *Cowdry's Problems of Aging,* 3rd ed. Baltimore, Williams and Wilkins, 1952.

McKeown, F.: *Pathology of the Aged.* London, Butterworths, 1965.

Shock, N. W., Ed.: *Aging—Some Social and Biological Aspects.* Baltimore, Horn-Shafer, 1960.

Shock, N. W., Ed.: *Biological Aspects of Aging.* New York, Columbia, 1962.

Strehler, B. L., Ed.: *The Biology of Aging—Symposium,* New York, Stechert, 1960.

Strehler, B. L.: *Time, Cells, and Aging.* New York, Academic, 1962.

Strehler, B. L., Ed.: *Advances in Gerontological Research.* New York, Academic, 1964, vol. 1.

Vedder, C. B.: *Gerontology: A Book of Readings.* Springfield, Thomas, 1963.

Verzár, F.: *Lectures on Experimental Gerontology.* Springfield, Thomas, 1963.

Wolstenholme, G. E. W., and Cameron, P., Eds.: *Aging—General Aspects.* Ciba Foundation Colloquia on Aging. Boston, Little, 1955, vol. 1.

Wolstenholme, G. E. W., and Millar, E., Eds.: *Ageing in Transient Tissues.* Ciba Foundation Colloquia on Ageing. Boston, Little, 1956, vol. 2.

Wolstenholme, G. E. W., and O'Connor, C. M., Eds.: *Ageing—Methodology of the Study of Ageing.* Ciba Foundation Colloquia on Ageing. Boston, Little, 1957, vol. 3.

Wolstenholme, G. E. W., and O'Connor, M., Eds.: *Water and Electrolyte Metabolism in Relation to Age and Sex.* Ciba Foundation Colloquia on Ageing. Boston, Little, 1958, vol. 4.

Wolstenholme, G. E. W., and O'Connor, M., Eds.: *Lifespan of Animals.* Ciba Foundation Colloquia on Ageing. Boston, Little, 1959, vol. 5.

Physiology and Biochemistry of Aging. Translation from Russian. Published for the National Science Foundation, Washington, D.C. by the Israel Program for Scientific Translations. Jerusalem, 1963.

VA *Prospectus Research in Aging.* Veterans Administration, Advisory Committee on Problems of Aging, U.S. Government Printing Office, 1959.

Review Articles

Bjorksten, J.: Aging: Present status of our chemical knowledge. *J. Amer. Geriat. Soc.,* 10:125, 1962.

Comfort, A.: The lifespan of animals. *Sci. Amer.,* 205:108, 1961.

Curtis, H. J.: Biological mechanisms underlying the aging process. *Science,* 141:686, 1963.

Krohn, P. L.: Review lectures on senescence. II. Heterochronic transplantation in the study of ageing. *Proc. Roy. Soc.* [Biol.], 157:128, 1962.

Sax, K.: Aspects of ageing in plants. In *Annual Review of Plant Physiology.* Mackis, L., Ed. Palo Alto, Calif., Annual Reviews, 1962, p. 489.

SINEX, F. M.: Biochemistry of aging. *Science, 134*:1402, 1961.

SINFEX, F. M.: Biochemistry of aging. *Perspect. Biol. Med.* 9:208, 1966.

SMITH, J. M.: Review lectures on senescence. I. The causes of ageing. *Proc. Roy. Soc.* [Biol.] *157*:115, 1962.

SZILARD, L.: On the nature of the ageing process. *Proc. Nat. Acad. Sci.,* U.S.A., *45*:30, 1959.

VERZÁR, F.: The ageing of collagen. *Sci. Amer., 208*:104, 1963.

The enigma of human aging. *Chem. Engin. News, 40*:138; (Feb. 12) (Feb. 19) 104, 1962.

Chapter 2

NUCLEIC ACIDS AND PROTEINS

M. EARL BALIS

INTRODUCTION

T HE PREEMINENT ROLE of nucleic acids and proteins as carriers of information in biological systems has quite naturally led many investigators to implicate them in theoretical considerations of aging. Such hypotheses presume that there are changes in the function of these molecules as transcribable depositories of information. These changes can occur because molecular structures have been altered by denaturation with the passage of time or by secondary action of external forces. A second possibility is that the mechanisms of synthesis or catabolism of these informational molecules has changed or been changed.

Current biochemical thinking maintains that proteins and ribonucleic acids (RNA) of living animals are in a state of dynamic equilibrium. However, the fact that deoxyribonucleic acid (DNA) is relatively stable has induced some to suppose that it is never renewed except during mitosis. This apparently is not so. Pelc (1964) has shown that there is at least a partial renewal of DNA in nondividing cells but at a rate much less than that observed with RNA and protein. From his data it is possible to calculate a half-life of 115 to 800 days for "stable" DNA of brain cells and 13 to 58 days for that of smooth muscle. These values, though small, suggest that errors in the synthesis of DNA could be responsible for the changes observed with aging. Aging changes could be due to direct effects on the mechanisms of polymerization which could, in turn, lead to improper sequences of monomers or to faulty secondary structures. Alternatively, changes in the rate of breakdown could be a primary source of variation in polymer homeostasis. This variation could mean that partially denatured macromolecules remain in the cell and prevent native molecules from functioning. On the other hand, variations in the metabolism of the monomers which are the precursors of the nucleic acids and proteins could produce such changes in the informational macromolecules as secondary responses. These several possibilities have been explored to a considerable extent; although the research is far from complete, there is a large body of data about changes in these parameters with aging.

AMINO ACIDS

The synthesis of protein is necessary for homeostasis as well as for growth. This synthesis consists of the polymerization of amino acids under the control of certain nucleic acids and enzymes. It is obvious that any alteration in the supply of the amino acid monomers, or any interference with their availability can, theoretically, influence protein synthesis. Several investigators have examined these possibilities, and certain relationships between amino acid pools and age have been demonstrated. Unfortunately, not all the workers agree on their findings. Riemschneider *et al.* (1961) examined the amino acids in the blood of young and old humans, rats, and guinea pigs and reported that old members of all these species had elevated glutamic acid and cystine levels, but lower levels of most other amino acids. Ackerman and Kheim (1964) measured levels of nineteen amino acids in young and old subjects and reported lower values in old people for eleven of the nineteen including valine, methionine, isoleucine, leucine, phenylalanine and lysine. These workers, as did Riemschneider *et al.*, found reductions in both essential and nonessential amino acids. On the other hand, Theimer (1964) found a different pattern. In his study, men with an average age of eighty-seven showed higher levels (from 19 to 39 per cent higher) of serine, glycine, alanine, lysine, threonine and glutamate than twenty-five-year old men, but decreases (from 25 to 33 per cent lower) in the amount of valine, leucine, and isoleucine with the net changes equaling essentially zero. Torre *et al.* (1954) measured levels of amino acids of humans aged twenty to thirty-nine years, forty to fifty-nine years, and sixty to eighty-eight years. They reported their data in terms of the fraction of the total represented by each amino acid. Their results were not consistent with those obtained by the others referred to. Interestingly, they found that with some amino acids the forty to fifty-nine-year age group was not intermediate between the older and younger groups. For example, glutamate was 16, 26 and 17 per cent of the total in the three groups of increasing age. The failure to recognize the possibility that changes in values between young and old are not necessarily a continuous function may well have vitiated several studies of the biochemistry of aging.

In view of the ease with which amino acids can be determined and the accuracy of the available methods, the spread of results is hard to understand. Certainly the variation is beyond experimental error, and normal "biological variation" should have been ruled out by the size of the samples studied. There are several possible explanations of these discrepancies that may account for the difference and indicate a possible fundamental significance. Wild *et al.* (1953) reported that older patients were less able than young ones to absorb amino acids fed to them. The nitrogen excretion of older subjects was greater and their blood levels of nonprotein nitrogen did not increase as much as did those of younger subjects after ingestion of a given amount of protein. Since certain digestive enzymes and B complex vitamins increased absorption by the older subjects, they apparently need more such factors in their diets. Thus, it is possible that the diets of the older subjects, though chemically equal, were not physiologically equivalent to those of the younger.

One difficulty in assessing the significance of serum levels of nitrogenous compounds is indicated by the work of Berger (1956) who postulated that despite great variations there is, in general, a decrease in the output of urinary amino acids after puberty. Relative to this aspect of the problem is the observation of Morgan *et al.* (1955) that nonprotein nitrogen in the serum of older people is usually somewhat higher than in younger subjects; uric acid and creatinine are exceptions to this generalization. The cause of this difference has been vaguely attributed to alterations in kidney function (Morgan *et al.*, 1955).

Another aspect of amino acid metabolism that could well

influence plasma-free amino acid levels is the apparent changes in nutritional requirements that are seen with aging. Forbes and Rao (1959) found a decreased need for lysine and tryptophane in old rats. Tuttle *et al.* (1957) reported apparent increases in requirement for one or more "essential" amino acids in older men. Carrying their studies further with men fifty to seventy years of age, in contrast to young men, Tuttle *et al.* (1965a) found that the older men had a greater need for "essential" amino acid nitrogen, but considerable uncertainty existed regarding the complete specificity of the requirement. Larger amounts of two amino acids, methionine and lysine, were required by older men (Tuttle *et al.* 1965b) in order to maintain nitrogen balance. The contrast between the findings of Tuttle *et al.* in man and Forbes and Rao in rats is at first disquieting. However, species differences in amino acid requirements are well known and the studies used diets of differing total composition. They do, however, both point to one common conclusion: that amino acids essential in the diet of old animals may well be different from those of young, just as those of adults differ from those of the very young (Holt *et al.*, 1960). Support of this concept also comes from the work of Schulze (1954) who showed that he could maintain old or young human adults in nitrogen balance with the same amount of protein. However, he had to use different proteins with different age groups. Milk was a better source of protein than wheat in the old; the reverse was true with the young. Since the amino acid composition of the two proteins is quite different, this is consistent with the concept of changed requirements with age. The one "essential" amino acid which is strikingly higher in milk than in wheat is lysine. Thus, Schulze's data are in clear agreement with the observations of Tuttle *et al.* and suggest that an alteration in lysine metabolism occurs with aging.

Several investigators have studied in some detail alterations in the metabolism of the thioamino acids in old animals. Oeriu (1958) found that with increasing age, cystine concentrations were higher and methionine levels lower. He also showed that there was more oxidized glutathione in old rats than in younger ones. These observations led Oeriu and Tigheciu (1964) to propose that the level of oxidized glutathione is a fundamental measure of senescence. They found that the concentration ranged from 3.9 mg per cent in weanlings to 6.2 mg per cent in 2 to 2½-year-old rats. The administration of cysteine to old rats caused the oxidized glutathione level to drop to that of young animals. These investigators were also able to reduce the level of oxidized glutathione of old human subjects from 6.8 to 3.9 mg per cent by the administration of cysteine. Riemschneider (1961, 1964) maintained that in old humans, rats, pigs and guinea pigs the level of aspartic was, in general, lower and that of glutamic higher. The serum concentrations of these compounds also changed towards normal if the animals were given cysteine or serine. Riemschneider reasoned that the alteration in these amino acids and their interrelationships support the concept that with aging there is an increase in disulfide bonds and the administration of mercaptans or precursors, thereof, reversed this trend. Certainly, the work of the several other investigators supports this premise. One might be tempted to extend the generalization further and to propose that basically the change is a general shift in oxidation potential, and that the proportion of -S-S-vs -SH bonds in serum peptides and amino acids is merely an oxidation-reduction indicator. Shifts in diet or intravenous administration of reducing agents (serine or cysteine) can mask this redox indicator but presumably cannot change the actual potential or alter the course of aging. However, even though it may be naive to suppose that the administration of cysteine will restore youth, the possibility that means could be found to influence this potential is real.

The concentration of amino acids in the serum is one reflection of the overall synthesis of proteins in the animal, and in an individual tissue the amounts present should be a reflection of the protein metabolism of that tissue. Torre *et al.* (1955) examined the amino acids of the cerebrospinal fluid and found aspartic acid present in old human subjects but not in young. The level of the other dicarboxylic amino acid, glutamic acid, was higher in these same old people. The free amino acids of brain have also been determined. Oeriu (1963) found that with aging, methionine, cysteine and glutamine decreased but free ammonia and cystine increased by as much as 30 percent. Brain and serum contained similar relative concentrations of free thioamino acids as did several other tissues. In connective tissues of old rats and rabbits there was an increase in cystine, and in males a general increase in free amino acids was seen (Boucek *et al.*, 1955).

There has been an understandable, practical interest in metabolic changes in those tissues which in humans are apparently directly involved in the deleterious aspects of aging. In arterial tissues (Wang and Kirk, 1960), an increase in glutathione levels of from 4.2 to 8.9 mg/g tissue nitrogen was observed in people sixty to seventy-nine years old compared to those under nineteen years of age. This change may be related to the shifts in cystine or oxidized glutathione seen in serum and other tissues. In both the testes and ovaries of aging rats there is a general increase in free amino acids (Oeriu and Tanase, 1964). In conformity with the general picture seen in serum and other tissues, there was an increase in cysteine; in the testes there was also a decrease in methionine.

The suggestion has been made (Balis and Samarth, 1962) that the total pool size is of at least equal importance to that of the instantaneous pool. Thus, at any instant the amount present may not be a measure of the total quantity of a given substance available during a finite period of time. This latter value is, perhaps, more significant than is the size of the instantaneous pool. It is not possible to determine the total pool size by simple assay of cell constituents, but it can be evaluated by measuring the rate of dilution of isotopically labeled substrates. In kidney of hamsters, for example, the pool size is essentially the same in young and old, but following the injection of glycine-

TABLE VII

EVALUATION OF TOTAL GLYCINE POOL SIZE OF KIDNEY[1]

	Non-Protein Glycine counts/min/μmole		
	1 hour	3 hours	5 hours
Young	2200	1520	630
Old	1500	730	240

Values are radioactivities of non-protein glycine at given times after injection of 0.1 mc/kg of glycine-[14]C.

[1]Balis and Samarth, 1962.

¹⁴C the rate of loss of activity in young animals is twice as great as in the old (see Table VII). Aging does not affect the pool size of this amino acid, but it does reduce the total supply extensively. Whether the small glycine supply contributes to aging or whether it is a result of the process is still an open question.

PROTEIN SYNTHESIS

The mechanism of protein synthesis, as understood today, involves several enzymes, each with its own specificity and also involves several nucleic acids which have individual functions. There is, thus, considerable chance for error in the reproduction of protein molecules since any change in the structures of any of these macromolecules is a potential source of error. The role of accumulated errors of transcription has been reexamined recently (Orgel, 1963) and their possible significance in the aging process considered. One should expect similar alterations to become evident in protein structures and functions in general, not only in enzymes or proteins of particular functions since all proteins and their synthesizing mechanisms are subject to the same controls and the same chances of mistakes. Thus, studies of the structure and concentration of proteins in various tissues are relevant to the evaluation of this potential mechanism of aging.

The protein content of tissues of young and old animals has been determined but the results have not been suggestive of a relationship to aging. The composition of veal versus beef reveals changes in water content but no evidence of changes in amino acid composition (Goll *et al.*, 1963). Similarly, no differences have been found in the amino acids of proteins of aortic tissue of young and old humans (Gortner, 1954). On the other hand, there has been a report of increases in mercapto groups of myosin with age (Khil'ko, 1965). This difference is of potential significance; it brings to mind the changes in free thioamino acid levels and also the role of sulfhydryl groups in determining secondary protein structure.

The obvious fact that the aging of humans is concomitant with a cessation in net protein synthesis has led many to examine the rate and mechanism of protein synthesis as a function of age. Certainly, some proteins are quite stable while others are rapidly renewed (Davison, 1961). Some of the proteins of both the central and peripheral nervous system and of muscle and tendon have extremely long half-lives.

The rate at which proteins are synthesized can be determined from studies of the incorporation of labeled precursors into protein or by evaluating the rate of disappearance of labeled material. The incorporation method suffers from the difficulty of determing the real activity of the precursor *in vivo* (Balis and Samarth, 1962). The disappearance method can be used by labeling proteins *in vivo* or by administration of prelabeled proteins. By the latter "disappearance methods", if one is able to compensate for any dilution of label due to growth, it is possible to determine the half-life of body proteins.

The synthesis of liver and muscle protein from radioactive glycine has been studied in young, young adults and old rats (Neuberger *et al.*, 1951). The rate of loss of label from these proteins when corrected for dilution due to growth, was the same for all three age groups. The data do not permit any conclusions regarding the direct synthesis of these proteins from the precursor, glycine. The total protein of kidney and heart are also equally labile in young adult (12 months) and old (24 months) rats (Barrows and Roeder, 1961). Following the administration of sulfur labeled methionine the rate of disappearance of radioactive sulfur from the soluble proteins of these tissues was determined. The decay constants were calculated (Table VIII), and they were not significantly different in the two age groups. In somewhat similar studies, the disappearance of ^{131}I-labeled albumin was determined

TABLE VIII

RATE OF DISAPPEARANCE OF RADIOACTIVITY FROM VARIOUS TISSUES OF YOUNG AND OLD RATS FOLLOWING ADMINISTRATION OF S[35]-LABELED METHIONINE[1]

Experiment	Age	N	Liver $k*$	Kidney $k*$	Heart $k*$	Muscle $k*$
I	Old (24 mos.)	11	0.298±0.080	0.299±0.029	0.162±0.024	0.034±0.031
	Young (12 mos.)	10	0.226±0.041	0.279±0.027	0.122±0.022	0.040±0.029
II	Old (24 mos.)	9	0.291±0.010	0.228±0.062	0.116±0.022	0.057±0.028
	Young (12 mos.)	13	0.237±0.056	0.227±0.042	0.115±0.017	0.014±0.020

*k from equation: log S.A. $= kt + b$
[1]Barrows and Roeder, 1961.

and old people (75 to 88 years) showed essentially normal turnover times (Cassassa *et al.*, 1962).

The several studies of protein decay appear to be in agreement in showing the rate of protein turnover to be generally the same in animals of several age groups. There are exceptions: Neuberger (1951) showed that collagen decay in young rats is almost entirely absent and that the synthesis of normal collagen is extremely small in old rats. The peculiarities of collagen metabolism and its relationship to aging are of such importance that they must be considered separately (Chapter 4).

It has long been appreciated that net changes in growth rates can be due to alterations in either synthesis or degradation or both (Shemin and Rittenberg, 1944). There is ample evidence that the changes that accompany aging are due to different rates of protein degradation. The question of synthesis cannot be answered so clearly. In an attempt to find possible differences with age, Barrows and Roeder (1961) measured the activity of several enzymes of liver, kidney and heart in rats, 3, 5, 12 and 24 months of age. They then placed groups of animals on a protein-free diet for three weeks. The loss of enzyme activity by representative members of the groups was determined and the rest of the animals were then placed on a complete diet. After appropriate times, enzyme levels were again determined. Animals of all three age groups showed the same loss of activity and all returned to normal at the same rate. Thus, no evidence of faulty protein synthesis was obtained.

Even though capacity for protein synthesis under stress was not diminished, it is possible that synthesis under normal conditions is reduced in old animals. The synthesis of protein from methionine-^{35}S was followed in 1-, 3- and 24-month-old rats by Silin (1960). He found the incorporation lowest in the youngest animals. In a similar series of experiments with 2-, 12- and 24-month-old rats the values for the 12- and 24-month-old groups were about the same (Oeriu *et al.*, 1963). Interestingly, Oeriu *et al.*, did not find much difference in the rate of synthesis in the intestines of the three age groups. The most labile portion of the intestines is the mucosa, and this tissue is less rapidly renewed in old age groups (Lesher *et al.*, 1961). Thus, to some extent, rate of protein synthesis is independent of renewal rate of tissues. Silin had attributed his results to greater dilution of the labeled protein by newly synthesized unlabeled material in the young animals, but a more likely explanation would be the dilution of precursor prior to polymerization. An interesting aspect of the work of Oeriu and his colleagues was their demonstration that the incorporation of methionine was increased by the administration of cysteine and folic acid. It will be recalled that the methionine level was low in serum and that cysteine and folic acid have been shown to normalize the level of thioamino acids in the serum. This work does not show whether the differences observed are due to fundamental changes in protein synthesis or to alterations in the methionine pool but does relate the metabolic shifts in serum to the act of protein synthesis.

Several groups of investigators have attempted to evaluate protein synthesis and age through the use of *in vitro* systems. The synthesis of protein by liver slices is a function of the age of the animal from which the tissue was obtained. The incorporation of glycine-^{14}C into protein of liver slices from rats 730 days old was between one-third and one-half that seen in slices from animals less than a month old (Bulankin *et al.*, 1960, 1962.) With labeled methionine as a precursor, the results were essentially the same (Bulankin and Parina, 1960) as those seen with glycine. *In vitro* studies with preparations of the aorta of young and old cattle (Mandel *et al.*, 1961) revealed the same pattern.

It is difficult to relate the observations of protein synthesis *in vitro* to that *in vivo*. Certainly, there is no unusual change in turnover rates with age. Changes in apparent utilization *in vivo* are in conflict with those seen *in vitro*. To a considerable extent this difference can be attributed to possible variations in free amino acid pool size and mobility. The reduced rate of synthesis exhibited in old tissues *in vitro* may be a reflection of reduced potential synthetic capacity per se. Alternatively, these changes may be secondary responses to energy mobilizing systems. For example, the synthesis of protein *in vitro* is responsive to the addition of ATP, and the magnitude of this effect decreases with age (Nikitin and Golubitskaya, 1959). Unfortunately, with the exception of the work of Barrows and Roeder, there is little data regarding the synthesis of protein under conditions of stress and aging. It is quite possible that the most significant changes in protein synthesis that accompany aging are not those seen in liver slices but rather those seen in animals under stress. On occasion all animals are under physical or emotional pressure, and the ability to synthesize proteins at these times may be significant. This is reminiscent of the work of Shock who has shown that normal function of many organs is unimpaired by age but that the ability to function under limiting conditions is reduced (Shock, 1960).

The concentration and properties of proteins of the serum are a reflection of, among other things, the animals' synthetic capacities. Several groups have examined the level of albumin and globulin in sera from a variety of animals of various ages. With rare exceptions (Kirk, 1954), they have agreed that with age there is a decrease in albumin concentration and an increase in that of the globulin (Vanzetti et al., 1952; Rafsky, et al., 1952). Though there is a fairly good agreement that globulins increase with age, there is no agreement as to which fraction is responsible. Some report big increases in α(Karel et al., 1956; Uebel, 1956). Some find major increases in β (Ghighliotti et al., 1956; Nöcker and Bemm, 1955; Rafsky et al., 1952.) Some find β down until puberty, then constant or slightly higher with increasing age (Falaschini et al., 1955; Uebel, 1956). Most workers find increases in γ globulin with age (Uebel, 1956; Ghigliotti et al., 1956; Goullet et al., 1964). It is quite possible that secondary pathological conditions have influenced the globulins and may explain some of the disagreement regarding which globulin fraction is increased. Variations in serum composition with pathological conditions are known (Cognasso and Costanzo, 1961).

Though there has been relatively little speculation about the significance of the increase in globulin production, there have been several hypotheses advanced to explain the decrease in albumin level. One theory holds that it is a manifestation of decreased liver function (Karel et al., 1956). The possibility that this deficiency is a result of the lessened synthetic capacity of liver has also been suggested (Bulankin et al., 1960). This latter suggestion is supported by the reduced synthetic capacity of liver slices coupled with the normal decay of serum albumin in old subjects. As so often occurs in the aging syndrome, the diet has a definite effect; the albumin level is especially sensitive to the protein intake (Acheson and Jessop, 1962), and any comprehensive explanation of the shift in serum protein concentrations must account for this fact. The reduction in albumin is real and consistent and its origin understandable kinetically; however, a causal relationship remains to be established.

SOLUBLE NUCLEOTIDES

Just as the synthesis of proteins is related to the metabolism of the free amino acid pool, so is the synthesis of the nucleic acids related to the metabolism of the soluble nucleotide pool. The concentration of nucleotides is, in general, easily determined, and the number of identified chemical individuals is large and steadily growing. The function of many nucleotides is not yet understood. The bulk of the simple mono-, di-, and triphosphates are primarily concerned with energy transport or are intermediates in nucleic acid synthesis.

The pool of nucleotides in mammals is largely formed by synthesis *de novo* from smaller molecules, and any alteration in their synthesis would naturally result in changes in the dynamic state of the pool. There has been no definitive study of the effect of age on the enzymes responsible for catalyzing the formation of these compounds. The levels of the molecules per se have been studied and have been found to vary from tissue to tissue in some instances. The cytidylic acid pool varies differently with age in each tissue (Wulff *et al.*, 1965). The adenine miscible pool in weanling hamsters varies from tissue to tissue, but in mature animals this is not so (Balis and Samarth, 1962).

Despite these problems in tissue individuality, there have been some generally consistent observations. The nucleotide concentrations are lower in old animals than in young. The bovine aorta has been studied extensively, and the concentration of adenylic, guanylic, uridylic, inosinic and cytidylic acid derivatives have been measured, and the concentration of each was lower in the old animals (Kempf and Mandel, 1961). In studies with rats, lower concentrations of free nucleotides were found in the skeletal and cardiac muscles of old animals (Bertolini *et al.*, 1962). The concentrations were about 30 percent less in 20-month old rats as compared with 4-month-old animals. The significance of these findings to the problem of aging is obscure since similar differences were not found in the brain. In a study of Devi *et al.*, (1963), a quite different picture was presented. They found no consistent pattern of nucleotides concentration with aging rats until the animals were almost a year old. After that there was an indication of a general decrease. Unfortunately, they discontinued their studies when the rats were only about a year old; thus, it is difficult to evaluate their work extensively.

The possibility that the major decrease in nucleotides is at the triphosphate level has been suggested by Mandel *et al.* (1961), who believed that the major reduction with age was in the triphosphate of adenosine and uridine. Thus, they have suggested a direct relationship of the reduction in nucleotide level to ribonucleic acid (RNA) synthesis, since the nucleosides triphosphates are the substrates for the synthesis of at least some RNA (Weiss and Gladstone, 1959; Hurwitz *et al.*, 1960). As will be seen below, the complexity of the RNA synthetic process makes evaluation of this intriguing proposal difficult.

DNA METABOLISM

There is an obvious possibility that the changes that occur with aging are due to alterations in DNA (see Chapter 6), and several investigators have examined the DNA of animals of various ages. One parameter that has been evaluated is the amount of DNA, and usually no change has been seen. Numerous tissues and animals have been analyzed: mouse uterus (Drasher, 1953); rat liver and kidney (Barrows *et al.*, 1960, 1962); and spleen, thymus, liver and kidney of the mouse (Kurnick and Kernen, 1962). The possibility that the change in DNA with age results in polyploidy with concomitant changes in function was examined by Falzone *et al.* (1959), who measured three quantities in rat liver: (1) DNA per nucleus, (2) mean volume of hepatic nuclei, and (3) number of nuclei. No difference with age was noted in any of these parameters. There have been some reports of changes but examination of the data shows primarily a difference between very young and mature but not old animals. For example, Devi *et al.* (1963) reported liver DNA values in embryonic rats as 7.5 mg/g; in 7 to 21 day-old rats, 4.9; in 150 to 200 g rats, 2.6; and 450 to 500 g rats, 2.7. Any evaluation of such changes relative to aging would require extensive data about cell types, water content, etc. Such data are of great value, but more as pertains to changes in development rather than aging.

A mature animal does not have as many dividing cells as a young growing animal, but it is not apparent that there is any great difference between mature and old animals in this regard. It would be expected that the incorporation of DNA precursors should be less in old animals; such incorporation should be roughly proportioned to growth rate. Experiments with mice 3 days, 2 months, 4 months and 13 months old revealed such decreasing synthesis of DNA with age (Litvak and Baserga, 1964). The animals received injections of tritiated thymidine, and the activity of the kidneys of the animals in the four age groups was in the ratio of 40:3:2:1. The results were the same in both renal cells and in the nephrons. The same general picture is seen in the mucosa of the mouse; this tissue is renewed with a cell generation time of 11.5 hours in 93-day-old animals and 15 hours in 940-day-old mice (Lesher *et al.*, 1961). An increase in intermitotic time was also noted. These *in vivo* data coincide with some earlier *in vitro* observations of Mukundan *et al.* (1963a) who found that extracts of the liver of old rats were less able to catalyze DNA polymerization than were those from younger animals if native DNA was used as the primer. On the other hand, if heat-denatured DNA was the primer employed, then the enzymatic activity was greater in old rats (Fig. 1). These data contrast the ability of extracts of liver of rats of various ages to catalyze the synthesis of DNA with the two primers. If "normal" DNA replication is measured by the ability of homogenates to catalyze polymer formation under the influence of native DNA, then there is a loss in DNA synthesizing capacity with age. The increased capacity to replicate denatured DNA could be a measure of alteration in the enzymatic specificity which could lead to the synthesis *in vivo* of DNA with new biochemical properties. The implications are obvious, but much more information is necessary before we can begin to assess the full significance. For example, the relationships of these systems to rates of growth of liver (and other tissues) must be evaluated; the synthesis of DNA in organs which are evidencing the functional deficiencies sometimes associated with aging should be related to these observations.

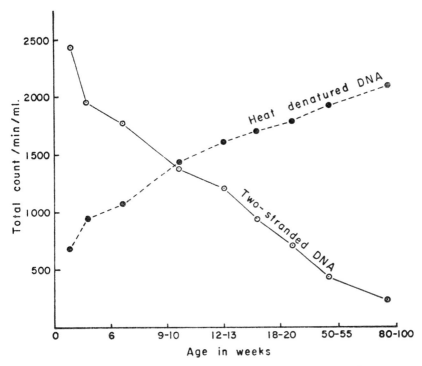

FIGURE 1. Effect of age on DNA polymerase activity in rat liver. The total counts in acid precipitable material is a measure of polymerase activity. (From Mukundan *et al.*, 1963.)

There are several enzymes capable of catalyzing the hydrolysis of DNA. The enzyme DNase II has been implicated in DNA metabolism as more than simply a catalyst of hydrolysis

(Allfrey and Mirsky, 1952). The activity of the enzyme is higher in rapidly growing tissues such as regenerating liver (Brody
and Balis, 1959), which leads to the belief that it has an anabolic
function. The enzyme might well play more than one role,
as a degradative enzyme in a salvage pathway and a primary
enzyme in the system of DNA replication. In the thymus and
spleen of mice, acid DNase increases several-fold during maturation, whereas in liver and kidney, the enzyme shows a
slight increase with age (Kurnick and Kernen, 1962). In similar
studies with rat liver, increases were noted in older animals
(Mukundan *et al.*, 1963b). There is an endogenous inhibitor
of DNase, the activity of which decreases with increasing
age in mice. The tendency of the enzyme to increase and the
inhibitor to decrease with age led to the hypothesis that this
enzyme plays a primarily catabolic role in old animals. If in
normal growth of DNase plays a necessary role, a shift in conditions so that the enzyme can no longer act may be related to
the apparent reduction of DNA replication. It is possible that
small changes in the cell pH or redox potential similar to the
shifts in mercaptan-disulfide equilibrium referred to above could
change the primary role of DNase and thus influence DNA
replication and ultimately cell viability.

DNA STRUCTURE

Permanent metabolic changes are often expressions of geno-
typic change. The molecular basis for such effects is a change
in DNA composition or structure. Such changes may come
about via errors in the copy mechanism, by any one of several
routes, or could result from external influences on already
formed DNA. Hahn (1963) has looked for potential aging
changes in DNA by studying the thermal denaturation and viscosity of preparations from young and old bovine thymus. He
found that crude preparations which contained 2 to 3 per cent
histone from young animals were different from those from old
animals in that the mean temperature of denaturation (T_m) and
the specific viscosity were lower. However, in more highly purified preparations which contained about 0.5 per cent histone, the
temperature of denaturation and the viscosity were higher in

the young animals although the difference in Tm was not statistically significant. These results led Hahn to postulate that the role of histone could be twofold in the aging process. First, the histone might stabilize structural alterations on or between DNA strands which had been brought about by other agents. Second, the histone itself might be involved in these structural alterations. An additional possibility must be considered; that the physical state of other proteins in older tissues may make preparation of nucleic acid free of extraneous protein difficult. Also, these different proteins might bind more firmly and, thus, affect the characteristics of the preparation. There are no unequivocal criteria for the ultimate purity of nucleic acids and there are few criteria of any kind for the purity of histone preparations. Hahn maintains that since the T_m is a measure of resistance to thermal denaturation, the higher T_m of the nucleohistone preparations from older animals is a measure of their stability and that, therefore, this linkage of histone and DNA stabilizes whatever changes may have occurred with time.

These speculations of Hahn are of particular interest at the present time because of the widespread belief that histones can suppress DNA function (Stedman and Stedman, 1961; Huang and Bonner, 1962). It is reasonable that alterations in histone-DNA binding might change with time and thus explain the observations of Hahn and the changes of aging. Further, evaluation of these possibilities requires a more thorough study of the histones. Perhaps, fractionations of the type described by Johns *et al.* (1960) will shed light on this possibility. These workers obtained fractions, some of which were lysine-rich and some arginine-rich. Fractions obtained in a similar manner have different abilities to inhibit nuclear RNA synthesis (Allfrey, 1963). Thus, it is possible that changes in various histone fractions with aging could explain reduced cell function and the different DNA-binding patterns.

A somewhat similar suggestion, that the control of gene function is exerted by small peptides, has also been proposed (Balis *et al.*, 1964). This concept was based on the finding that with bacteria grown in different media, the amount of amino acids bound to the DNA was inversely proportional to the number of enzymes functioning. The peptides were seen as de-repressors of regulatory genes (Pardee *et al.*, 1959). Extrapolation of this concept suggests a generalized mechanism of control of gene function in such processes as aging. Thus, loss of certain DNA-bound peptides could lead to loss of the ability to synthesize the molecules coded for by that particular gene. This could lead to the observed sequence of events called aging.

One readily obtained analytical value from DNA is the base composition. Chargaff (1955) postulated that within a given species the base composition of DNA is constant. Nevertheless, the possibility that shifts might occur in the liver of old animals led to a series of analyses (Nikitin and Shereshevskaya, 1962) summarized in Table IX. It is quite evident in these studies that aging does not lead to fundamental changes in DNA composition. In a similar series of experiments, Khilobok (1965) isolated DNA from the intestinal mucosa of rats of 1,6, and 30 months of age. He examined the purine-pyrimidine ratio of his isolated DNA and found no difference in the DNA obtained from the animals from the three age groups. On the other hand, if he used a procedure involving sodium pyrophosphate at a high temperature, he found the purine-pyrimidine ratio varied from 1.9 to 2.2, and 3. With the same extraction medium at low temperature he obtained a DNA with ratios of purine to pyrimidine of 1.1, 2.6, and 5.3. These differences may be real, but one is inclined to suspect that in the salt extractions he was fractionating the DNA in a manner similar to that reported by Bendich *et al.* (1953). Any evaluation of these conflicting data must await resolution of the procedural differences.

TABLE IX

BASE COMPOSITION OF DNA FROM RAT LIVER[1]

Age (days)	Guanine	Adenine	Cytosine	Thymine
30	18.6	30.9	18.7	31.8
730	19.0	31.6	19.1	30.3

[1]Nikitin and Shereshevskaya, 1961.

One of the most fascinating experiments in the study of aging is that described by Crowley and Curtis (1963), who studied two strains of mice, one (C57BL/6J) having a 600-day normal life expectancy, the other (A/HEJ) having a 395-day lifespan. Animals of the two strains were given carbon tetrachloride to cause liver damage and subsequent regeneration was permitted. Squashes of liver cells were examined for chromosomal aberrations. At equal chronological ages, the A/HEJ showed many more abnormal chromosomes than did the C57 (Fig. 2). Thus, the DNA seemed to age, not relative to time but relative to fraction of lifespan; or conversely the lifespan was proportional to the rate of DNA damage. These data lend strong support to the concept that damage to DNA is the prime step in aging. They also indicate the value of the use of inbred strains of known life expectancy in gerontological research.

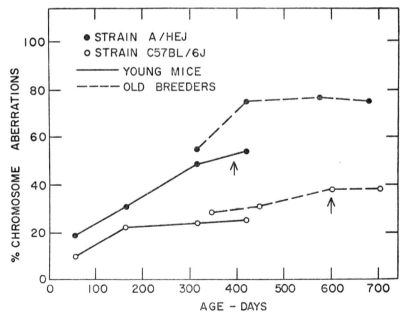

FIGURE 2. Chromosome aberrations in regenerating liver cells. The median lifespan of each strain is indicated by the arrows. In each case, the solid lines represent animals 8 weeks of age at the start of the experiment, and the broken lines old breeding animals about 1 year old at the start of the experiment. (From Crowley and Curtis, 1963.)

RNA METABOLISM

The concept that alterations in the synthesis or function of RNA are responsible for the changes of aging has also received considerable attention. According to modern interpretation of protein synthesis in general, and enzyme synthesis in particular, at least three kinds of RNA are involved. Any alteration in the rate of synthesis or catabolism of RNA could affect cell function in a variety of ways. Unfortunately, most of the studies of RNA have been carried out on total cell material rather than on individual RNA's since methods of fractionating are new and somewhat complicated. Unequivocal interpretation of the data is, therefore, difficult.

The simplest parameter of RNA to determine is the total amount in the tissues. Sergienko (1947) claimed that the RNA content of tissues decreases with age. Other workers maintain that in brain, liver and kidney there is a decrease in RNA after birth and a slight increase well after the animals reach maturity (Stavitskaya, 1956; Devi *et al.*, 1963). In a cytospectrophotometric study of the nucleic acid content of several rat tissues, Wulff *et al.* (1963) showed in some tissues increases with increasing age; in others, decreases; and in still others, no change in RNA content with age. They also found that most decreases occurred too early in the lifespan to be considered true age effects, but rather to be related to maturation. Though there may be gross changes in the amount of RNA with age, it is not possible, on the basis of data presently available, to consider altered RNA content a fundamental property of aging cells.

It is quite possible that the apparent changes in RNA content are reflections of changes in the concentration of subcellular particulates. Older liver cells have a lower total nitrogen content which has been attributed to loss of microsomes and mitochondria (Detwiler and Draper, 1962). The microsomes are particularly high in RNA; thus, relative RNA composition could change with age. Detwiler and Draper (1962) found an increase in nuclear RNA but a decrease in total RNA. Since nuclear RNA has a high cytidylic acid content, they expected and found a shift in this direction in the total RNA. Other workers (Nikitin and Shereshevskaya, 1962) found no such shift (Table X) in the livers of rats 30 and 730 days old. In all studies of this nature, there is a need for adequate weight controls since with rats, at least, a weight loss tends to accompany aging (Everitt, 1957) and there is a close relationship between nutritional status, as reflected in weights and RNA content (Leslie, 1955).

TABLE X

BASE COMPOSITION OF RNA FROM RAT LIVER[1]

Age (days)	Guanine	Adenine	Cytosine	Uracil
30	33.6	18.8	28.3	19.4
730	34.0	19.0	27.4	19.5

[1]Nikitin and Shereshevskaya, 1961.

The fact that in many tissues there is an apparent change in RNA content with aging led several investigators to examine possible biochemical bases of these events. The incorporation of inorganic radiophosphorous into RNA apparently decreases with the age of the animal (Bulankin and Parina, 1960). The maximum incorporation into both RNA and DNA after a single injection of $^{32}PO^4$ is reached later in old rats than in month-old animals, and the labeled phosphorous is lost at a slower rate in the older animals (Shereshevskaya, 1962a). However, no simple interpretation of these observations is available since no values were reported for the activity at various times of the immediate precursor, viz. the soluble nucleotides which were very highly labeled. In a more recent study, Shereshevskaya (1962b) has shown that age has no effect on total soluble phosphorylated compounds and that the entire time course of nucleic acid synthesis is slowed down with age. Hence, in older animals there would be less turnover of nucleic acids *in toto*. These data do not indicate whether the reduced nucleic acid turnover is a direct function of age or is a secondary result of changes in diet, protein synthetic activity, etc. Evidence that suggests it is a primary event comes from the observation that intraperitoneal injections of ATP stimulate liver RNA synthesis more in young than in old rats (Nikitin and Golubitskaya, 1960). Thus, one would be inclined to believe that total capacity for RNA synthesis is lower in old animals.

Wulff and his associates have studied quite intensively the question of the changes in RNA synthesis with age. The technique employed was primarily to follow incorporation of isotopically labeled cytidine into ribonucleic acid. In one of their first experiments they noted that in some tissues of mice there was a higher incorporation of cytidine in old animals than in young; in others, the opposite was found (Wulff *et al.*, 1961). They noted that it would be necessary to follow the size of the pool of more immediate precursors before any definite conclusions could be drawn. With adenine and with glycine as precursors, others have found higher incorporation into RNA of old animals, but examination of pool size did indeed show that here, at least, the difference in apparent rate of synthesis of RNA could be explained in terms of altered pool metabolism (Balis and Samarth, 1962). Recent work by Wulff *et al.* (1965) indicates a similar situation relative to cytidine metabolism.

Regardless of whether the reduced incorporation is due directly to changes in RNA synthesis or to change in nucleotide metabolism, certain patterns appear in the incorporation data. Wulff *et al.* (1962) noted that those cells with lower RNA content incorporated less exogenous cytidine whereas those with higher RNA content incorporated more. This striking parallel between synthetic rate as measured directly and indirectly led them to infer that this change was indeed fundamental to aging. They postulated that with aging, sites for RNA synthesis sustain damage from continual use and synthesize defective, short-lived messenger RNA; thus, the symptoms of age might appear. Unfortunately, the theory is in conflict with some of the observations concerning RNA content and incorporation data. It also fails to provide any explanation of the mechanism by which RNA synthesizing systems age. Though this theory may not be correct, it represents an excellent attempt to correlate various aspects of aging and to interrelate them biochemically and may serve as a point of departure for further research.

SUMMARY

The hypothesis that the physiological manifestations of aging are related to corresponding changes in the informational macromolecules has been assessed from several directions.

Changes in the relative or absolute composition of the monomeric precursors have been detailed. There is evidence that with increasing age, there are changes in the essential amino acids. Similarly, there appear to be changes in absorption and retention of nitrogen with age. These differences could be the basis for many of the conflicting reports in the literature. One of the more intriguing observations is that changes in the amount of oxidized thioamino acids are concomitant with aging. These may be related directly to protein synthesis since treatment, which appears to reverse the trend in free amino acids, reverses corresponding decreases in protein synthesis which occur with age. On the other hand, the possibility that a shift in redox potential is fundamental to all these observations must be considered.

The synthesis of proteins in older animals may occur at the same rate as in young animals. However, even if this is true, the ability of tissues of older animals to synthesize proteins under nutritionally limiting conditions or under physiological stress may be less than that of younger animals. This may explain the abnormalities of serum protein levels of older animals. These differences are real, though their nature and significance is not completely understood.

There is evidence also of differences in biosynthesis and structure of DNA. The rate of synthesis of DNA with different templates by tissue extracts from young animals varies considerably from that seen with preparations from older animals. The DNase activity of young and old animals is different. The stability of certain DNA-protein complexes is not the same in animals of different ages. An interrelationship among these several manifestations of age-related alterations in DNA metabolism is, thus, clearly indicated.

The several changes in the metabolism of the nucleic acids and proteins that accompany aging suggest that these substances play a major role in the process. The exact nature of the relationship among these variations is not readily apparent. Several of the studies of metabolism of animals of different ages have led to the observation that many systems undergo continual changes through development, maturation, and aging. These reports suggest the possibility that aging is one phase of the differentiation and development of tissues. Both of these processes probably are concerned with control of and by the nucleic acids and proteins of the cell. The elucidation of the exact interrelationships between these molecules and the maturation and aging of cells presents one of the most challenging and optimistic problems of the immediate future.

REFERENCES

ACHESON, R. M., and JESSOP, W. J. E.: Serum proteins in a population sample of males aged 65-85 years; a study by paper electrophoresis. *Gerontologia (Basel)* 6:193, 1962.

ACKERMANN, P. G., and KHEIM, T.: Plasma amino acids in young and older adult human subjects. *Clin. Chem.,* 10:32, 1964.

ALLFREY, V. G.: Nuclear ribosomes, messenger-RNA and protein synthesis. *Exp. Cell Res.,* suppl., 19:183, 1963.

ALLFREY, V. G., and MIRSKY, A. E.: Some aspects of desoxyribonuclease activities of animal tissues. *J. Gen. Physiol.,* 36:227, 1952.

BALIS, M. E.; SALSER, J. S., and ELDER, A.: A suggested role of amino acids in deoxyribonucleic acid. *Nature* (London), 203:1170, 1964.

BALIS, M. E., and SAMARTH, K. D.: Influence of age on glycine and purine metabolism. *Arch. Biochem.,* 99:517, 1962.

BARROWS, C. H., JR.; FALZONE, J. A., JR., and SHOCK, N. W.: Age differences in the succinoxidase activity of homogenates and mitochondria from the livers and kidneys of rats. *J. Geront.,* 15:130, 1960.

BARROWS, C. H., JR., and ROEDER, L. M.: Effect of age on protein synthesis in rats. *J. Geront.,* 16:321, 1961.

BARROWS, C. H., JR.; ROEDER, L. M., and OLEWINE, D. A.: Effect of age on renal compensatory hypertrophy following unilateral nephrectomy in the rat. *J. Geront.,* 17:148, 1962.

BENDICH, A.; RUSSELL, P. J., JR., and BROWN, G. B.: On heterogeneity of desoxyribonucleic acids. *J. Biol. Chem.,* 203:305, 1953.

BERGER, H.: Die amino-stickstoff-ausscheidung im harn in ablängigkeit vom lebensalter (ein beitreg zur physiologie der aminoacidurie). *Ann. Paediat. (Basel),* 186:338, 1956.

BERTOLINI, A. M.; QUARTO DIPALO, F. M., and SPINNLER, H. R.: Variations, during aging, of the content of nucleotides and free pentoses in the muscular and cerebral tissues of rats. *G. Gerontol.,* 10:341, 1962.

BOUCEK, R. J.; NOBLE, N. L., and KAO, K. Y. T.: Conjugated lipids of connective tissue of rat and rabbit. *Circ. Res.,* 3:519, 1955.

BRODY, S., and BALIS, M. E.: Mechanism of growth. I. Interrelation between deoxyribonuclease and deoxyribonucleic acid synthesis in nonmalignant growth. *Cancer Res.,* 19:538, 1959.

BULANKIN, I. N., and PARINA, E. V.: Protein synthesis changes in relation to age. II. Incorporation of methionine-^{35}S into liver-slice proteins.

Uch. Zap. Khar'kovsk. Gos. Univ. 108, *Tr. Nauchnoissled. Inst. Biol. i Biol. Fak.*, 29:23, 1960.

BULANKIN, I. N.; PARINA, E. V., and GOLOVKO, N. I.: Synthesis of albumin in white rat liver slices at various ages. *Dok. Akad. Nauk. S.S.S.R.*, 134: 1461, 1960.

BULANKIN, I. N.; PARINA, E. V., and GOLOVKO, N. I.: Protein synthesis changes in relation to age. III. Protein synthesis in liver slices of animals of various ages. Uch. Zap. Khar'kovsk. Gos. Univ. 131, *Tr. Nauchnoissled. Inst. Biol. i Biol. Fak.*, 33:21, 1962.

CASASSA, P. M.; GHEMI, F., and TURCO, G. L.: Preliminary note on the metabolism of serum albumin tagged with I131 radioactive serum albumin in the aged. *G. Geront.*, 10:35, 1962.

CHARGAFF, E.: Isolation and composition of the deoxypentose nucleic acids and of the corresponding nucleoproteins. In *The Nucleic Acids.* Chargaff, E., and Davidson, J. N. Eds. New York, Academic, 1955, vol. I, p. 307.

COGNASSO, P. A., and COSTANZO, F.: Serum glycoproteins in old age. *G. Geront.*, 9:573, 1961.

CROWLEY, C., and CURTIS, H. J.: The development of somatic mutations in mice with age. *Proc. Nat. Acad. Sci., U.S.A.*, 49:626, 1963.

DAVISON, A. N.: Metabolically inert proteins of the central and peripheral nervous system, muscle and tendon. *J. Biochem.*, 78:272, 1961.

DETWILER, T. C., and DRAPER, H. H.: Physiological aspects of aging. IV. Senescent changes in the metabolism and composition of nucleic acids of the liver and muscle of the rat. *J. Geront.*, 17:138, 1962.

DEVI, A.; MUKUNDAN, M. A.; SRIVASTAVA, U., and SARKAR, N. K.: The effect of age on the variations of deoxyribonucleic acid (DNA), ribonucleic acid (RNA), and total nucleotides in liver, brain, and muscle of rat. *Exp. Cell. Res.*, 32:242, 1963.

DRASHER, M. L.: Aging changes in nucleic acid and protein-forming systems of virgin mouse uterus. *Proc. Soc. Exp. Biol. Med.*, 84:596, 1953.

EVERITT, A. V.: The senescent loss of body weight in male rats. *J. Geront.*, 12:382, 1957.

FALASCHINI, A.; BIONDO, G., and LEONTI, F.: Modification of the blood proteins in kids in relation to their age and alimentary regime. *Biol. Soc. Ital. Biol. Sper.*, 31:306, 1955.

FALZONE, J. A., JR.; BARROWS, C. H., JR., and SHOCK, N. W.: Age and polyploidy of rat-liver nuclei as measured by volume and deoxyribonucleic acid content. *J. Geront.*, 14:2, (1959.

FORBES, R. M., and RAO, T.: Effect of age on the net requirements for nitrogen, lysine, and tryptophan for the well-fed rat. *Arch. Biochem.*, 82:348, 1959.

GHIGLIOTTI, G.; COSTA, U.; ASTENGO, F., and VIALE, L.: Blood protein picture in old people. *G. Geront.*, 4:493, 1956.

GOLL, D. E.; BRAY, R. W., and HOEKSTRA, W. G.: Age-associated changes in muscle composition. Isolation and properties of a collagenous residue from bovine muscle. *J. Sci. Food Agri.*, 28:503, 1963.

GORTNER, W. A.: Effect of age on enzymic release of amino acids from aorta tissue. *J. Geront.*, 9:251, 1954.

GOULLET, P.; CALVARIN, R.; SANDIER, S., and KAUFMANN, H.: Physiologie—Augmentation des y–globulines "naturelles" selon l'age chez le rat. *C. R. Soc. Biol. (Paris)*, 158:1220, 1964.

VON HAHN, H. P.: Age-dependent thermal denaturation and viscosity of crude and purified desoxyribonucleic acid (DNA) prepared from bovine thymus. *Gerontologia (Basel)*, 8:123, 1963.

HOLT, L. E., JR.; GYORGY, P.; PRATT, E. L.; SYNDERMAN, S. E., and WALLACE, W. M.: *Protein and Acid Requirements in Early Life.* New York, N. Y. U., 1960, p. 1.

HUANG, R. C., and BONNER, J.: Histone, a suppressor of chromosomal RNA synthesis. *Proc. Nat. Acad. Sci. U.S.A.*, 48:1216, 1962.

HURWITZ, J.; BRESLER, A., and DIRINGER, R.: Enzymic incorporation of ribonucleotides into polyribonucleotides and the effect of deoxyribonucleic acid. *Biochem. Biophys. Res. Commun.*, 3:15, 1960.

JOHNS, E. W.; PHILLIPS, D. M. P.; SIMSON, P., and BUTLER, J. A. V.: Improved fractionations of arginine-rich histones from calf thymus. *Biochem. J.*, 77:631, 1960.

KAREL, J. L.; WILDER, V. M. and BEBER, M.: Electrophoretic serum protein patterns in the aged. *J. Amer. Geriat. Soc.*, 4:667, 1956.

KEMPF, E., and MANDEL, P.: Free nucleotides in bovine aortas obtained from adult and aged animals. *C. R.*, 253:2155, 1961.

KHIL'KO, O. K.: Age changes in the contents of sulphhydryl groups and the ATPase activity of myosin. *Ukr. Biokhim. Zh.*, 37:8, 1965.

KHILOBOK, I. Y.: Age changes of some properties of the DNA of the intestinal mucosa of albino rats. *Ukr. Biokhim. Zh.*, 37:43, 1965.

KIRK, J. E.: Blood and urine vitamin levels in the aged. *Nutrition Symposium Series*, 9:73, 1954.

KURNICK, N. B., and KERNEN, R. L.: The effect of aging on the desoxyribonuclease system, body and organ weight, and cellular content. *J. Geront.*, 17:245, 1962.

LESHER, S.; FRY, R. J., and KOHN, H.: Age and the generation time of the mouse duodenal epithelial cell. *Exp. Cell Res.*, 24:334, 1961.

LESLIE, I.: The nucleic acid content of tissues and cells. In *The Nucleic Acids.* Chargaff, E., and Davidson, J. N., Eds. New York, Academic, 1955, vol. II, p. 1.

LITVAK, R. M., and BASERGA, R.: An autoradiographic study of the uptake of 3H-thymidine by kidney cells of mice at different ages. *Exp. Cell Res.* 33:540, 1964.

MANDEL, P.; FONTAINE, R., and PANTESCO, V.: Incorporation of (S-35)-methionine into the aorta of young and old bovine animals. *Biochim. Biophys. Acta, 49*:580, 1961.

MORGAN, A. F.; MURAI, M., and GILLUM, H. L.: Nutritional status of aging; serum protein, blood nonprotein nitrogen, uric acid and creatinine. *J. Nutr., 55*:671, 1955.

MUKUNDAN, M. A.; DEVI, A., and SARKAR, N. K.: The effect of age on the variations of nuclease activities and their possible functions in rat liver. *Exp. Cell Res., 32*:251, 1963.

MUKUNDAN, M. A.; DEVI, A., and SARKAR, N. K.: The effect of age on the incorporation of C14-thymidine into DNA, catalysed by soluble extract of rat liver. *Biochem. Biophys. Res. Commun. 11*:353, 1963.

NEUBERGER, A.; PERRONE, J. C., and SLACK, H. G. B.: Relative metabolic inertia of tendon collagen in rat. *Biochem. J., 49*:199, 1951.

NIKITIN, V. N., and GOLUBITSKAYA, R. I.: The stimulation of ontogenetic protein synthesis in liver homogenates by ATP. *Biokhimiia, 24*:1023, 1959.

NIKITIN, V. N., and GOLUBITSKAYA, R. I.: Age-dependent influence of ATP injections on NAS in rat liver. *Uch. Zap. Khar'kovsk Gos. Univ. 108, Tr. Nauchnoissled Inst. Biol. i Biol. Fak.* 29:103, 1960.

NIKITIN, V. N., and SHERESHEVSKAYA, T. M.: The nucleotide composition of liver ribonucleic and deoxyribonucleic acids from animals of different ages. *Biokhimiia, 26*:918, 1962.

NÖCKER, J., and BEMM, H.: Einwirkung von alter und geschlecht auf die serum-proteine. *Z. Alternsforsch, 9*:222, 1955.

OERIU, S. Correlation between the thioamino acids in the animal and vegetable organism. Acad. rep. populare Romine Inst. Biochim. *Stud. Cercet. Biochim., 1*:321, 1958.

OERIU, S.: The aging process in the central nervous system. *Fiziol. Norm. Pat.* 9:331, 1963.

OERIU, S.; PARTENIE, L.; COVASNEAU, Z.; TIGHECIU, M., and DINU, V.: The effect of sulfhydryl groups on the methionine-^{35}S incorporation in the tissue proteins of old rats. *Fiziol. Norm. Pat., 9*:339, 1963.

OERIU, S., and TANASE, I.: Metabolic processes in endocrine glands during aging. I. Action of cysteine and vitamins involved in methylation reactions and in sulfur and amino acid metabolism in ovaries and testes of variously aged animals. *G. Gerontol., 12*:681, 1964.

OERIU, S., and TIGHECIU, M.: Oxidized glutathione (I) as test of senescence. *Gerontologia, 9*:9, 1964.

ORGEL, L. E.: The maintenance of the accuracy of protein synthesis and its relevance to aging. *Proc. Nat. Acad. Sci., 49*:517, 1963.

PARDEE, A. B.; JACOB, F., and MONOD, J.: Genetic control and cytoplasmic expression of inducibility in the synthesis of β-galactosidase by Escherischia coli. *J. Molec. Biol., 1*:165, 1959.

50 *Aging Life Processes*

Pelc, S. R.: Labeling of DNA and cell division in so-called nondividing tissues. *J. Cell. Biol.* 22:21, 1964.

Rafsky, H. A.; Brill, A. A.; Stern, K. G., and Corey, H.: Electrophoretic studies on serum of "normal" aged individuals. *Amer. J. Med. Sci.*, 224: 522, 1952.

Riemschneider, R.: Amino acids. V. The age dependence of the content of some amino acids in the blood and normalization through supply of cysteine. *Z. Naturforsch. [B]*, 16b:142, 1961.

Riemschneider, R.: Amino acids. XI. Intermediary metabolism and age. 5. Amino acid content of human and animal blood in relation to age. *Monatsh. Chem.* 95:184, 1964.

Riemschneider, R.; Göehring, O., and Froeomming, E.: Amino acids. VI. Alteration of the amino acid content of blood with old age. *Z. Naturforsch [B]*, 16:704, 1961.

Schulze, W.: Untersuchungen uber den Eiweiss-Stoff-wechsel im alter. *Z. Alternsforsch.* 8:65, 1954.

Sergienko, E. F.: *TR. N.-1 ta Biologii*, 25:75, 1947.

Shemin, D., and Rittenberg, D.: Some interrelations in general N metabolism. *J. Biol. Chem.*, 153:401, 1944.

Shereshevskaya, T. M.: Age differences in the turnover rate of phosphorus fractions of liver tissue, *Biokhimiae* 26:618, 1962a.

Shereshevskaya, T. M.: Age characteristics of nucleic acid turnover and their qualitative composition in liver. *Vop. Geront. Geriatrii*, 30, 1962b.

Shock, N. W.: Age changes in physiological functions in the total animal: The role of tissue loss. In *The Biology of Aging*. Strehler, B. L., Ed. New York, 1960, p. 258.

Silin, O. P.: Rate of restoration of proteins in muscle and liver during ontogenesis. *Uch Zap. Khar'kovsk Gos. Univ. 108, Tr. Nauchnoissled. Inst. Biol. i Biol. Fak*, 29:53, 1960.

Stavitskaya, L. I.: Changes in tissue ribonuclease activity with age. *Uch. Zap. Khar'kovsk Gos. Univ. im A.M. Gor'kogo* 24, 68:59, 1956.

Stedman, E., and Stedman, E.: The basic proteins of cell nuclei. *Phil. Trans. Roy. Soc. London, Ser. B.*, 235:565 1951.

von Theimer, W.: Quantitative changes in free amino acids in serum in old age. *Naturwissenschaften*, 51:465, 1964.

Torre, M.; Baggio, G. F.; Scarzella, R., and Zanalda, A.: Gli amino-acidi liberi del sangue in soggetti di varia eta studiati con metodo cromatografico. *G. Gerontol.*, 2:389, 1954.

Torre, M.; Scarzella, R., and Zanalda, A.: Chromatographic investigation of the free amino acids in the cerebrospinal fluid of normal senile subjects. *Bull. Soc. Itul. Biol. Sper.*, 31:64, 1955.

Tuttle, S. G.; Swenseid, M. E.; Mulcare, D. B.; Griffith, W. H. and Bassett, S. H.: Study of the essential amino acid requirements of men over 50. *Metabolism*, 6:564, 1957.

TUTTLE, S. G.; BASSETT, S. H.; GRIFFITH, W. H.; MULCARE, D. B., and SWENDSEID, M. E.: Further observations on the amino acid requirements of older men. I. Effects of nonessential nitrogen supplements fed with different amounts of essential amino acids. *Amer. J. Clin. Nutr.* 16:225, 1965a.

TUTTLE, S. G.; BASSETT, S. H.; GRIFFITH, W. H.; MULCARE, D. B., and SWENDSEID, M. E.: Further observations on the amino acid requirements of older men. II. Methionine and lysine. *Amer. J. Clin. Nutr.,* 16:229, 1965b.

UEBEL, H.: Changes in serum proteins of Wistar rats with age. Z. *Alternsforsch, 10:*149, 1956.

VANZETTI, G.; MARS, G., and FORMIGA-ORAZI, G.: Investigation of the protein fractions and of the polysaccharides bound to the protein in the serum of elderly persons. *Minerva Med., 431:*1052, 1952.

WANG, I., and KIRK, J. E.: The total glutathione content of arterial tissue in individuals of various ages. *J. Geront.* 15:35, 1960.

WEISS, S. B., and GLADSTONE, L.: A mammalian system for the incorporation of cytidinetriphosphate into ribonucleic acid. *J. Amer. Chem. Soc., 81:*4118, 1959.

WILD, C. I.; REYMOND, C. I., and VANNOTTI, A.: Amino acid absorption. *Schweiz. Med. Wschr.,* 83:894, 1953.

WULFF, V. J.; PIEKIELNIAK, M., and WAYNER, M. J., JR.: The ribonucleic acid (RNA) content of tissues of rats of different ages. *J. Geront. 18:* 322, 1963.

WULFF, V. J., QUASTLER, H., and SHERMAN, F. G: The incorporation of H3-cytidine in mice of different ages. *Arch. Biochem.* 95:548, 1961.

WULFF, V. J.; QUASTLER, H., and SHERMAN, F. G.: An hypothesis concerning RNA metabolism and aging. *Proc. Nat. Acad. Sci., U.S.A., 48:* 1373, 1962.

WULFF, V. J.; QUASTLER, H.; SHERMAN, F. G., and SAMIS, H. V., JR.: The effect of specific activity of H3-cytidine on its incorporation into tissues of young and old mice. *J. Geront. 20:*34, 1965.

Chapter 3

ENZYMES AND CELLULAR METABOLISM

ANITA ZORZOLI

INTRODUCTION

IN THE PREVIOUS CHAPTER, it was pointed out that DNA dictates the sequence of purine and pyrimidine bases in the ribonucleic acid (RNA) templates attached to the ribosomes of the endoplasmic reticulum. The sequence of purines and pyrimidines of the RNA, in turn, dictates the sequence of amino acids in proteins. An important group of proteins are the enzymes which are found in all living cells. Enzymes are biological catalysts which serve to increase the rate of chemical reactions in the body. Enzymes are involved in the metabolism of protein, fat, and carbohydrates. They are involved in digestion and absorption of food, excretion of carbon dioxide; transport of oxygen, blood clotting, muscle contraction, calcification, etc. Without enzymes, reactions would occur at too slow a rate to maintain body processes.

It has been clearly demonstrated that aging is accompanied by decline in the physiological performance of many organs and organ systems. Man, the object of intensive study, may undergo reductions as large as 50 per cent in certain renal, respiratory and cardiovascular functions (Shock, 1961). To account for such age-related alterations one must consider, among other things, the possibility that there has been age-related change in biochemical mechanisms operative at the cellular level. The logic behind this choice is simply the time-honored idea that the cell is the basic unit of living tissue. Its activity determines not only the nature but the extent of function at the tissue, organ, and system levels.

In addition one must consider that age-related changes in

physiological performance may result from the actual loss of functioning tissue. For example, death of irreplaceable cells, changes in the numbers of subcellular particulates, replacement of cytoplasm by metabolically inactive material—all phenomena known to occur in living organisms obviously would affect the functional capacity of the tissue or organ.

Enzyme-catalyzed reactions, which form the basis for biochemical mechanisms, have been investigated in some detail as a function of the age of the organism. The bulk of the studies has been carried out in mammals and has been aimed at determining and quantitating changes in enzymatic activities which occur with age. A few studies have been concerned with senescent changes in cellular metabolism under experimental conditions.

This chapter will review the studies of enzyme activity and cellular metabolism in aging. Where necessary for clarity, the exact ages used will be reported, for there appear to be differences in the literature in the use of the word *old*. The ages considered by some authors to be old ages are regarded by others as young or adult ages. For example, Devi *et al.* (1963) compared rats of young age, middle age, and old age. Their *old* animals had a maximum chronological age of fourteen months. On the other hand, Barrows and Roeder (1961) considered twenty-four-month-old rats to be *old* animals and twelve-month-old rats to be *young* animals. Where possible, information on the number of cells or cell particulates will be correlated with the biochemical data. Investigations centering solely on the time of growth and development will not be included.

It is general biochemical practice to express enzyme activity with reference to one or more of a number of different parameters: wet weight; dry weight; protein content; nitrogen content and DNA content of tissue; organ weight and body weight; average cell, cell fraction, and number of cell particulates. In studies where organisms of different ages are used it is important to determine if age has any effect on the parameter itself, for it is obvious that changes will influence the interpretation of the data.

When DNA is used as an index of cell number the assumption must be made that the amount of DNA per nucleus does not change in senescence. In rat liver (Falzone *et al.*, 1959) and rat kidney (Adams and Barrows, 1963) this appears to be true; other tissues have not been specifically investigated. Another point which must be considered when making biochemical studies is the possible effect of age on the character of the cell population. There is some evidence that one cell type may replace another in senescence, e.g., replacement of neuronal elements by glial cells in the brain (Himwich, 1962), and that changes in the connective tissue elements may occur, e.g. in the small intestine (Andrew, 1962b). This is an area in which correlation of biochemical studies and anatomical studies is of great value.

TABLE XI

NORMAL ARTERIAL TISSUE: ENZYMES WHICH DO NOT CHANGE IN ACTIVITY WITH AGE

Enzyme	Range of Ages Studied (years)	Species
Hexokinase[1]	0.2-87	Human
Phosphoglucoisomerase[1]	0.2-87	Human
Enolase[2]	0.0-79	Human
Glucose 6-phosphate dehydrogenase[1]	0.3-85	Human
6-Phosphogluconate dehydrogenase[1]	0.3-85	Human
Aconitase[3]	0.0-85	Human
Isocitric dehydrogenase[4]	0.0-85	Human
Malic dehydrogenase[1]	0.2-83	Human
NADP-Malic enzyme[4]	0.0-85	Human
Leucine aminopeptidase[5]	0.0-79	Human
Cathepsin[6]	0.0-87	Human
Acid phosphatase[1]	0.0-85	Human
Adenyl pyrophosphatase[1]	0.0-85	Human
Inorganic pyrophosphatase[1]	0.0-85	Human
Purine nucleoside phosphorylase[7]	0.0-87	Human
Carbonic anhydrase[8]	0.0-87	Human
Succinoxidase[9]	0.4-2.5	Rabbit
Succinoxidase[9]	0.4-2.5	Dog
Aspartic-a-ketoglutaric transaminase[10]	young-old	Cattle

[1]Kirk, J. E.: *Ann. N.Y. Acad. Sci.*, 72:1006, 1959.
[2]Wang, I., and Kirk, J. E.: *J. Geront.* 14:444, 1959.
[3]Laursen, T. J. S., and Kirk, J. E.: *J. Geront.* 10:26, 1965
[4]Kirk, J. E.: *J. Geront.*, 15:262, 1960b.
[5]Kirk, J. E.: *J. Geront.*, 15:136, 1960a.
[6]Kirk, J. E.: *J. Geront.*, 17:158, 1962.
[7]Kirk, J. E.: *J. Geront.*, 16:243, 1961.
[8]Kirk, J. E., and Hansen, P. F.:*J. Geront.* 8:150, 1953.
[9]Maier, N., and Haimovici, H.: *Proc. Soc. Exp. Biol. Med.*, 95:425, 1957.
[10]Mandel, P., and Kempf, E.: *C.R. Soc. Biol.*, 154:791, 1960.

CIRCULATORY SYSTEM

Arteries

Much of the information on enzyme systems in arterial tissue has come from the work of Kirk and collaborators over a period of many years. These studies have revealed that the vascular wall contains enzymes of the major metabolic pathways identified in other tissues, i.e. glycolysis, hexose monophosphate shunt, tricarboxylic acid cycle, oxidative chain. In addition, enzymes which are part of a variety of other pathways have been reported (Kirk, 1963). Some enzymes show significant changes in activity with age; other enzymes are apparently unaffected by the passage of time.

In all studies of enzyme activity in the arterial wall the tissue used has been taken from the intimal and medial layers. Aorta, pulmonary arteries, and coronary arteries have been investigated in man. In other species only the aorta has been studied.

Table XI contains a list of arterial wall enzymes, studied by the Kirk group and other investigators, which do not change significantly in activity in individuals of different ages. It will be noted that the list is a very varied one containing enzymes of different metabolic pathways.

Figures 3 and 4 show the changes in enzyme activities which have been reported in normal human arterial tissue as a function of age. The childhood years during which growth and development occur have been omitted and the mean values for enzyme activities (calculated on the basis of wet weight of tissue) in the second decade of life have been taken as the reference point (100 percent activity) with which to compare activity at older ages.

Lactic dehydrogenase and aldolase (Fig. 3), both of which are enzymes of glycolysis, exhibit increased activity from the reference base to fifty to fifty-nine and seventy years of age, respectively. Then the activity declines, especially in the case of lactic dehydrogenase which again reaches the reference level. It is known that the rate of glycolysis is comparatively high in arterial tissue (Kirk, 1963). Of the five glycolytic enzymes

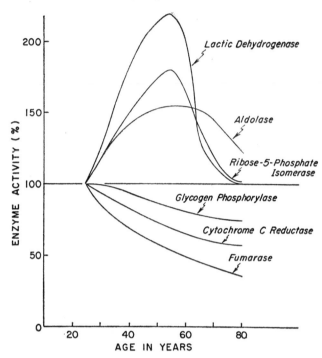

FIGURE 3. Effect of age on enzyme activities of normal human aortic tissue. (Kirk, J. E.: In *Fundamentals of Vascular Grafting*, S. A. Weslowski and C. Dennis, Eds. New York, McGraw-Hill, 1963, p. 32.

which have been studied in arterial tissue, hexokinase, phosphogluco-isomerase and enolase do not show change in activity with increasing age (Table XI), whereas lactic dehydrogenase and aldolase do. It would be tempting to speculate that the last-named are rate-limiting in this type of tissue and increase in activity when physiological stresses make greater demands. However, the activity data (Kirk, 1963) do not bear out this idea.

It has been reported that aldolase (Mandel *et al.*, 1959) and lactic dehydrogenase (Mandel and Kempf, 1960) activities are significantly lower in the aorta of old cattle as compared with young animals. It is difficult to determine if these findings are really of the same nature as those for the human since specific ages were not given. All that can be said is that, at the two ages selected, the older group exhibited lower enzyme activity than the younger group. Mandel and Kempf (1960) also

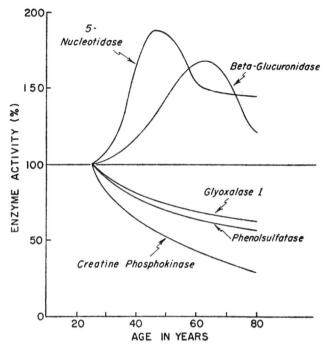

FIGURE 4. Effect of age on enzyme activities of normal human aortic tissue. (Kirk, J. E.: In *Fundamentals of Vascular Grafting*. S. A. Weslowski and C. Dennis, Eds. New York, McGraw-Hill, 1963, p. 32.

reported that malic dehydrogenase activity is lower in old animals; for human tissue, age-related changes in this enzyme do not occur (Table XI).

Ribose 5-phosphate isomerase (Fig. 3) exhibits a pattern of age changes very similar to that noted before (LHD), i.e. an increase in activity followed by a decline to the base level. Other enzymes of hexose monophosphate shunt, glucose 6-dehydrogenase and 6-phosphogluconate dehydrogenase, do not show age changes (Table XI).

The phosphatase, 5-nucleotidase (Fig. 4), increases in activity up to about age fifty, then declines and finally levels off in the sixth and seventh decades of life. Beta-glucuronidase (Fig. 4) activity increases to the ages of fifty to sixty-nine years and then declines, but not down to the reference base.

Six enzymes of normal human arterial tissue have been

shown to decrease significantly with age (Figs. 3 and 4). Of
these, creatine phosphokinase and glycogen phosphorylase are
the most interesting. It is likely that they are associated mainly
with the smooth muscle of the arterial wall, for considerably
higher activity is found in the muscular coronary and brachial
arteries than in the elastic aorta. The decline in activity noted
with age may be associated with the reduction in muscle fibers
which is known to occur with increasing age (Kirk, 1963).

Fumarase activity (Fig. 3) declines sharply until about
fifty-nine years and more slowly at older ages. Other enzymes
of the citric acid cycle—aconitase, isocitric dehydrogenase, succinic dehydrogenase, malic dehydrogenase—do not change with
age (Table XI).

Mallov (1964) reported that lipoprotein lipase activity in the
aorta of old male Holtzman albino rats and old male New Zealand
white rabbits is significantly lower than in young animals of the
same species. The young animals studied were 4 to 5 months;
the old animals, over one year of age. It would seem more appropriate to refer to the latter as adult animals rather than old
animals for neither the rat nor the rabbit enters the period of
senescence before two years of age.

Succinoxidase activity, determined by the utilization of succinate and p-phenylenediamine, has been demonstrated in human aortae of two age groups: one-day-old to seventeen-years,
and twenty-one to seventy-three years. Activity was higher in the
younger group (Maier and Haimovici, 1957). It is unfortunate
that the authors pooled material from such widely differing ages.
Certainly in the older group, young adult, adult, and senescent
tissues were present, making it impossible to determine if any
change occurred with aging.

Heart

In contrast to the detailed analysis of the enzymology of
the arterial wall, very few studies have been made on metabolism of heart tissue as a function of age. Monoamine oxidase, an
enzyme involved in the catabolism of catecholamines, appears
at four weeks of age in the rat heart and increases steadily in
activity with age (Novick, 1961; Gey *et al.*, 1964). DOPA de-
carboxylase, which is concerned with the synthesis of catechol-

amines, decreases significantly in the first year of life in the rat (Gey *et al.*, 1964). The total level of catecholamines also decreases significantly but not until 17 months of age (Gey *et al.*, 1964). It seems likely that the decrease in catecholamines is related to the changes in enzyme activity but not exclusively so, since the former occurs well after the changes in enzyme activity.

Succinoxidase activity of rat heart homogenates has been variously reported to remain unchanged from 2 months to 12 months of age (Shirley and Davis, 1959), to increase slightly up to 12 months of age (Barrows and Roeder, 1961), and to decrease slightly from 12 to 24 months of age (Barrows *et al.*, 1958b; Barrows and Roeder, 1961).

Nikitin and Pashkova (1963) investigated the rate of caprylic and acetic acid oxidation by cardiac tissue homogenates in albino rats of several age groups. A significant decline of oxidation rate occurred for both caprylic acetic acids in the age interval between three months and 12 months. Further reductions occurred at 24 months of age, particularly for caprylic acid which decreased 50 per cent. Endogenous respiration of heart muscle did not vary with age.

A very interesting phenomenon observed in cardiac muscle is the accumulation of lipofuscin granules with increasing age. This subject will be reviewed in the section on the neuromuscular system.

Blood

Erythrocytes

The mammalian erythrocyte has a finite lifespan, amounting in the human to approximately 120 days. At the termination of its lifespan it is removed from the circulation and destroyed. Indeed, there is a constant turnover of cells in the blood and an ordinary peripheral blood sample contains a mixture of erythrocytes of all ages.

Much effort has been devoted to study of the changes which occur with age in the erythrocyte. The findings were reviewed recently by Harris in an elegant monograph on the red cell and to which the reader is referred (Harris, 1963). However, it will not be amiss to point out here that many alterations in cell energetics and levels and activities of various enzymes have been reported. It is not known if these changes actually constitute the aging process in the erythrocyte *in vivo* or if they are merely concomitant alterations.

In addition to studies of the metabolism of young and old erythrocytes, investigators have been concerned with the enzymatic activities of erythrocytes taken from organisms of different chronological ages. Much of this work is the result of the efforts of Bertolini and collaborators and has been reviewed by Bertolini recently (1964a). In general it can be said that enzyme activities of red blood cells from aged human subjects, compared with young subjects, display multidirectional changes. It is not possible at the moment to interpret the results in terms of mechanisms of aging.

Plasma

Many different enzymes can be detected in plasma, i.e. acid phophatase, alkaline phosphatase, glutamic-aspartic transaminase, and lactic dehydrogenase, but it is unlikely that they play any specific metabolic role in plasma (with the exception of the coagulation process) (White *et al.*, 1964). Nevertheless, measurements of enzyme activities have definite value as aids to diagnosis in clinical medicine.

Some studies of blood enzymes in senescent humans and other mammals have been made over a period of years. These were reviewed by Oeriu (1964). Once again it appears that a variety of alterations occur which cannot, at the moment, be fitted into a meaningful pattern.

DIGESTIVE SYSTEM

Liver

Parenchymal cells constitute 90 to 95 per cent of the cellular mass of the liver (Bucher, 1963) and are the sites of the many diverse metabolic activities of this organ. They undergo some anatomical change as a result of aging but not striking ones (Andrew, 1962a,b). There is little evidence of a decline in cell number with increasing age (Shock, 1964).

Oxidative Metabolism

Among the enzymes involved in oxidative metabolism,

succinic dehydrogenase, fumarase, and the succinoxidase system have been investigated in different species. Barrows *et al.* (1958b; 1960) measured succinoxidase activity in both homogenates and mitochondria of old rats (24 to 27 months) as compared with young rats (12 to 14 months) and were unable to demonstrate any age-related differences. Ross and Ely (1954) did not find a change in succinic dehydrogenase activity in old (21 months) rats. On the other hand, Oeriu (1964) reported that progressive decreases in the activation energies of succinic dehydrogenase and the succinoxidase system in liver of albino rats of various ages from 15 days to 26 months have been observed.

More recently Tauchi *et al.* (1964) made a study correlating succinic dehydrogenase activity with the number and size of mitochondria in hepatic cells of rats of different ages. Numbers of mitochondria per cubic hepatic cell were counted at 3,439.6±566.6 in the center of the lobule of young adult animals (4 to 6 months); 4,358.7±302.0 in the periphery of the lobule of young adults; 1,900.8±213.7 in the center of the lobule of old rats (over 24 months); 2,548.7±183.3 in the periphery of the lobule of old rats. The differences in mitochondrial numbers in old and young animals were significant to the 5 per cent level for the center of the lobule and to the 1 per cent level for the periphery of the lobule. Mitochondria of the parenchymal cells of old rats were shown to be significantly larger in size than those of young adult animals. Succinic dehydrogenase (per mg N) which is associated with mitochondrial structure did not exhibit age-related differences in activity. The decrease in mitochondrial number, increase in mitochondrial size, and lack of change of succinic dehydrogenase activity were interpreted as indicating an increase in enzyme activity in each mitochondrion of the old rats. It might be noted here that Andrew (1962a), in light and electron microscope studies of senescent mouse liver, also found evidence of a decrease in the number of mitochondria in parenchymal cells.

The specific activity of fumarase in mouse liver has been found to rise approximately twofold from late prenatal life to one month of age and then to remain essentially constant through 24 months of age (Zorzoli, unpublished data). Mitochondrial counts were not made in this study. However, if one extrapolates from

Andrew's work, which also was on the C57B1/6 mouse, fumarase activity per mitochondrion is higher in senile liver than in adult liver.

Studies of changes with age in total oxygen uptake in tissue slices and tissue homogenates were reviewed by Barrows (1956). Conflicting evidence and the need for additional data were noted. Since then several studies have appeared. Robillard *et al.* (1956) reported that there is no difference in the oxygen consumption of liver homogenates, nuclei or mitochondria (using glucose and succinate as substrates) in two-year-old rats as compared with nuclear and mitochondrial numbers per unit of wet liver in one-year-old animals. They also reported the absence of change the old rats.

Barrows *et al.* (1958b) were unable to detect changes in endogenous uptake of oxygen by liver slices of old rats (24 to 27 months). No agewise differences were noted in oxidative phosphorylation (stimulated by succinate) of homogenates prepared from livers of 12 to 14-month-old and 24 to 27-month-old rats (Barrows *et al.*, 1960). Weinbach and Garbus (1956, 1959) reported that the amount of phosphate esterified and the amount of B-hydroxy-butyrate oxidized by liver mitochondria isolated from 24-month-old rats was 30 per cent lower than similar preparations from 3-month-old rats. These authors were not able to detect age decrements in the rate of phosphorylation and P/O ratios using succinate, a-ketoglutatate, glutamate or malate in fresh preparations. Age-related differences were evident after prolonged storage of the mitochondria at 4°C or after receiving other pretreatments, e.g. freezing and thawing (Weinbach and Garbus, 1959).

Thus, there is some lack of agreement relative to oxidative metabolism in liver. However, it is fair to say that none of the data provide striking evidence in favor of changes in oxidative metabolism during senescence.

Amino Acid and Protein Metabolism

A number of enzymes associated with various aspects of amino acid and protein metabolism have been studied in aging. The specific activity of tryptophan peroxidase more than doubles from 38 days to 400 days of age in the rat (Rivlin and Knox,

1959). Then from 12 to 13 months to 24 to 26 months there is no further change (Gregerman, 1959). Tyrosine transaminase also does not change in senescence as compared with adult life (Gregerman, 1959).

The concentration of D-amino acid oxidase in rat liver, calculated per gram of wet weight of tissue, increases from 1 to 12 months of age and then decreases about 12 per cent in 24-month-old animals (Barrows and Roeder, 1961). In this study a decrease in the number of cells, as estimated by the concentration of DNA, was noted. The change in enzyme activity could be accounted for by the change in DNA. Cathepsin, on the other hand, was unchanged in animals up to 12 months of age but was strikingly elevated in senescent rats. This suggested an increased rate of protein catabolism in aging. However, study of the rate of disappearance of radioactivity from liver following administration of S35-labeled methionine did not indicate anything more than a slight elevation of protein breakdown in senescence (Barrows and Roeder, 1961).

Several studies have been made to test the ability of senescent tissue to synthesize protein (see Chapter 2, Nucleic Acids and Proteins). Gregerman (1959) measured the adaptive synthesis of tryptophan peroxidase and tyrosine transaminase resulting from hydrocortisone or tryptophan treatment. His conclusion was that the senescent rat liver is capable of responding with an increase in protein synthesis equivalent to that of younger animals.

In an experiment of different design, Barrows and Roeder (1961) also demonstrated unimpaired enzyme synthesis in senescent animals. They maintained rats of different ages (3.5, 12, and 24 months) on a protein-free diet for 21 days (depleted). Then the animals were refed a normal diet (repleted) for 3 and 7 days. The concentrations of succinoxidase, pyprophosphatase, D-amino acid oxidase and pseudocholinesterase decreased markedly during depletion (Fig. 5). These enzymes were restored to their original levels or almost so in seven days of repletion. No age-related differences in enzymatic activities were evident either during depletion or repletion with the exception of D-amino acid oxidase, the activity of which was higher in young than in adult or senescent animals. Catheptic activity was

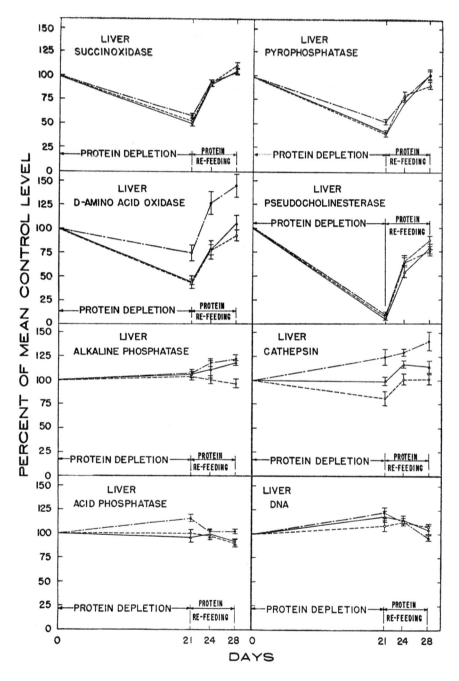

←————————

FIGURE 5. Enzymatic activities in liver of fed, protein-depleted and protein-depleted refed rats of different ages. The mean enzymatic activities for
the depleted, 3-day repleted, and 7-day repleted animals are expressed as the
percentage of the mean enzymatic activity of the normal animals of corresponding age. Vertical bars represent the standard errors of the mean.
(— · — = 3.5-month-old animals, - - - = 12-month-old animals, ———— =
24-month-old animals). (Barrows, C. H., and Roeder, L. M.: *J. Geront.*,
16:321, 1961.)

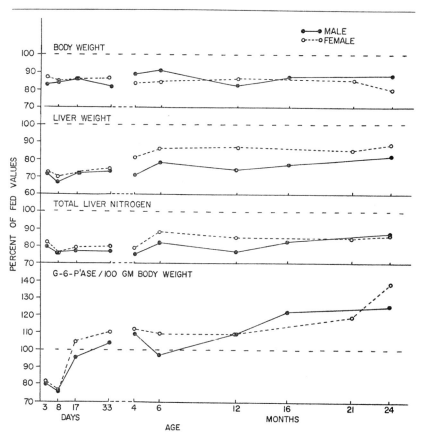

FIGURE 6. Effects of 24-hour fasting in mice of different ages. At each age
the data are plotted as mean values for fasted animals expressed as a
per cent of the mean values for fed animals of the same age. For the sake
of clarity the data for 16-day-old animals which parallel those for 17-day-
old animals have been omitted. (Zorzoli, A.: In *Age With a Future*, P. F.
Hansen, ed. Copenhagen, Munksgaard, 1964, p. 175.)

different for each age group but rose during repletion in each case.

Recently Zorzoli (1964) demonstrated age differences in the response of mouse liver glucose-6-phosphatase to 24-hour fasting. However, once again it was clear that senescent liver synthesized enzyme protein at a rate equal to that of younger ages. Animals ranging in age from 3 days to 24 months were fasted for 24 hours and then were sacrificed immediately. Significant decreases in body weight, liver weight, and liver nitrogen occurred at each age studied (Fig. 6). In young animals, 3 and 8 days of age, the total available glucose-6-phosphatase activity (activity per 100 grams body weight) of fasted animals was significantly lower than for fed controls of the same ages. At 16, 17, and 33 days; 4, 6, and 12 months of age, small but not significant changes occurred. In senile animals the glucose-6-phosphatase activity per 100 grams of body weight was significantly elevated after 24-hour fasting.

These results confirmed Weber and Cantero's (1957) conclusion, based on studies of adult rats, that liver glucose-6-phosphatase is preferentially maintained after 24-hour fasting. Furthermore, these results suggested that ability of C57B1/6 mice to maintain liver glucose-6-phosphatase in the face of loss of nitrogen due to fasting is developed in the period between the 8th and 16th days of life. The significant increase in total available activity occurring in senile animals indicated that more enzyme is available in these animals after fasting than in younger animals. It was concluded that senescent mouse liver retains the ability to synthesize enzyme protein to the same degree as that of younger animals.

Enzyme Studies

Nonspecific alkaline phosphatase activity changes very little from 1 to 12 months of age but rises significantly in senescence (Zorzoli, 1955). Acid phosphatase, on the other hand, shows a downward trend in activity from 11 to 24 months of age, but the differences are not significant (Zorzoli, 1955). Glucose-6-phosphatase, which is present in low concentrations in fetal animals, rises, reaching a peak a few days after birth, and then declines to the adult level which is maintained into senescence (Zorzoli, 1962). The activity of each of these enzymes was calculated per unit of tissue nitrogen in mouse liver.

In rat liver, total acid phosphatase activity does not change in senescence (Barrows and Roeder, 1961; Franklin, 1962); pyrophosphatase (Barrows and Roeder, 1961) increases from 1 to 3.5 months of age but does not change at older ages. Cholinphosphatase (Barrows and Roeder, 1961) declines from 1 to 3.5 months of age but does not change at older ages. Choinesterase activity does not change in senescence (Barrows *et al.*, 1958a; Bertolini, 1964b). Pseudocholinesterase also does not change in senescence, but increases from 1 to 12 months of age (Barrows and Roeder, 1961). Hexokinase activity is unchanged in the liver of old rats (Bertolini, 1964b).

Acid DNAase and alkaline DNAase have been studied in mouse liver (Kurnick and Kernen, 1962). The acid DNAase activity bears a low correlation with age. Alkaline DNAase reaches a peak of approximately 2.5 times the level at 10 days on the 147th day of life and then gradually falls with advancing age.

Intestine

Enzyme activity in the intestine of senescent animals has not received much attention. A recent study of mucosal preparations from the proximal two-thirds of the mouse small intestine revealed that fumarase activity does not change with increasing age (Zorzoli, unpublished data). This is not surprising since intestinal epithelial cell renewal, even in senescence, occurs within a matter of days and therefore the cells are not of the same chronological age as the organism (Lesher, 1961).

The absorption of glucose in the small intestine is linked to the metabolism of the epithelial cells. Calingaert and Zorzoli (1965), using an *in vitro* method, measured the uptake of 6-deoxy-D-glucose by the small intestine of mice ranging in age from late gestation to senility. At all ages studied (including fetal), accumulation occurred against a concentration gradient. During the third week, uptake of the sugar was elevated. By the fourth week, the level of absorption was higher than at all younger ages and was equal to that of adult animals. Senile animals, 21 to 24 months of age, maintained the adult level of absorption.

Thus, oxidative metabolism of the mucosa, as indicated by fumarase activity, does not change during early postnatal life, but the transport of sugar undergoes developmental increases. Neither changes in senescence as compared with adult life.

URINARY SYSTEM

Kidney

The kidney is one of the organs, especially in the human, which exhibits decreases in functional capacities with increasing age. For example, there are decreases in renal blood flow, glomerular filtration rate, maximum excretory rates for diodrast, and maximum resorptive rate of glucose (Shock, 1961). The close relationship between the age decrements in these parameters suggests that nephrons disappear with increasing age (Shock, 1960).

Histological studies provide some evidence for renal changes with age. Using Wistar rats, Arataki (1926) found that the number of glomeruli increases progressively from birth, achieving the maximum number of 100 days. From this age to 350 days, no significant change occurs. However at 500 days, when the animals are beginning to senesce, the number of glomeruli is greatly reduced. Tubular changes, including some of atropic nature, have been reported by a number of investigators (Andrew and Pruett, 1957; Durand *et al.*, 1964; Kennedy *et al.*, 1960).

Barrows *et al.* (1958b) and Adams and Barrows (1963) have reported a small but significant decline in the concentration of DNA in kidney cortex of senile rats (26 to 33 months). Since there is no evidence that age influences the DNA content of kidney nuclei, the decrease in DNA content suggests fewer cells per unit wet weight in old animals. However, the results of DNA measurements are not unequivocal, for Barrows and his collaborators have not been able to detect significant age-related changes in DNA in all of their studies (Barrows *et al.*, 1960; Barrows and Roeder, 1961).

The rate of respiration of slices of kidney cortex was found to be lower in senile female rats than in adult animals. This decrement was paralleled by a change in DNA concentration, suggesting therefore, that the respiration per cell was not affected by age (Barrows *et al.*, 1958b). Interestingly, the same authors found decrements in the concentrations of succinoxidase, succinic dehydrogenase and cytochrome oxidase of kidney cortex homogenates which exceeded the reduction in the concentration of DNA (Barrows *et al.*, 1958b). A subsequent study showed that the succinoxidase activity of mitochondria isolated from kidney cortex was not different in senile animals from adult animals. These data suggested that the agewise decrement in the metabolic activity noted for whole homogenates of kidney cortex resulted from a loss of mitochondria from the tissue rather than from changes in the concentration of the enzymes per mitochondrion (Barrows *et al.*, 1960).

In the section on liver an experiment involving protein depletion and repletion of rats of different ages was described. Study of the effects of these procedures was also made for kidney enzymes. As in liver, no marked age differences were noted. These data were interpreted as offering no evidence of an impairment in enzyme synthesis in senescent animals (Barrows and Roeder, 1961).

Alkaline DNAase has been found to rise approximately seven fold during maturation of the kidney. In senescence the activity is slightly lower than the peak value (Kurnick and Kernen, 1962).

Total acid phosphatase activity per unit nitrogen decreases in the rat kidney from 10 to 15 weeks of age to 23 to 25 months. The difference between adult animals (12 to 14 months) and senile animals (23 to 25 months) is statistically significant, P <.001 (Franklin, 1962).

It was noted earlier that active transport has been studied in the small intestine as a function of age. The accumulation of p-aminohippuric acid (PAH) by kidney cortex slices, also an energy requiring process, was investigated recently in rats (Adams and Barrows, 1963) and mice (Berech and Curtis, 1964). In both species no age differences were noted when the incubation medium contained low concentrations of PAH. However, when senescent rat kidney cortex slices were incubated in a system containing a high concentration of PAH (200 μg/cc) the accumulation after sixty minutes was markedly lower than in either young or adult animals. Thus, the senescent kidney slices were not able to meet the greater energy demands imposed by this system (Adams and Barrows, 1963).

DNA measurements indicated that fewer cells were present per unit wet weight of the kidney slices, a fact which could account for the age decrement in active transport. However, the senescent alteration in PAH accumulation greatly exceeded the DNA change. Thus, it can be suggested that kidney cortex cells undergo some biochemical changes either in the energy-producing system or in a specific PAH transport system during senescence.

It is apparent that the kidney shows age-related changes at the biochemical level as well as at the physiological level. There is evidence not only of cell loss as a function of age, but also of decrease in cell particulates, the mitochondria, in those cells remaining. However, the changes at the biochemical level, with the possible exception of maximum active PAH accumulation, are of a considerably smaller order of magnitude than those observed at the organ level.

NEUROMUSCULAR SYSTEM

Nerve and muscle cells were classified many years ago by Cowdry (1952) as fixed postmitotic cells. These units do not have the ability to divide during the postnatal existence of the organism. Therefore, unlike other types, e.g. intestinal epithelial cells, which retain the ability to divide throughout the lifespan of the organism, they are presumably of the same chronological age as the organism itself. Study of the metabolism of nondividing cells is clearly of special interest in the elucidation of the mechanism(s) of aging. Unfortunately, however, very little has been done on any but young and adult ages.

Brain

It is of some importance in the study of the neurochemistry of aging to determine if a loss of neurons occurs with increasing age. According to Himwich (1962), there is much information from histological studies indicating that this does indeed occur in the human brain. The loss of neuronal elements is followed by replacement with glial cells, although not in a quantitative fashion. Wright and Spink (1959) have suggested that neuronal loss is a constantly occurring process which does not increase with increasing age.

Oxidative Metabolism

Although the literature is not extensive, there are several types of studies which indicate a decline in oxygen consumption with age. Kety (1955) and Himwich and Himwich (1959) have reviewed the results of the work on whole human brain. According to these authors, there is a rapid fall in oxygen utilization of brain from childhood through adolescence followed by a more gradual but progressive reduction through the remainder of the lifespan.

In homogenates of rat brain, oxygen consumption per unit dry weight rises to the adult level during the first month of postnatal life, is maintained until 24 months of age, and then drops to a considerably lower level (Reiner, 1947).

In mice the respiration of brain suspensions, calculated either on the basis of fresh or dry weight, increases sharply with age to a maximum during the third month, after which there seems to be a slight decline with advance in age to 586 days (Desbarats-Schonbaum and Birmingham, 1959).

When the oxygen utilization of parts of the brain is measured, a decrease with age is seen to occur. Bürger (1962) reported a significant reduction in oxygen consumption (per unit of wet weight) of cortex, thalamus, medulla oblongata, and caudate nucleus in senile dogs as compared with adult animals.

It is not known yet whether the age-related decrements in oxygen consumption are due to changes in the metabolism of the brain cells or are merely the result of loss of cells. The observations that mitochondrial preparations from senescent rat brain do not differ significantly from those of young animals with respect to oxygen utilization and P:O ratio (Weinbach and Garbus, 1959) support the latter hypothesis.

Enzyme Studies

Starting from the finding that the glutamine content of the

brain is decreased in old rats, Oeriu (1964) studied glutaminase activity in rats of various ages. The amount of NH_3 released as a result of enzyme action was more than twofold higher in adult than in young animals and almost fourfold higher in old than in young animals.

Phenolsulfatase, glutamic-oxaloacetic transaminase and glutamic-pyruvic transaminase activities have been recorded as decreasing in old rat brain (Bertolini, 1964b). Aldolase, on the other hand, was reported to increase in activity in old brain (Bertolini, 1964b).

Although this chapter is concerned chiefly with mammalian species, it is not inappropriate to mention Rockstein's (1950) very interesting study of the relation of cholinesterase activity to change in cell number with age in the brain of the worker honeybee. It was found that a steady decrease occurred in the number of brain cells beginning at the time of emergence of the bees and continuing to old age. Cholinesterase activity, on the other hand, increased significantly during the first week after emergence and continued undiminished until extreme old age. How the increased enzyme activity was mediated while the cell number continued to decrease was open to speculation.

Spinal Cord

It was pointed out recently by Bondareff (1964) that Nissl substance, which is influenced by the physiological and metabolic states of neurons, has been variously reported to decline in aging, or not to be affected by age. In his own studies of the second cervical ganglion of the rat, Bondareff (1962) noted that cytoplasmic basophilia (primarily a function of Nissl substance staining) was lower in 20-month-old animals than in 3-month-old animals. Furthermore, when such animals were forced to swim to exhaustion, there was a difference in the ability of young and old animals to recover, as indicated by the pattern of distribution of Nissl substance. This difference was attributed to the older animals' inability to recover from the metabolic demands, i.e., synthesis, imposed by the experimental procedure.

Striated Muscle

It has already been noted that certain tissues, e.g. liver,

do not undergo loss of cells with aging, whereas tissues composed of nondividing cells, e.g. nervous tissue, exhibit age-dependent changes in cell number. Skeletal muscle, a tissue composed of fixed postmitotic cells, has also been shown to undergo loss of functioning protoplasm during aging. Using McCollum strain rats, Yiengst *et al.* (1959) demonstrated a significant decline in muscle mass (total skeletal muscle was removed from the hip to the knee of the hind limbs) and in the percentage of muscle mass to body weight in old (24 to 27 months) male rats. In the females similar changes occurred but were of smaller orders of magnitude. These authors also demonstrated a small but significant decrease in intracellular components in the aged rats using potassium as a tissue index of intracellular water. From the results of histological study, Andrew *et al.* (1959) also concluded that there is a decline in skeletal muscle mass in senescence.

Rockstein and collaborators studied enzyme changes in muscle, not only of mammalian forms (Rockstein and Brandt, 1961, 1963), but also of insects (Rockstein 1956, 1964; Rockstein and Brandt, 1962). In male Sprague-Dawley strain rats, gastrocnemius Mg-activated adenosine triphosphatase (ATPase) activity (calculated per gram fresh muscle) dropped in senile animals (26 months) to about 47 per cent of the activity of adult

TABLE XII

AGE CHANGES IN Mɢ-ATPᴀsᴇ ACTIVITY AND WEIGHT OF
GASTROCNEMIUS MUSCLE OF THE MALE WHITE RAT

	1	2	3	4
Strain	*Median age* *Mos.*	*ATPase Activ.*	*Muscle Wt.* *Grams*	*Muscle Wt./* *Body Wt.* *x* 10^{-3}
Sprague	9.5 (7-12)	.69($\pm$ .13)	4.58	11.93
Dawley	16.5 (13-20)	.51($\pm$ .18)	4.63	9.47
	26.0 (23-28)	.24($\pm$ .07)	2.45	6.69
CFN	8.0 (5-12)	.79($\pm$ .15)	4.10	8.92
	17.5 (14-18)	.58($\pm$ .10)	4.89	9.34
	26.0 (24-33)	.37($\pm$ .05)	4.55	7.91

Values in parentheses, column 1, show actual ranges of ages for the various median age groups. Data in columns 2 and 3 represent median enzyme activity and gastrocnemius muscle mass values for 10 animals of each median age group. ATPase activity is expressed in μg of P released in 15 minutes, per gram of fresh muscle mass. Values in parentheses in column 2 are probable deviation. (From Rockstein and Brandt, 1961).

animals (16.5 months). The total gastrocnemius muscle mass fell about 47 per cent and the muscle weight:body weight ratio declined approximately 27 per cent from the adult level. Thus, the loss of Mg-activated ATPase in senile animals was even greater on an absolute body weight basis than on a muscle weight basis (Table XII).

In CNF strain rats, there was about a 50 per cent decrease in enzyme activity, no change in muscle mass, and virtually no change in muscle:body ratio. Therefore, the enzyme activity on a body weight basis in the senile CFN males was more than twice that found in the Sprague-Dawley animals. In this connection, it is of interest to note that CFN rats are longer-lived than Sprague-Dawley ones and do not show signs of the muscular failure of the hind limbs at advanced age characteristic of Sprague-Dawley rats (Rockstein and Brandt, 1961).

The diaphragm, a thin layer of skeletal muscle separating the thoracic and abdominal cavities, has been used to study the activity of a respiratory enzyme during fetal and postnatal life of the mouse. It was found that the specific activity of fumarase rises slowly from prenatal levels to 6 months of age, the increase being about threefold. Older adult anmials and senile animals (24 months) do not show further change in activity (Zorzoli, unpublished data). It is not known if there is a loss of functional elements in the diaphragm in aging. However, there is no reason to assume that these muscles must respond to aging in the same fashion as do the locomotor muscles.

Age Pigment—Lipofuscin

Interest has developed in recent years in a category of intracellular bodies, lipofuscin granules, which are very notably present in neurons and cardiac muscle and also in other tissues, e.g. liver. These particulates, mainly lipoprotein in nature, are known to accumulate with age. In human myocardium, for example, the pigment increases at the rate of approximately 0.6 per cent of the total intracellular volume per decade (Strehler, 1964).

On the basis of combined light microscope, electron microscope, and histochemical observations it has been shown that acid phosphatase, β-glucuronidase, and other enzymes known to be characteristic of lysosomes can be identified at sites of lipofuscin accumulation (Strehler, 1964). It has been suggested that lysosomes are involved in the formation of lipofuscin pigment (see Samarajski *et al.*, 1964) and the reviews of Strehler (1964) and Bjorkerud (1964).

Several procedures have been developed for the isolation of lipofuscin granules. Consequently it has been possible to measure enzyme activity in this pigment in quantitative fashion. In isolated lipofuscin granules from cardiac muscle, acid phosphatase, cathepsin, acid desoxyribonuclease and acid ribonuclease have been detected (Bjorkerud, 1964).

It is not known if lipofuscin age pigments represent a causative factor in the aging process at the cellular level.

CONCLUSION

Biochemical studies of the effects of aging on different tissues and organs have been reviewed here. It was noted that in many instances age-related changes did not occur, e.g. protein synthesis was unaltered in senescent liver; in other instances declines in metabolic activities accompanied aging, e.g. decline of oxygen consumption of brain; finally, in a few cases, increases in activities occurred, e.g. elevation of catheptic activity in senescent liver.

In general, the changes noted at the biochemical level were of small order of magnitude. Some could be accounted for by cell loss or mitochondrial loss; others could not and appeared to be real age-related impairments at the biochemical level.

At the moment, the biochemical changes do not fall into discernible patterns which suggest specific mechanisms. However, it is of importance to note that the most striking changes in metabolic activities are found in those organs, e.g. kidney, which shows pronounced age-related decrements in physiological function.

REFERENCES

ADAMS, J. R., and BARROWS, C. H., JR.: *J. Geront.* 18:37, 1963.
ANDREW, W.: *Amer. J. Anat.* 110:1, 1962a.
ANDREW, W.: In *Biological Aspects of Aging."* Shock, N. W., Ed. New York, Columbia, 1962b, p. 123.
ANDREW, W., and PRUETT, D.: *Amer. J. Anat.* 100:51, 1957.

ANDREW, W.; SHOCK, N. W.; BARROWS, C. H., and YIENGST, M. J.: *J. Geront.,* 14:405, 1959.

ARATAKI, M.: *Amer. J. Anat.,* 36:399, 1926.

BARROWS, C. H., JR.: *Fed. Proc.* 15:954, 1956.

BARROW, S. H.; SHOCK, N. W., and CHOW, B. F.: *J. Geront.* 13:20, 1958a.

BARROWS, C. H.; YIENGST, M. J. and SHOCK, N. W.: *J. Geront.* 13:351, 1958b.

BARROWS, C. H.; FALZONE, J. A., and SHOCK, N. W.: *J. Geront.* 15:130, 1960.

BARROWS, C. H., and ROEDER, L. M.: *J. Geront.* 16:321, 1961.

BERECH, J., and CURTIS, H. J.: *Radiant. Res.,* 22:95, 1964.

BERTOLINI, A. M.: In *Age with a Future.* Hansen, P. F., Ed. Copenhagen, Munksgaard, 1964a, p. 165.

BERTOLINI, A. M.: Cited by Oeriu, S., in *Advances in Gerontological Research.* Strehler, B. L., Ed. New York, Academic, 1964b, vol. 1, p. 50.

BJORKERUD, S.: In *Advances in Gerontological Research.* Strehler, B. L., Ed. New York, Academic, 1964, vol. 1, p. 257.

BONDAREFF, W.: In *Biological Aspects of Aging.* Shock, N. W., Ed. New York, Columbia, 1962, p. 147.

BONDAREFF, W.: In *Advances in Gerontological Research.* Strehler, B. L., Ed. New York, Academic, 1964, vol. 1, p. 1.

BUCHER, N. L. R.: *Int. Rev. Cytol.,* 15:425, 1963.

BÜRGER, M.: Cited by Himwich, H. E.: *Geriatrics,* 17:89, 1962.

CALINGAERT, A., and ZORZOLI, A.: *J. Geront.* 20:211, 1965.

COWDRY, E. V.: In *Cowdry's Problems of Ageing,* 3rd ed., Lansing, A. I., Ed. Baltimore, Williams and Wilkins, 1952, p. 53.

DESBARATS-SCHONBAUM, M., and BIRMINGHAM, M. K.: *J. Geront.* 14:284, 1959.

DEVI, A.; MUKUNDAN, M. A.; SRIVASTAVA, U., and SARKAR, N. K.: *Exp. Cell Res.,* 32:242, 1963.

DIXON, M., and WEBB, E. C.: *Enzymes,* 2nd ed. New York, Academic, 1965, p. 672.

DURAND, A. M.; FISHER, M., and ADAMS, M.: *Arch. Path.* (Chicago), 77: 268, 1964.

FALZONE, J. A.; BARROWS, C. H., and SHOCK, N. W.: *J. Geront.,* 14:2, 1959.

FRANKLIN, T. J.: *Biochem. J.,* 82:118, 1962.

GEY, K. F.; BURKARD, W. P., and PLETSCHER, A.: In *Age With a Future.* Hansen, P. F., Ed. Copenhagen, Munksgaard, 1964, p. 181.

GREGERMAN, R. I.: *Amer. J. Physiol.* 197:63, 1959.

HARRIS, J. W.: *The Red Cell.* Cambridge, Harvard, 1963.

HIMWICH, H. E.: *Geriatrics,* 17:89, 1962.

HIMWICH, W. A., and HIMWICH, H. E.: In *Handbook of Aging and the Individual.* Birren, J. E., Ed. Chicago, Univ. of Chicago, 1959, p. 187.

KATO, R.; VASSENELLI, FRONTINO, G., and CHIESARA, E.: *Biochem. Pharmacol.* 13:1037, 1964.

KENNEDY, G. C.; FLEAR, C. T. G., and PARKER, R. A.: *Quart. J. Exp. Physiol.*, 45:82, 1960.

KETY, S. S.: In *Biochemistry of the Developing Nervous System.* Waelsch, H., Ed. New York, Academic, 1955, p. 208.

KIRK, J. E.: *Ann. N.Y. Acad. Sci.* 72:1006, 1959.

KIRK, J. E.: *J. Geront.* 15:136, 1960a.

KIRK, J. E.: *J. Geront.* 15:262, 1960b.

KIRK, J. E.: *J. Geront.* 16:243, 1961.

KIRK, J. E.: *J. Geront.*, 17:158, 1962.

KIRK, J. E.: In *Fundamentals of Vascular Grafting.* Wesolowski, S. A., and Dennis, C., Eds. New York, McGraw, 1963, p. 32.

KIRK, J. E., and HANSEN, P. F.: *J. Geront.* 8:150, 1953.

KURNICK, N. B., and KERNEN, R. L.: *J. Geront.* 17:245, 1962.

LAURSEN, T. J. S., and KIRK, J. E.: *J. Geront.* 10:26, 1955.

LESHER, S.; FRY, R. J. M., and KOHN, H. I.: *Lab. Invest.*, 10:291, 1961.

MAIER, N., and HAIMOVICI, H.: *Proc. Soc. Expj. Biol. Med.*, 95:425, 1957.

MALLOV, C.: *Circ. Res.*, 14:357, 1964.

MANDEL, P. and KEMPF, E.: *C. R. Soc. Biol.*, 154:791, 1960.

MANDEL, P.; PANTESCO, V.; KEMPF, E., and FONTAINE, R.: *C. R. Soc. Biol.* 153:343, 1959.

NIKITIN, V. M., and PASHKOVA, A. O.: *Ukr. Biokhim. Zh.* 35:580, 1963. (*Fed. Proc.* [*Transl. Suppl.*], 24:T 65-T 67, 1965.

NOVICK, W. J., JR.: *Endocrinology*, 69:55, 1961.

OERIU, S.: In *Advances in Gerontological Research.* Strehler, B. L., Ed. New York, Academic, 1961, vol. 1, p. 23.

REINER, J. M:. *J. Geront.* 2:315, 1947.

RIVLIN, R. S., and KNOX, W. E.: *Amer. J. Physiol.*, 197:65, 1959.

ROBILLARD, E.; DUBUC, J., and DYRDA, I.: *Rev. Canad. Biol.*, 15:207, 1956.

ROCKSTEIN, M.: *J. Cell. Comp. Physiol.*, 35:11, 1950.

ROCKSTEIN, M.: *J. Geront.*, 11:282, 1956.

ROCKSTEIN, M.: In *Age With a Future.* Hansen, P. F., Ed. Copenhagen, Munksgaard, 1964, p. 148.

ROCKSTEIN, M., and BRANDT, K. F.: *Proc. Soc. Exp. Biol. Med.*, 107:377, 1961.

ROCKSTEIN, M., and BRANDT, K. F.: *Nature* (London) 142:142, 1962.

ROCKSTEIN, M., and BRANDT, K. F.: *Science*, 139:1049, 1963.

ROSS, M. H., and ELY, J. D.: *J. Franklin Inst.*, 258:63, 1964.

SAMORAJSKI, T.; KEEFE, J. R., and ORDY, J. M.: *J. Geront.* 19:262, 1964.

SHIRLEY, R. L., and DAVIS, G. K.: *J. Nutr.* 67:635, 1959.

SHOCK, N. W.: In *The Biology of Aging.* Strehler, B. L., Ed. New York, Stechert, 1960, p. 258.

SHOCK, N. W.: *Ann. Rev. Physiol.*, 23:97, 1961.

SHOCK, N. W.: In *Age With a Future.* Hansen, P. F., Ed. Copenhagen, Munksgaard, 1964, p. 13.

STREHLER, B. L.: *Time, Cells and Aging.* New York, Academic, 1962.

STREHLER, B. L.: *Adv. in Geront. Res.*, *1*:343, 1964.

TAUCHI, H.; SATO, T.; HOSHINO, M.; KOBAYASHI, H.; ADACHI, F.; AOKI, J.: and MASUKO, T.: In *Age With a Future*. Hansen, P. F., Ed. Copenhagen, Munksgaard, 1964, p. 203.

WANG, I., and KIRK, J. E.: *J. Geront.*, *14*:444, 1959.

WEBER, G., and CANTERO, A.: *Amer. J. Physiol.*, *190*:229, 1957.

WEINBACH, E. C., and GARBUS, J.: *Nature*, *178*:1225, 1956.

WEINBACH, E. C., and GARBUS, J.: *J. Biol. Chem.*, *234*:412, 1959.

WHITE, A.; HANDLER, P., and SMITH, E. L.: *Principles of Biochemistry*, 3rd ed. New York, McGraw, 1964, p. 642.

WRIGHT, E. A., and SPINK, J. M.: *Gerontologia*, (Basel) 3:277, 1959.

YIENGST, M. J.; BARROWS, C. H., and SHOCK, N. W.: *J. Geront.*, *14*:400, 1959.

ZORZOLI, A.: *J. Geront.*, *10*:156, 1955.

ZORZOLI, A.: *J. Geront. 17*:359, 1962.

ZORZOLI, A.: In *Age With a Future*. Hansen, P. F., Ed. Copenhagen, Munksgaard, 1964, p. 175.

Chapter 4

CONNECTIVE TISSUES

DAVID A. HALL

INTRODUCTION

In the preceding chapters, it was pointed out that DNA not only carries the heredity information, but also determines the type of RNA; RNA governs protein synthesis. Enzymes are proteins and undergo alterations with age. The connective tissues are extracellular and support or bind other tissues of the body. It is found in tendons, ligaments, skin, blood vessels, bone, teeth, cartilage, lining of the gastrointestinal tract and in lung. In fact it surrounds or is located in close proximity to practically all cells of the body. The connective tissues are usually divided into three chemical categories: collagen, elastin, and mucopolysaccharides. Collagen is the most abundant protein in the body, comprising about 30 per cent of all body protein. Elastin is present in high concentration in blood vessels. These fibrous proteins are embedded in the ground substance which has a high content of mucopolysaccharide.

In some cases, established lines of research have been expanded by studies of factors associated with the aging process; in others, considerations of age changes in particular bodily functions have arisen *de novo*, either in response to the demands of clinicians for new therapeutic techniques, or as the result of completely new approaches to biological topics.Typical of the latter has been the advance which has been made over the past twenty years in studies on the age changes apparent in connective tissues. At the beginning of this period connective tissue research was in the main confined to histological observations on a limited number of tissues, and the whole concept of gerontological research as an experimental science had still to be developed. Since the middle 1940's, both lines have developed rapidly, and it is not surprising that one has had its effect on the other. As will be demonstrated later, early methods of analysis were often so limited in their selectivity and accuracy that longitudinal surveys over protracted age ranges from which trends in analytical values could be deduced often represented the only way in which results, which were at best only comparative, could be displayed. In this chapter, therefore, it will be necessary to consider the general theories of connective tissue structure as well as the effects of aging, since historically the two have been so closely knit together and knowledge about the former is inextricably bound up with theories about the latter. The base line from which age changes can be measured has in fact not yet been determined with any degree of accuracy.

THE GROSS STRUCTURE OF CONNECTIVE TISSUE

The animal body contains a limited number of highly specialized structures with digestive, respiratory, or reproductive function, together with organs which produce a variety of secretions, the function of which is to maintain the physiological tone of the organism. Many of these structures are highly cellular and thus have a low solid content. In unicellular and poikocellular organisms of little mass, this fact is of small significance; but in more complex organisms such as the vertebrates, the very size of the organism necessitates a structural framework in which the more delicate structures can be supported. Thus, the connective tissue can have a supportive, protective, or connective role in the body and occur in a variety of forms.

Where its function is one of support, it exists in the form of rigid essentially nonextensible rods, or when acting as a matrix for the deposition of calcium salts, assists in the provision of a rigid frame on which other structures can hang or against which they can exert specialized tensile effects. Another form of supporting structure lies within the various organs themselves. Here connective tissue elements support and separate the cellular components, permitting them to carry out their synthetic activities in a correct spatial orientation to one another. There are fundamental differences between the functions of supporting structures such as the loose fascia locating the kidney or the spleen within the peritoneal cavity and the organic matrix of a bone or the basement membrane of a nephron. Even supporting connective tissues therefore differ in their structures. Other connective tissues can differ to an even greater extent. For instance, in the case of connective tissues with protective or containing roles such as the skin, elasticity without undue distortion is provided by an interwoven network of fibres. The containing function of the vascular wall on the other hand is provided by peri-luminar sheets of highly elastic tissue interleaved with a network of less extensible material. In highly specialized organs such as the umbilical cord and the eye, fibrous components are not required, and Wharton's jelly in the former and the vitreous humor in the latter take the form of completely transparent gels.

The varied properties of different connective tissues can be ascribed in the main to differing proportions of the extracellular components. Although the cellular fraction is of great importance, since it is this fraction which determines the nature of the extracellular material, the latter is responsible for the appearance, integrity, elasticity, and hence the general function of the tissue. The extracellular portion consists of fibrous and nonfibrous components, and their qualitative and quantitative relationships with one another affect the properties of the tissue.

The fibrous elements of connective tissue are essentially four in number: collagen fibers, the yellow fibrous tissue of the histologists; elastic fibers, or white fibrous tissue; reticulin, which is either an immature form of collagen ultimately to be transformed into recognizably collagenous structures or to remain in its *immature* state throughout life as the basement membrane of some specialized organ; and the so-called *cellulose-containing fibers*, which have in recent years been shown to occur especially in aged tissues (Hall *et al.*, 1958, 1960). To study changes in these varied tissues it will be necessary to consider first the intact structures, and then to examine changes in their relative compositions before finally dealing with such changes as may occur in the individual component elements. The time has not yet come when it will be possible to reverse this analytical process and predict from the properties of the elemental structures how a given tissue may be expected to react. This is the ultimate aim of research on connective tissue aging and we can look forward with hope.

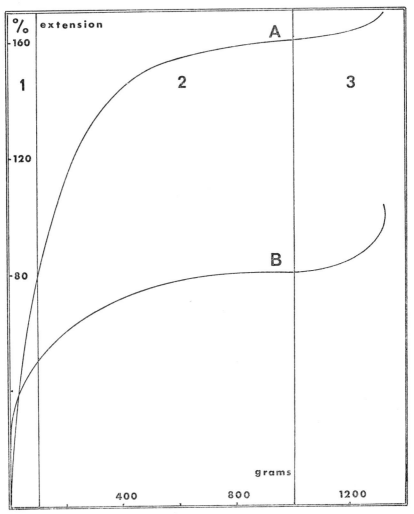

FIGURE 7. Load extension curves for young and aged skin derived from the observations of Ridge and Wright. Both curves are for abdominal skin for male subjects cut at the same angle to the midline of the body. The three portions of the curves are, respectively, 1) The extension due to orientation of the fibre bundles; 2) The extension of the individual collagen fibres; and 3) The slip and ultimate rupture of the sample. A.) Age 3½ months; B) Age 82 years.

Physical Properties of Whole Tissue

In the main, studies on whole connective tissue have been restricted to examination of the skin, arterial tissue and ligaments, and to a lesser extent, the lungs. Tendon represents a special case, since so great a proportion of it is composed of collagen, and changes that occur in this tissue may be regarded as being due to alterations in the collagen fibers themselves and will be dealt with as such in another section.

Dermal Changes

Ridge and Wright (1964, 1965, 1966) and Ridge (1965) have recently described studies of the load extension relationships of the skin. They have demonstrated that the normal load extension curve of a skin sample can be divided into three sections (Fig. 7) The first is associated with the straightening out of the collagenous network; the second with the extension of the collagen fibers themselves and the final section with slip, plastic deformation, and ultimately with rupture of the tissue. They have as yet dealt mainly with the age relationships of the second portion of the curve which can be expressed as a power function.

$$E = kL^b \tag{1}$$

In this equation, E is the extension, L the load, and k and b are constants; k, which appears to be associated with the number and size of the collagen fibers, decreases steadily with age, falling to a quarter its initial value between ten and eighty years. The constant b, on the other hand, increases with age during the first four decades, reaching a value about four times that for infant skin. This rise is followed by a steady fall over the rest of the age range studied. In view of the very low values for Young's Modulus exhibited by elastic fibers (300 times smaller than that for collagen), Ridge and Wright suggest that these alterations in the values of the constant b reflect changes in the properties of the individual collagen fibers. Any changes which can be ascribed to the elastin content of the tissue will in the main affect the first section of the overall curve. The increasing value of b during the first four decades, indicates a marked stiffening of the fibres due no doubt to the formation of an increasing number of cross linkages. This is in close agreement with the observations made by chemical means, but in this respect these physical studies are of greater import than the chemical ones since the latter do not provide evidence for subsequent degradation such as may be deduced from the physical studies.

Arterial Changes

The most obvious changes to be observed in the artery wall as the subject ages are also those associated with decreased tensile strength. These are especially apparent during the relatively early stages of arterial disease. Later, massive calcification causes considerable restriction to flow which results in hypertension. Various workers (Hallock and Benson, 1937; Wilens, 1937; Wiggers, 1938; Krafka, 1937; Saxton, 1942; and Burton, 1954) have reported on the properties of intact artery walls and have employed a range of methods of tensile analysis. This has led to considerable confusion in the assessment and comparison of their findings. Two forms of experiment have provided the majority of the results. Rings of artery have been cut and extended as loops, or segments of artery have been distended either pneumatically or hydrolically. The former records what is essentially a tangential extension, whilst the latter is concerned solely with radial extension. Analysis of the extension curves so obtained indicates that contributions are derived from both collagenous and elastic components. Many workers have claimed that their particular experimental technique demonstrates a progressive decrease with age in load extension relationships. It has, however, proved difficult to correlate such changes with alterations in any one of the structural components. Hass (1943) suggested that the decrease in tensile strength might be regarded as being due to the fracture of a limited number of the elastic elements which make up a three-dimensional network throughout the arterial wall. More recently, Ayer *et al.* (1958) have succeeded in separating the effects due to collagen and elastin by removing the collagen fibers with formic acid, following the changes in load extension curves as the contribution due to this component is removed. The sigmoid relationship characteristic of the complex structure changes to a more or less linear form as the extensibility of the tissue approaches that normally associated with elastic fibers alone. Hass suggested that the whole tissue may be regarded as an elastic three-dimensional structure maintained in a semiextended state by the presence of the relatively inextensible collagen fibers. Changes in the structure of either of these components would of necessity result in quite radical alterations in the physical properties of the tissue as a whole.

Ligaments

Similar suggestions have been made by Wood (1954) to explain the particular load-extension relationships apparent in ligament, another two-component system. Here, however, the roles are reversed. Considerable extension occurs when very low loads are applied to ligament strips, but at later stages in the extension cycle the rate of increase of load with extension rises rapidly, especially in the case of old tissues. Wood explains this phenomenon as being due to the fact that the collagen fibers, which make up about 20 per cent of the bulk of the ligament, tend to slip past one another during the numerous extension cycles which the ligament undergoes during life and are then held in a crumpled state by the network of elastic fibers. When a load is applied to a piece of old ligament, the first stage of the extension merely entails the straightening out of the collagen fibers and the extension of highly extensible elastic fibers (Young's Modulus for this component is 3×10^6 dynes/cm^2). Following this relatively easy extension, the collagen fibres themselves are lengthened, but this requires a far greater load (Young's Modulus for collagen: 1×10^9 dynes/cm^2).

Since the tensile properties of any particular connective tissue depend to such a great extent on the contributions derived from the two major fibrous components, it is apparent that changes either in the relative amounts of these components or in their individual structure can play a major role in determining age changes in efficiency or even in gross function of the tissue.

The Nonfibrous Component
The Ratio of Fibrous to Amorphous Components

Although the fibrous components of connective tissues are of considerable importance in determining their function, the amorphous ground substance can be shown to be equally important. The amorphous phase provides a metabolic environment bathing the fibers and acting as a link between the cellular and extracellular phases. Sobel and Marmorsten (1956) measured changes in the relative amounts of fibrous and amorphous material by assessing changes in the hydroxyproline and hexosamine contents of tissues. The amino acid is characteristic of collagen, whereas the amino sugar level is proportional to the mucopolysaccharide content. They showed that as rats increase in weight there is a disproportionate increase in the amount of collagen synthesized in the skin, femurs, and lungs of the animals; whereas the mucopolysaccharide level rises at a rate comparable to that of animal's own weight increase. If as has been suggested (Moon and Rinehart 1952), the presence of the polysaccharide is essential for fiber growth, this decrease in fiber-gel ratio with age may explain the nature of the control mechanisms which determine the ultimate size of an animal by limiting further production of the fibrous elements of its connective tissue.

As will be shown in a later section, the nature of the polysaccharide in a tissue may be equally as important as its total amount, and it is conceivable that changes in the physical properties of a tissue as the fibers become more closely packed may affect the passage of nutrient material to the cells.

It has been suggested that both fibrous and amorphous components of connective tissue are synthesized by one strain of tissue cells, the fibroblasts. This may be so, or it may be that the cells commonly referred to as fibroblasts consist in fact of a group of closely related cells, so similar in appearance as to be histochemically identical but each having a different enzymic make up which enables it to specialize in the synthesis of collagen, elastin, mucopolysaccharides, cholesterol, or such other components of connective tissue as appear at times to be products of fibroblastic activity. Whichever of these two hypotheses is correct, marked changes are obviously apparent with age. Either the environment changes in such a fashion that the single strain of cells alters its synthetic capabilities, or cells of one strain are inhibited whilst cells of another strain are activated.

Proof of one or other of these hypotheses awaits the production of either one only, or all of the apparent products of fibroblastic activity from a single cell culture affected by the appropriate stimulus. Since the nature of the stimulus necessary for an alteration in activity, either by activation of enzyme systems in a single cell species or activation of a new cell line is still in doubt, many negative results will no doubt be reported before this question is answered.

The Ground Substance

The nature of the ground substance polysaccharides has been dealt with in considerable detail by Muir (1964). One of the difficulties attendant on an assessment of age changes in tissue polysaccharides is that there is still little evidence on the basis of which the location of the polysaccharide can be unequivocally ascertained. Polysaccharides are known to exist either free or protein-bound in the ground substance itself, but they also exist in combination with the structural proteins. There are two ways in which the problem can be solved: either all the polysaccharides can be extracted from the tissue and then fractionated to facilitate their identification and characterization, or attempts may be made to separate the components and to identify the individual polysaccharides attached to each protein species. In practice, except in certain highly specialized instances, this later approach has not proved possible. All methods for the separation of collagen, elastin, and ground substance, of necessity result in a certain amount of degradation. Although polysaccharides have been identified in firm combination with both collagen and elastin, a neutral glycan in the case of collagen (Schultz-Haudt and Eeg-Larson, 1961), and a neuraminic acid containing polysaccharide in the case of elastin (Banga, 1963; Czerkawski, 1962) it has also become apparent (Banga and Balo, 1960; Loeven, 1960) that both species of structural protein contain other polysaccharides which are more loosely bound to the protein. Hall (1958, 1964) has suggested that all questions regarding the overall composition of the elastic fiber as distinct from the elastin molecule itself depend to a considerable extent on where one draws the hypothetical cylindrical boundary between the fibre and the surrounding ground substance. Thus the loosely bound polysaccharide may be regarded as firmly adhering ground substance, or it may be considered that at least part of the polysaccharide complement of the ground substance is derived by partial degradation of the fibrous components. Until methods are available which will permit the exact identification of individual polysaccharides in the electron microscope, it will not prove possible to pass from the chemical to the topographical characterization of the fibre-ground substance relationship in connective tissues.

The tensile properties of connective tissue depend in the main on the fibrous components, but the ground substance provides the correct colloidal properties as lubricant and stabilizer for the tissue as a whole. Changes in the physical properties of the ground substance will bring about marked alterations in the load extension relationships of the whole issue. The nature, degree of polymerization, and polarity of the mucopolysaccharide components of the amorphous mass will effect its thixotropic properties, and these in their turn will alter the rheological properties of the tissue. Referring again to the analysis of the load extension curves put forward by Ridge and Wright (Fig. 7) the portions of the curve which will be most affected by changes in the ground substance are the first and third. In the first, during the alignment of the collagen fibers, highly polymerized polysaccharide will tend to restrict the movement of the fibers and will prolong the curve along the load axis. Similarly at the other end of the extension cycle, highly viscous ground substance will tend to increase the load at which final rupture occurs. In the experienments of Ridge and Wright constant conditions of loading were applied; but in life, sharp discontinuities occur in rates of loading. Massive increases in cardiac output, such as may accompany excessive exertion, will result in great increases in the stress exerted on the vascular wall. Excessive distension of an artery resulting in a dissecting aneurysm may be due ultimately to rupture of the fibrous components of the tissue, but the properties of the ground substance which bathe these fibers may have an equally important part to play. Highly thixotropic solutions of mucopolysaccharide are particularly resistant to shear, and will hence act as a buffer between applied stress and resultant strain on the relatively inextensible collagen fibers such as may be caused by a rapidly applied load. The same solution, however, will shear easily under the action of less rapidly applied stress and thus considerable changes in extension can be permitted where gradually increasing loads occur.

Kirk and Dyrbye (1957) have not been able to identify marked changes in the hexosamine content of the aorta with increasing age. This may indicate that there is little change in the overall amount of mucopolysaccharide in the tissue, but does not preclude changes in the nature of the individual components. Meyer *et al.* (1957) and Happey *et al.* (1953) have demonstrated differences in the polysaccharide content of other connective tissues, and Saxl (1957) has shown that the region of the aortic media immediately below the intima loses a considerable proportion of its free metachromatic material as age advances. There are two possible explanations for this decrease; either there may be an actual drop in the polysaccharide level with age or increasing amounts of the polysaccharide may become attached to protein and hence not be stainable by metachromatic dyes. Recent observations by Slater (1966) appear to indicate that the latter may be the most likely reason, since she has been able to observe no change in the degree of Alcian blue staining of aortic tissue with age. Hall (1964) demonstrated that the relative amounts of neutral and acidic polysaccharides extractable from human aorta with 2% acetic acid fall proportionately over three successive twenty-four hour periods of extraction independent of age. Subsequent extractions with boiling 40% urea solution result in the removal of greater amounts of neutral polysaccharide from elderly aortas than from young ones, indicating an increase in this particular polysaccharide fraction with age. Nemeth-Csoka (1965) has studied the age changes of hexosamine and hexuronic acid in costal cartillage, aorta and skin, and reports that appreciable changes only occur in the case of cartilage, where losses in both types of sugar indicate a decrease of up to 75 per cent in the mucopolysaccharide content.

Hakamori (1962), using slightly more sophisticated methods for the extraction and fractionation of polysaccharides from human aorta, reports a marked decrease in the hexose and methyl pentose content of the aorta of cattle between the two groups;

six months to a year, and ten to fifteen years. Hexosamine and
uronic acid figures do not change by anything like the same
extent. This would appear to indicate changes in the neutral
glycans but a relatively constant level for the glucosaminoglycans
or mucopolysaccharides. He also reports similar changes in rat
skin polysaccharides over the range from birth to three years.
It may be that the different methods of extraction—hot urea
solution in the case of Hall's experiments, and cold Tris/EDTA
buffer, pH 9, in the case of Hakamori's method—can explain the
differences observed. Hakamori reports that after the extraction
with Tris buffer, there remains further polysaccharide which is
difficult to remove from the tissue even with strong alkali. This
would appear to be the material which Hall reports as increasing with age. There is considerable evidence that this neutral
polysaccharide is in fact bound to the material of intermediate
amino acid composition to which Hall has given the name pseu-
dolastin.

The Relative Amounts of Collagen and Elastin

Quantitative studies on the collagen-elastin ratios in tissue
are dependent on the accuracy and selectivity of methods of
collagen and elastin analysis. From this point of view it is therefore unfortunate that elastin is so resistant to solution and can
only be estimated in tissue by subtractive processes. Collagen,
on the other hand, has proved relatively easy to estimate by
methods based on its dissolution from tissue with hot water,
boiling dilute acetic acid, or alkali, followed by hydroxyproline
determinations. This method is highly accurate when normal tissues are being examined, since the hydroxyproline content of
collagen is a well-characterized value. However, in pathological
or aged tissues collagen degradation products may be present
and the hydroxyproline content of such species of protein is unknown. Hall (1957a) showed that treatment of collagenous tissues with phthalate buffer (pH 5) results in the extraction from
the tissue of a hydroxyproline-rich fraction. This can be removed
from the tissue without a complete disruption of structure; and
although the hydroxyproline-deficient residue is more resistant
to hot water than normal collagen and hence will be retained
with the elastin fraction, it is soluble in dilute acetic acid and

hence may contaminate and disproportionately lower the apparent collagen content of the tissue if this method of obtaining gelatin for analysis is employed.

In contrast to collagen, elastin is estimated in the residue remaining after extraneous material has been removed by processes which it is hoped will do so without affecting the elastin in any way. Even in normal tissues there is still no unequivocal evidence that any such selctive methods are available. One of the most commonly used is the removal of ground substance with salt solutions followed by treatment with either boiling water, dilute acetic acid, or alkali, as mentioned above. The elastin is then estimated either directly or after dissolution with elastase, by gravimetric means, or by an estimation of the hydroxyproline content. The relatively small amounts of elastin in most connective tissues and the exceedingly low hydroxyproline level in this protein render these methods of doubtful accuracy even when performed on essentially pure elastin. The differences which exist between the various methods of purification introduce even more errors. Hot water has been employed for the purification of elastin (Partridge *et al.*, 1955) for chemical studies and provides an essentially polysaccharide-free preparation. Acetic acid (Hall *et al.*, 1952, Hall, 1955), on the other hand leaves behind an appreciable amount of polysaccharide, the origin of which is still in doubt. It may be a component of the ground substance or an integral part of the elastic fiber (Hall 1959b, 1964). Alkali treatment can result in marked alterations in the susceptibility of elastin to elastase (Hall and Gardiner, 1955) and if carried on for prolonged periods (Wood 1958; Hall and Czerkawski, 1961a) can result in the complete solution of the protein. It is therefore difficult to ascertain how comparable the results reported by different groups of workers really are in view of widely differing methods of analysis currently in use, and no individual value can be regarded as absolute. Even figures obtained by a single worker for a variety of tissues or for tissues with widely differing histories of disease or of different age may not necessarily be comparable. Bearing this in mind it is of interest to consider the figures for the elastin-collagen ratios in different tissues reported by various groups of workers.

Harkness *et al.* (1957) studied the amount of elastin in the arteries of the dog and its change with age. Expressed as a percentage of the total fibrous protein, the elastin content falls as the vessels leave the thorax. The proportion of elastin in the interthoracic aorta falls from around 70 per cent in a young dog to between 50 and 60 per cent in an adult animal. Changes in the peripheral vessels are even more pronounced. A newborn dog has over 60 per cent elastin in its peripheral vessels, but this falls to 35 per cent after six weeks and to between 25 and 30 per cent in the adult animal. When similar observations have been made on human aortic tissue, a variety of results has been obtained. Lansing and his colleagues (1951) reported very slight differences between the elastin levels in the pulmonary arteries and the aorta in youth and little change thereafter. Kramer and Miller (1953) reported a similar constancy in elastin content, but other workers record significant decreases. Thus Faber and Møller-Hou (1952) reported a drop in the elastin content of the aorta from 35 per cent at the end of the second decade to 22 per cent by the end of the seventh. A similar drop of 37 to 27 per cent is reported by Myers and Lang (1957) but according to these workers this occurs during early middle age and is followed by a long period during which no changes are apparent. Bertolin (1958) also observed a pronounced drop, but contrary to the observations of Myers and Lang, suggested that it was most pronounced during the fifth decade. Scarcelli (1961) whose results are more recent and hence potentially more dependable since he has been able to avoid many of the errors of which earlier workers were unaware, reported a 25 per cent increase during the first two decades but suggested that this was followed by an even greater drop (50%) than those reported by other workers.

It is possible that the considerable differences between these recorded values are due to differences in technique.

CHANGES IN INDIVIDUAL COMPONENTS
Collagen

Physical Properties

Age changes in collagen fibers appear to be restricted, as

far as gross structure is concerned, to alterations in size until degradation sets in due to the combined action of age and, in the case of the dermis, of exposure. Changes in the size of the collagen molecule are also dependent on the site in which the collagen fibers are laid down. In tendon, although there is a tendency for all fibers to increase in size with age (Fitton-Jackson, 1957), fibers obtained from a single piece of tissue demonstrate marked variations in cross-sectional dimensions. In the skin, however, (Tunbridge *et al.*, 1952) collagen fibers of identical cross-sectional area are to be found in a given sample, ranging with age from 300 to 1300 A (Banfield, 1952). Wood and Keech (1960), while studying the effect of polyelectrolytes on the formation of collagen fibers from soluble collagen solution (Wood 1960), demonstrated that different polysaccharides present in tissues at various stages in their development have varying effects as initiators, activators, and inhibitors of fiber nucleation and growth. It may be that changes in the environment, as exemplified by alterations in the polysaccharide content of the ground substance, may determine the rate of growth and the ultimate dimensions of collagen fibers in various tissues.

Since collagen fibers act as the relatively inextensible framework of most conective tissue structures, any changes in their physical properties might be expected to result in marked alterations in the function of organs of which they form a major part. Banga *et al.* (1956) and Verzar (1955, 1963) have developed methods for demonstrating changes in the physical properties of collagen fibers. The latter are characterized by their ability to contract when subjected to thermal or chemical denaturation. It is possible to measure the tension induced in the fiber during this contraction and to determine the load required to inhibit contraction entirely. Using this technique, (Verzar (1955) demonstrated that significantly greater weights were required to inhibit the contraction of collagen fibers from the tails of aged rats than from those of young animals. Later it was shown that this is a universal property of collagen fibers. Verzar and Meyer (1959, 1961) showed that thermal contraction is associated with the release into solution of appreciable amounts of protein-bound hydroxyproline.

The nature of cross-linking in collagen fibers and tendons has been studied by Ciferri and co-workers (Rajagh *et al.*, 1965; Puett *et al.*, 1965; Ciferri *et al.*, 1965; Ciferri and Rajagh, 1964). Interpretation of the results of their work indicates that the cross-links in tendons are of a much weaker nature than covalent bonds.

Degradation of Collagen Fibers

A similar type of reaction had also been shown to occur during chemical denaturation (Banga *et al.*, 1956). They suggested that a so-called *procollagen* fraction is dissolved from the collagen fibers, leaving an insoluble residue to which they gave the name *metacollagen*. The amino acid analysis of both these fragments from collagen are essentially the same, but the appearance of the metacollagen has many points of resemblance to a substance reported by Keech (1954) as remaining after the exhaustive treatment of young adult collagen with the bacterial collagenase derived from *Clostridium histolyticum*. When old collagen is treated with collagenase and the progress of the reaction followed in the electron microscope, the fibers fragment along diagonal lines resulting in the formation of *tactoid* units pointed at either end but still retaining the characteristic 640 A spacings of normal collagen. At a later stage these units break down further with the production of an array of small beads as the penultimate stage prior to complete dissolution. Youthful and young adult fibers (5 to 30 years), on the other hand, degrade in a different fashion. Even after prolonged exposure to the enzyme, a high proportion of the tissue remains undissolved, and this residue appears in the electron microscope as an amorphous mass which on subsequent heat treatment assumes many of the morphological properties of elastin (Keech, 1958). Very young tissues (fetal and infant) dissolve rapidly without the appearance of any amorphous masses. The question of the origin of these variations with age will be dealt with in detail in a later section in which the concept of cross-linkages is considered. Here it is only necessary to say that infant tissue has apparently few, if any, cross-links, and is easily attacked by the enzyme. Mature, but not aged tissue, contains sufficient cross-linkages to prevent rapid dissolution, but the molecules still retain an adequate number of reactive centers for interaction between adjacent parts of the molecule resulting in the formation of an amorphous mass when the initial fission of a limited number of cross-links permits the secondary structure of the collagen molecule to collapse. Aged collagen, on the other hand, is either so heavily cross-linked that it is impossible for there to be a rearrangement of the secondary structure until so many linkages have broken that the resultant products of enzyme action are soluble, or the reactive sites which enable the partial degradation products to reform in an amphorous state are blocked in such a way as to render them inactive.

Cross-Linkages

Ever since it was observed that a portion of the collagen present in various connective tissues could be dissolved (Nageotte 1927) and fibrous elements reconstituted from it following precipitation (Wyckoff and Corey, 1936; Schnitt *et al.*, 1902), it has been assumed (Orekhovitch and Shpikiter, 1955) that this soluble fraction represents the precursor of the intact collagen fiber. Gross *et al.* (1954) postulated the existence of a fundamental particle to which they gave the name *tropocollagen,* and such an entity has been proved to exist and has been characterized by Boedtker and Doty (1956). This particle consists of a triple helix, the individual components of which are held together by hydrogen and other bonds. The extractable citrate-soluble human skin collagen decreases with age and the amount decreases in an exponential manner in the interval between zero and sixty years (Bakerman, 1962). Early studies on the cross-linking of collagen were confined to determinations of the type of linkage which could be assumed to form microfibrils and fibrils from the tropocollagen molecules. Nishihara and Doty (1958) reported that the reactivity of the tropocollagen molecules could be ascribed in part to the presence of short appendages at either end. These, to which they gave the name *telopeptides,* were easily damaged both enzymically and by ultrasound with a resultant failure on the part of the treated collagen to form normal microfibrils (Schmitt and Hodge 1960). The nature of the linkages between the telopeptides will proably not be fully understood until the general architecture of the tropocollagen molecule itself has been elucidated.

Denaturation of tropocollagen at 40° results in the separation of the three individual helices (Boedtker and Doty, 1956). The mixture of protein chains can be fractionated either by electrophoresis on starch (Näntö *et al.*, 1963) or acrylamide gels, or by chromatography on carboxymethyl polysaccharide ion exchangers (Kessler *et al.*, 1959; Piez *et al.*, 1960; Kulonen *et al.*, 1962). In the case of tropocollagen preparations derived from the majority of tissues, the resulting subfractions are four in number. Two of these have double the molecular weight of the other two (Orekhovitch and Shpikiter, 1957) and can be classified as molecular species formed by the retention of linkages between pairs of smaller molecules. Quantitative studies of most mammalian collagens indicate that there is twice as much of one of the smaller molecules as the other, thus indicating that the tropocollagen molecule is made up of two of the so-called $\alpha 1$ chains and one of the $\alpha 2$ chains. The ratio of the cross-linked chains to the non-crosslinked chains remains unaltered with age (Bakerman, 1964) but changes with disease (Bakerman, 1965).

A new molecular species, isolated by Bakerman and Hersh (1964), apparently has a total of four αchains, two of which are paired to form two β chains. In codfish skin collagen, a third component ($\alpha 3$) differing from the other two can be found (Piez 1964). When whole collagen containing only the $\alpha 1$ and $\alpha 2$ species of subunit is denatured, dimers from all possible intramolecular configurations, and also the $\beta 221$ species which can only be derived from intermolecular cross-linking can be observed (Veis and Anesey 1965). It appears likely therefore that the same type of linkage is responsible for the interconnection of adjacent tropocollagen molecules as provides the linkages between the individual subunits. That these linkages are easily broken during the process of thermal denaturation would indicate that they are not particularly strong bonds, and they certainly would not appear to be the ones solely responsible for the relative metabolic inertia of the mature collagen fiber. They do, however, increase either in number or strength with age. Keikkinen and Kulonen

(1964) have demonstrated that denaturation of collagen from subjects of increasing age provides increasing amounts of the βspecies of unit and two other species which cannot be observed in young tissues. The first of these, the so-called γform of tropocollagen (Altgelt *et al.*, 1961) would appear to represent intact triple helical tropocollagen molecules. The other group of fractions, the X fractions, may represent fragments from adjacent tropocollagen molecules still bound together by link-ages too strong to be broken during the normal processes of thermal denaturation.

Studies at lower levels in the molecular structure may cast light on the nature of these stronger bonds. Treatment of collagen with hydroxylamine or hydrazine, both reagents for ester groups, indicates the presence of these potential cross-linking groups in the molecule. Gustavson (1956), Grassman *et al.* (1954), and Konno and Altmann (1958) had suggested, on the basis of the production of excess carboxyl groups following alkaline hydroly-sis and the reduction of collagen with lithium borohydride to give amino alcohols, that esters might be involved in the fine structure of the molecules. Gallop *et al.* (1959) showed that the effect of hydroxylamines is to form five or six protein-bound hydroxamic acids per α-chain, dividing it into smaller subunits. The distribu-tion of these ester linkages in the subunits is still not clear. Gal-lop's original studies were performed on whole tropocollagen preparations, and there is no direct way in which the distribution between α1 and α2 chains can be deduced without similar reac-tions being performed on bulk separations of each species. This is awaited with some interest. Petruska and Hodge (1964), using five subunits and each α2 chain, seven. Gallop (1964), on the other hand, suggested that the ester links are in pairs and hence with an average of three pairs per chain, that there are on average four subunits per chain.

The point of attachment of these ester links is relatively easy to determine insofar as the carboxyl side of the link is concerned. Half of the carboxyls have been identified as being contributed by the αgroups of aspartic acid and half by the βcarboxyl end of the same molecule. That these groups have a role to play in the increasing cross-linkage of collagen with age can be demonstrated by a consideration of the age changes in the staining properties of collagen fibers. Saxl (1957) has shown that aged, degenerate collagen can be stained with elastic tissue stains, especially with those modifications of Weigert's stain which employ very acidic conditions (Hart, 1908). Under these conditions the few carboxyl groups which remain unblocked are easily back-titrated. Fullmer and Lillie (1957) have shown that staining, even with the less acidic forms of Weigert's stain, is possible if the collagen is modified by esterification of all free carboxyl groups.

The other side of the ester linkage is more doubtful. A variety of hydroxyl groups are available in the molecule: serine, threonine, tyrosine, hydroxyproline, and hydroxylysine. None of these has been unequivocally implicated or ruled out as yet, nor is there conclusive evidence that one or more of these reactive hydroxyl groups are blocked to a greater extent in aged collagen.

Hydrogen ion titration data (Hartman and Bakerman, 1966; Bakerman and Hartman, 1966) have been obtained for both salt- and acid-soluble collagen molecules in undenatured and denatured states. Heat denaturation resulted in the release of carboxyl and ε-amino groups for the two different types of molecules with separation of the polypeptide chains. However, not all groups known to be present from amino acid analyses were titrated in the acid-extracted molecules. These marked groups, carboxyl and ε-amino groups are thought to be involved in interchain bonds between the polypeptide chains which make up the cross-linked β-components.

A further possible contributor to age-dependent cross-linking in collagen is provided by the variable amount of carbohydrate which is present in collagen preparations. It appears likely that glycoproteins, in which glucose and galactose together with small concentrations of other sugars are bound by glycosidic linkages to the collagen, possibly through the telopeptides, will ultimately be shown to contribute increasingly to the cross-linkage of the molecule as it ages.

A definition of the way in which collagen becomes more stable and less extensible with age has been attempted from another direction as well as from the direct identification of cross-links in partially hydrolysed tissue. Bjorksten (1959), as a corollary to his suggestion (1951) that the aging process as a whole depends on the immobilization of macromolecules by the formation of resistant cross-links, looked for possible cross-linking reagents in the normal metabolic products of the organism. Aldehydes, especially those with bifunctional activity are produced in considerable amounts during the normal catabolism of carbohydrates (Milch, 1963). Milch *et al.* (1963) examined the effect of a number of aldehydes and showed that the physical properties of collagen fibers treated with such reagents resembled quite closely those of aged collagen (Milch and Murray, 1962). Rojkind *et al.* (1966) have isolated a peptide from a collagenase digestion of ichthyocol which contains an aldehydic component as an α, 4-dinitrophenylhydrazone.

Elastin

Changes in the Amino Acid Composition of Elastic Fibers

The first direct evidence that elastic fibers suffer changes with age was provided by Lansing and his colleagues between 1948 and 1954 (Lansing *et al.*, 1948; Lansing *et al.*, 1950; Lansing 1954). Studying the elastic component of the human coronary vessels they showed that the material remaining after the removal of collagen and ground substance by treatment with hot dilute acetic acid becomes more heavily impregnated by calcium salts as the age of the subject increases (Lansing *et al.*, 1950), rising to ten times the youthful value between the first and eighth decade.

When the elastin remaining after the removal of the collagen and the ground substance is ground finely and suspended in sucrose solution (s. g.:1.30), it can be fractioned by centrifugation into two distinct components, a heavy, highly calcified fraction and a light, relatively calcium-free fraction. The proportion of the former increases with age, nearly all the elastin being present in this fraction in elderly subjects. The calcium content of the old elastin, (6.39%) is five and a half times that of young elastin.

Lansing *et al.* (1951) also observed that the old, heavy

fraction has a markedly different amino acid analysis from the young, light preparation. The major differences between the two are in their relative contents of polar amino acids. The heavy fraction contains 4.11 grams of aspartic and glutamic acid nitrogen per 100 g of protein nitrogen and 6.27 g of basic amino acid nitrogen (lysine, arginine, and histidine), The comparable figures for the young elastin fraction are 2.21 and 1.99, respectively.

Hall (1951, 1955), using boiling forty per cent urea solution as a solvent for the extraneous proteins, showed that contrary to the findings of Stein and Miller (1938), the resistance of elastin to this reagent is only relative, being dependent on a low, liquor-solid ratio. If treatment with urea is maintained for prolonged periods, not only does all the collagen and ground substance pass into solution, but ultimately this is followed by all the elastin as well. In the case of young elastic tissue, the material passing into solution at all times after the removal of the collagen is of similar composition. (Hall used a semiquantitative method of analysis based on a visual assessment of one- and two-dimensional paper chromatograms, but this was sufficiently sensitive to distinguish between the amino acid compositions of young and old elastins.) Old elastin preparations, on the other hand, can be fractionated by the removal of the urea-soluble material after successive periods of time into material having the classical elastin composition which passes into solution last and another substance with a different amino acid analysis. This material has a high content of basic and acidic amino acids and a high hydroxyproline level. On the basis of these observations, Hall suggested (1951, 1959, 1964; Hall *et al.*, 1955) that aged elastic tissue contained a third component in addition to the native collagen and elastin. This material was given the name *pseudoelastin.*

The Relationship with Collagen

Unna (1896) had suggested that proteins other than collagen and elastin could exist in elastic tissues. He was primarily interested in the skin, and in pathological conditions described the presence of at least three other components to which he gave the names *collastin, collacin, and elacin.* These he regarded as being derived either from collagen or elastin. Burton *et al.* (1955) and Hall *et al.* (1955) suggested that as a result of combined morphological and biochemical studies on the degradation of collagen by a variety of reagents, a substance having many of the properties of elastin can be derived from collagen. Further electron microscope studies by Keech (1958) and Keech and Reed (1957) supported these suggestions, and Hall (1956, 1957) demonstrated that the formulation of substances with many of the physical and tinctorial properties of elastin is accompanied by the extraction from collagen of a protein fraction rich in hydroxyproline and deficient in valine. The concept that collagen and elastin are more closely related than might at first be apparent is dependent on the hypothesis that the former is not homogenous in composition. Appreciable evidence has already been advanced from which this might be deduced, but other aspects of the chemical and physical structure of the collagen fiber support the hypothesis.

Early physical studies on collagen (Astbury, 1940) indicated that a relatively high degree of order existed in the molecule. To explain the very marked reflections observed in wide-angle x-ray diffraction patterns, Astbury ascribed a repeating triad structure to the molecule. Of every three amino acids, one was to be glycine, a second either proline or hydroxyproline, and the third could be any of the other amino acids present in the molecule. Later sequence studies on some of the smaller peptides isolated from partial hydrolysates of collagen or gelatin led Schroeder *et al.* (1953) to suggest that the true structure might be a repeating tetrad rather than a repeating triad. At the time when Hall and his colleagues were contemplating the possible conversion of collagen to an elastin-like structure, only Cowan *et al.* (1955) had suggested that the collagen molecule might in fact not consist of the same rigid structure throughout. On the basis of their interpretation of the x-ray data, they suggested that at least one of the three chains in the collagen molecule might be different from the other two. Since that time, evidence for heterogeneity in the collagen molecule has been provided by many workers. Grassmann and his colleagues (Grassmann *et al.*, 1957; Hanning, 1960) and Gallop and his colleagues (Seifter *et al.*, 1961; Franzblau *et al.*, 1964), using enzyme methods of hydrolysis, obtained larger peptides, and the former group were able to demonstrate that whereas some of these peptides were highly polar, others contained disproportionate amounts of the amino acids proline and hydroxyproline. This could also be deduced from the fine striations appearing when collagen is stained with acidic compounds such as phosphotungstic acid. Presumably those regions which stain heavily with this type of reagent are rich in basic groups. Bear (1952) has suggested that the nonpolar amino acid-rich regions represent highly crystalline areas, whereas the acidophilic regions are amorphous. It now appears (Seifter and Gallop 1966) that these nonpolar crystalline regions consist essentially of a series of repeating triads:

Gly-P-X

where P is normally proline, but may also be hydroxyproline; X, on the other hand, is most frequently alanine or hydroxyproline, but may also be serine, threonine, leucine, or one of the other nonpolar amino acids. The only exception to this rule is the amino acid arginine which has been identified as the C-terminal amino acid in a small number of peptides of this type. This is believed to represent the junction between a nonpolar and a polar crystalline region.

The amorphous regions, which tend to remain relatively intact after treatment with *Clostridial* collagenase and hence can be recovered as large peptide units, also contain almost one-third glycine, but in addition contain most of the basic and acidic amino acids and nearly all the tyrosine. It appears that the telopeptides, which it is suggested (Hodge and Schmitt 1958) protrude beyond the trihelical portion of tropocollagen and act as potential links between tropocollagen molecules, are in fact portions of these amorphous polar regions. Recently, as mentioned earlier, the three-stranded tropocollagen molecules have been denatured and dissimilar subunits separated. The disruption of any one of these could result in the collapse of the molecule without it passing into solution but with a marked change in amino acid composition.

As yet, the values obtained for the amino acid analyses do not indicate a sufficiently great difference to justify the assumption that a complete conversion to elastin occurs, but in the case of the majority of amino acids, the alteration is in the right direction (Table XIII). Very recent work on the nature of the subunits themselves (Gallop, 1964), however, has shown that they can be considered as ester-linked polymers of even smaller subunits. As yet, the fractionation of the mixtures of fragments obtained after hydroxylaminolysis has not been accomplished with sufficient accuracy to justify amino acid analysis. It may be, however, that when this is possible it will be found that the individual sub-units differ from one another to an even greater extent and that conversion to structures closely resembling that of elastin may be possible by a selection from the mixture. Hall *et al.* (1955) suggested that the site of the biosynthetic origin of collagen and elastic fibers might be located in the same cell and that environmental changes could effect a choice of subunits from a selection synthesized on different microsomal particles in the cells with the production of either protein. Pseudoelastin, with an amino acid composition part way between these two extremes, could originate either in cells which have suffered defective differentiation or are surrounded by an aberrent environment; or on the other hand, the protein could be derived by the selective degradation of specific parts of either collagen or elastin.

TABLE XIII

PARTIAL AMINO ACID COMPOSITION
OF SUBUNITS OF THE COLLAGEN MOLECULE FROM RAT SKIN
Residues/1000 Total Residues

	$\alpha 1$	$\alpha 2$
4-Hydroxyproline	96.0	86.0
Valine	19.6	32.0
Methionine	8.0	6.1
Isoleucine	6.4	16.4
Leucine	18.1	32.4
Hydroxylysine	4.3	8.0
Lysine	30.4	22.4
Histidine	1.9	8.5

Biochemical Assessment of Elastic Tissue Aging

Tunbridge and his colleagues (Tunbridge *et al.*, 1950, 1952) subjected exposed dermal tissue from aged subjects to electron microscopical examination. It had long been recognized that the dermis from the cheeks and the outer aspects of the forearms of aged subjects demonstrates a particularly abnormal histochemical appearance (Kissmeyer and With, 1922; Ejiri, 1936, 1937). In place of the fine strands of elastic tissue which can be observed in skin from all sites in young subjects and from covered sites even in elderly subjects, masses of elastica staining material with a gross fibrous structure can be observed. In the electron microscope it can be seen that the areas concerned contain considerable amounts of broken and degraded collagen fibers. (Tunbridge *et al.*, 1952). When these studies were being made, techniques of tissue preparation for electron microscopy were relatively primitive, and the pictures obtained were all from teased material which had been finally prepared for the microscope by grinding it in a Potter Elvehjem mill. More recent studies in which the sections have been examined (Banfield and Brindley, 1963) do not indicate the presence of so much degraded collagen. It is possible therefore that the appearance of degraded fibers as reported by Tunbridge and his colleagues may be an artefact. This does not imply, however, that the collagen in the exposed sites is in the same state as in young or unexposed sites, since exactly similar treatment of such tissue does not result in any degraded fibers being selected for the microscope. A limited amount of mechanical damage is unavoidable during the teasing-grinding process, and Keech has shown (1961) that similar changes can be observed when freshly reconstituted collagen is prepared in a similar fashion. Since it is well known that reconstituted fibers of this type are completely devoid in cross-linkages, it could be assumed that such is also the case with the preparations from old tissues. However, since there is no evidence for *de novo* fibrillogenesis in aged tissues, it is not likely that the labile nature of aged collagen fibers is due to the absence of the same cross-linkages which are missing in reconstituted collagen. A far more likely reason for the trauma-sensitive nature of the fibers would appear to be that main-chain degradation has occurred in one or more of the subunits

Contrary to these findings, Lansing *et al.* (1953) and Findlay

(1954) suggested that the extra elastica staining material in senile dermis is in fact true elastin. This point of view has been developed by Smith and his colleagues (Smith, 1963) basing their beliefs on the fact that the new elastica which has the morphological, tinctorial, and physical properties of elastin, is also elastase susceptible, (Lansing *et al.*, 1953) but not affected by either collagenase or trypsin (Loewi *et al.*, 1960). There are one or two doubtful assumptions in this theory. Firstly, as has been mentioned above, the elastica of senile dermis is much more gross in its appearance than the "delicate, straight, freely branching fibers" (Smith, 1963) which are characteristic of the elastin of young skin. It is therefore incorrect to say that the new elastica has the same morphological appearance as that present in youth. The size of the individual elastica staining elements is closer to that of a typical collagen bundle than a fine elastic fiber. Secondly, by visual assessment, it would appear that the amount of elastica staining material increases up to fifty-fold. Estimating the elastin content of alkali-extracted dermis, Smith *et al.* (1962) observed between 8 and 13 mg of elastin per 100 mg dry weight of dermis. Control dermis contains (Smith *et al.*, 1962) 2.4 ± 1.7 mg per cent and (Varadi and Hall, 1966) 2.78 − 3.17 per cent. Therefore, it appears likely that the method of estimation based on the removal of extraneous protein with alkali may give results which are low by a factor of between five and ten. As mentioned in a previous section, it has been shown (Hall, 1955) that prolonged treatment with alkali can result in the solution of the whole of the dermis, elastin included.

The elastica staining material increases in amount following exposure of the dermis to ultraviolet radiation (Smith and Lansing, 1959; Smith *et al.*, 1962) but only when such treatment is carried out *in vivo*. Keech (1961) has demonstrated that the electron microscopic appearance of dermal collagen is unchanged when it is subjected to prolonged irradiation after death. It would appear therefore that two factors, age and exposure, are essential for the degradation which is typical of senile elastosis. Smith (1963) has tended to ascribe all the changes to the irradiation and has renamed the condition *actinic elastosis*, but Slater

(1966) considers the effect to be dual in nature and has demonstrated slight age changes even in covered skin. The effects of the latter have been, in the main, minimized by Smith (1963). Although Smith *et al.* (1963) suggests that the amino acid analyses of elastin preparations from normal and aged skin are identical, their results show some rather interesting differences, all of which could indicate that part at least of the material included in their analytical sample might be derived from collagen. For instance, there is a 12 per cent decrease in the valine content, a 54 per cent decrease in the tyrosine content, and a 108 per cent increase in the basic and acidic amino acids, arginine, lysine, aspartic and glutamic acids. The combined serine and threonine content also increases by 47 per cent. Further speculation as to whether a material similar to *pseudoelastin* postulated by Hall (1964) exists in these preparations is rendered doubtful on account of the slight increases which are to be observed in the leucines. However, it does not appear justifiable to ascribe all the increase in the elastin fraction in senile dermis to true elastin.

Slater (1966) has examined the elastin content of human aging skin using preparations of pancreatic elastase to remove elastin specifically. It has been known for some time (Banga, 1953; Hall *et al.*, 1953) that pancreatic elastase can bring degraded collagen into solution, and Banga has shown (Balo and Banga, 1954) that it does so at a greater rate than that at which true young elastin is solubilized. It should therefore be possible to ascertain whether elastin or denatured collagen is being dissolved from a particular tissue specimen by studying the rate at which the dissolution occurs. Slater observed that there is a slight increase in the percentage of abdominal skin dissolved by elastase over the age range zero to eighty-three years. The average amount dissolved, however, 7.25 mg./100 mg tissue, is significantly lower than that for forearm skin (10.1) or for cheek and for forehead skin from which 18.7 per cent is dissolved.

Slater has also reported figures (1966) for the aorta in which changes in the elastin content and the possible involvement of collagen may also occur.

Fitzpatrick and Hospelhorn (1965) have compared the amino acid composition of alkali- and enzyme-purified elastins from aortas of different ages. They report the presence in the enzyme-treated material of an alkali-soluble fraction containing a collagenase-resistance-collagen-like protein together with sialic acid, hexose, and fructose, but no uronic acid.

Two forms of the pancreatic enzyme elastase exist (Hall, 1968), and they apparently react differently with elastic tissue. It is therefore of considerable interest to note (Hall, 1966) that differences can be shown to exist in the susceptibility of elastic tissues of different ages to the two enzymes. The two extremes in severity of purification procedure are represented by extraction of elastic tissue with boiling $1N$ NaOH (Banga and Schuler, 1953) and mild treatment at or below body temperature using various proteolytic enzymes to remove the extraneous material (Hospelhorn and Fitzpatrick, 1961; Czerkawski, 1962). Aortic tissues from fetal, two, four, and seven-year-old cattle treated by these two extreme purification procedures demonstrate completely different susceptibilities to preparations of elastase consisting in the main of monomer and dimer, respectively. Over the whole age range the caustic soda treated substrates are one quarter as susceptible as the mildly treated ones to either enzyme. This observation is in agreement with that of Labella and Lindsay (1963) who, however, only employed one enzyme species. The monomeric enzyme is 43 per cent more active than the dimer on foetal elastin purified by enzyme treatment. This increased susceptibility falls gradually with age to a value of 29 per cent higher than that of the dimer when tissue from a seven-year-old animal is used as substrate. At the other end of the scale, the susceptibility of the alkali-treated elastin to the monomer increases relatively to its susceptibility to the dimer as the age of the animal increases. Both enzymes are equally active against the alkali-purified fetal elastin, but the seven-year-old tissue is 80 per cent more susceptible to the monomer than the dimer.

The monomer attacks those sites on the elastin molecule which are cross-linked by coordinately bound calcium atoms (Hall 1966), whereas the dimer attacks sites on the periphery of the fiber where free carboxyl and hydroxyl groups are available (Hall, 1964; Hall and Czerkawski, 1961). Therefore, in view of the changes in susceptibility reported above it would appear that the number of coordinately bound calcium atoms in elastin increases with age, a fact which has been demonstrated by Yu and Blumenthal (1960) using extraction with chelating agents to fractionate the calcium content of elastic tissues. In addition to these linkages, however, others must be formed to account for the decreased susceptibility of the alkali-treated tissues, especially in old age, to attack by either enzyme. These hypothetical age-dependent noncalcarious cross-links may well be those described by Partridge and Thomas—the desmosines.

The Structure of the Elastic Fiber and of Elastin as Revealed by Elastase

Hall (1957) proposed a structure for elastin based on the light and electron microscopic appearance of elastic tissues following treatment with elastase and the biochemical analysis of the products of elastolysis. He suggested that the fibre comprises a microfibrillar core consisting entirely of the protein elastin, surrounded by an amorphous sheath composed of the same protein subunits, joined together in this instance, however, by polysaccharide. He suggested that the outer sheath is susceptible to attack by a mucolytic component of the pancreatic elastase complex, whereas the protein core is attacked preferentially by the component of the complex. Recently Benga *et al.* (1965), using particularly pure preparations of the mucolytic and proteolytic components of the elastase complex, have confirmed these observations in part, although their observations would appear to indicate that the nature of the two fractions in the elastic fiber is in fact reversed as compared with the hypothesis put forward by Hall. Whichever of these two concepts is correct, it appears that the idea that elastic fibers consist of two different components is justified.

Balo and Banga (1955) were the first to report that the susceptibility of elastic tissue to elastase is markedly affected by age, old elastic tissue being more easily solubilized than young elastin. Hall (1959) suggested that this might be due to the fact that an appreciable portion of the material isolated with the elastin fraction from old sources is in fact not elastin, but pseudoelastin. Banga (1953) and Hall *et al.* (1953) demonstrated that degraded collagen is more susceptible to elastase than elastin. Since Hall *et al.* (1965) and Burton *et al.* (1955) suggested that pseudoelastin could be derived from the partial degradation of collagen, it appears likely that the retention of material with these properties together with true elastin would in fact increase the apparent susceptibility of this elastin-plus-pseudoelastin fraction. Recent observations on the plural nature of elastase can shed light on this fact.

Elastase can exist in at least two isoenzymic forms (Hall, 1965; Hall, 1966). The first of these to be isolated (Hall and Czerkawski, 1959) was the monomer, although it is now apparent that the preparations of the enzyme available at that time were in fact contaminated with about 20 per cent of the second form; the dimer. Evidence for the existence of this second form was obtained during the preparation of pure enzymes with mucolytic and lipolytic properties from crude elastase preparations. Under normal conditions of extraction using pH 4.7 acetate buffer as extractant and acetone defatted hog pancreas as the source, much of the monomer can be segregated in the euglobulin fraction when the extractant buffer salts are removed by dialysis. The precipitated enzyme is no longer soluble in water, requiring up to 1 per cent for its solution (Balo and Bango, 1950). If the pancreas powder is serially extracted with the acetate buffer, the yield of euglobulin decreases in all extracts after the first, and negligible amounts are present in the third and subsequent extracts. On the other hand, the elastolytic activity of the albuminoid fraction of the extract increases through the second and third extracts, and although it decreases thereafter, small but significant amounts are still present in a sixth extract. This enzyme differs from the water in soluble form in its reaction with the plasma elastase inhibitor, being virtually unaffected by this protein, and also has a different set of kinetic constants (Hall, 1968).

The two enzymes would appear to be associated in their activity with two forms of substrate (Hall, 1964, 1965). A combination of physical and enzymic studies has demonstrated that at least some of the protein chains in the elastin molecule are joined together by coordinately bound calcium atoms. The formation of the enzyme-substrate complex also appears to be through a coordinately bound calcium atom. Where such a linkage exists between elastin chains, the active complex can be formed by interaction with the monomeric form of the enzyme. This results in the formation of an enzyme substrate complex with the enzyme molecule attached to one of the elastin chains and the other elastin chain remaining free.

$$S\text{-}Ca\text{-}S + E = S\text{-}Ca\text{-}E + S \qquad (2)$$

The symbols S and E in equation 2 refer to a substrate chain and an enzyme monomer, respectively, the crosslink being indicated by the calcium atom -Ca-. For the interaction of enzyme and substrate, the same types of groups, namely carboxyl and hydroxyl, are essential on both surfaces (Hall and Czerkawski, 1961b; Tolnay and Bagdy, 1962). Where free carboxyl and hydroxyl groups occur, especially at the periphery of the fiber, they present what is essentially a substrate monomer. These centers are most readily approached and attacked by enzyme dimers, and the reaction can be indicated as follows:

$$E\text{-}Ca\text{-}E + S = E\text{-}Ca\text{-}S + E \qquad (3)$$

TABLE XIV
A COMPARISON OF THE CALCIUM CONTENT OF VARIOUS ELASTIN PREPARATIONS FROM CATTLE AORTA AND THE RATIO OF THEIR SUSCEPTIBILITIES TO MONOMERIC AND DIMERIC ELASTASE.

Method of Purification	Age	Calcium Content %	Ratio monomeric susceptibility: dimeric susceptibility
Enzyme treatment	Fetal	0.693	1.43
	2 yrs	0.125	1.41
	4 yrs	0.250	1.32
	7 yrs	0.375	1.29
Boiling decinormal alkali	Fetal	0.817	1.02
	2 yrs	0.500	1.00
	4 yrs	0.550	1.14
	7 yrs	0.712	1.80

These figures indicate that an appreciable amount of the calcium present in the enzyme purified elastase is not in the form appropriate for the formation of the active complex between enzyme and substrate.

Here again an active enzyme substrate complex is formed but with the liberation in this case of a free monomer of the enzyme. The relative susceptibility of elastin preparations of different ages to the two enzyme species indicates that changes may occur in the degree of calcium cross-linkage, or possibly in the degree of blockage of the peripheral acidic and hydroxyl groups by other compounds. The values reported in Table XIV indicate that the former is the more likely.

Desmosine Cross-linkages

Partridge *et al.* (1955) demonstrated that the soluble protein derived from elastin by treatment with oxalic acid has 26 free amino groups, a molecular weight of 60,000 to 80,000 and appears to consist of 17 chains each containing 35 residues. They considered all the normal linkages known to maintain the secondary structure of proteins and decided that none of the common cross-links could account for the unique resistance of elastin to attack by most chemical reagents. The soluble derivatives of elastin, whether obtained by controlled elastolysis (Hall and Czerkawski, 1961a; Labella, 1962; Loomeijer, 1961), by partial hydrolysis with sulphuric acid (Hall and Czerkawski, 1961a; Kärkelä and Kulonen, 1959), dilute oxalic acid (Partridge *et al.*, 1966), alkali (Hall and Czerkawski, 1961a), or alkaline urea solution (Hall, 1951; Bowen, 1953), retain the yellow pigmentation which is characteristic of intact elastin in the fraction containing material of relatively high molecular weight. It has been suggested (With, 1947) that this yellow coloration is due to the uptake during life of porphyrin pigments from the circulation, but extraction procedures carried out by a variety of workers proved that the pigmentation is in fact an integral component of the peptide chains themselves. Partridge and Davies demonstrated a marked ultraviolet absorption between 275 and 315 Mμ, over and above that which could be ascribed to the relatively low tyrosine and phenylalanine content of the protein. Partial hydrolysis of elastin with 1 N HCl (Loomeijer, 1961) both in aqueous and ethanolic solution results in the concentration of the pigment in the form of a peptide. Loomeijer was able to separate the pigment from known amino acids which constituted the peptide, Gly, Leu, and Val in the ratio 2.1.1 with an N-terminal alanine. The pigment is acidic and titrates to give an equivalent weight of between 220 and 280. This substance is highly fluorescent but does not demonstrate any marked ultraviolet absorption. In this it differs from the material extracted by Thomas and Partridge from elastase- and papain-treated elastin which, as mentioned above, has a high absorption in this region. Partridge *et al.* (1963) separated a quadridentate peptide from their hydrolysates by adsorption and elution on divinyl benzene polymers of different porosities. This, the so-called H-peptide, contains Gly, Pro, and Ala in the ratio 1.1.2, two carboxyl and two amino groups, and appears to be derived from two peptide chains. The rest of the molecule forming the actual cross-link was suggested by Partridge and his colleagues to consist of a new form of amino acid having four carboxyl-amino doublets. By further controlled hydrolysis, Thomas *et al.* (1963) established that two forms of this central compound exist, both having a molecular weight of 540. Of the five

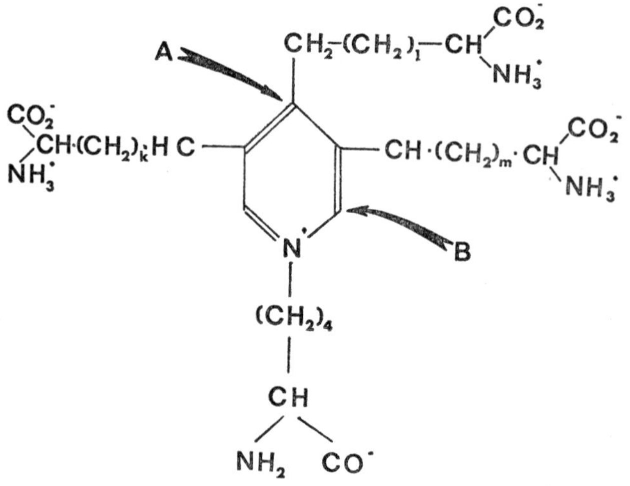

FIGURE 8. The polyfunctional amino acids desmosine and isodesmosine. The numbers of methylene groups in the substituent side chains is as yet unknown and is represented here by the letters *k*, *l* and *m*. The formula shown in that of desmosine. Isodesmosine is the isomer with the substituent at carbon atom A moved to position B.

nitrogen atoms which can be demonstrated, four are present in α-amino groups and the fifth as a quaternary nitrogen. On the basis of ultraviolet spectra, infrared spectra, and proton magnetic resonance studies, together with the probable value for molecular weight, these molecules were ascribed structures (Fig. 8) which indicated that they are quaternary salts of substituted collidines. Degradation of the molecules releases lysine, indicating that the quaternary nitrogen is substituted with the group $(CH_2)_4CH$-$(NH_2)COOH$. The two isomeric forms of the compound were identified by a comparison of their ultraviolet spectra with those of various tetramethyl pyridinium compounds and finally characterized as the 1.3.4.5 and the 1.2.3.5. substituted pyridinium compounds and were given the names desmosine and isodesmosine.

Soon after the identification of these complex cross-linking agents, Miller *et al.* (1964) studied their incidence in chick embryos and in newly hatched and adult chickens. They showed

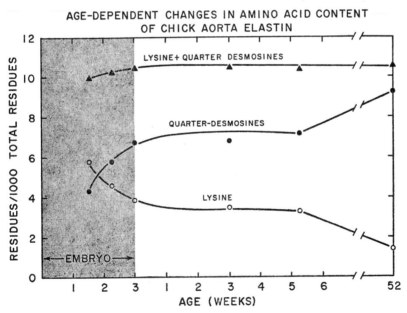

FIGURE 9. Age-dependent changes in amino acid content of chick aorta elastin. (Kindly supplied by Dr. E. J. Miller.)

that the only major difference between embryonic and more adult elastins lies in an increase in the total desmosine content accompanied by a decrease in the lysine content. Twelve-day embryo elastin contains less than half the amount of desmosine (both forms added together) present in the elastin from a one-year-old bird, but over half this difference is eliminated three weeks after hatching. The lysine, on the other hand, falls from 5.7 residues per 1000 in twelve-day embryo elastin to 1.6 in the one-year-old chicken. These results are shown in Figure 9 which was kindly supplied by Dr. E. J. Miller. A useful review on the chemistry of elastin has been published by Piez *et al.* (1965).

Cellulose Containing Fibers

The first evidence for fibrous components in connective tissue other than collagen and elastin came with the observations by Hass (1943) of structures which he termed *anisotropic splints* in the aortic media of middle-aged subjects. Later Hall *et al.* (1958, 1960) isolated highly anisotropic structures from human dermis following the removal of ground substance, collagen, and elastin by successive treatment with salt solutions, collagenase, and elastase. These structures contain a high concentration of carbohydrate together with a protein moiety. Under certain conditions, it can be observed that they consist of two phases; an inner isotropic core and an outer highly anisotropic sheath. In some fibers in which the outer sheath is not complete, it can be seen to consist of a pair of helices wound round the core in opposite directions at an angle to the axis, which in eighty-nine per cent of the fibers, is 72°. When the core is completely covered, the sheath retains its anisotropy at all settings of the polarizers, indicating that the structure consists of a series of anisotropic micelles each alligned at a slightly different angle. Chemically and by x-ray diffraction criteria, the polysaccharide component of the fibers was identified as cellulose. (Hall *et al.*, 1956, 1960; Hall and Saxl, 1960, 1961) The protein moiety has an amino acid analysis midway between that of collagen and elastin, similar in many respects to that of pseudoelastin. Hall and Saxl demonstrated that degradation of collagen under conditions similar to those earlier shown to result in the formation of elastinlike structures (Burton *et al.*,

1956; Hall *et al.*, 1966) results in the formation of similar aniso-tropic bodies. An examination of skin preparations from human subjects of a range of ages demonstrated that cellulose-contain-ing fibers are apparent in small numbers in the dermis of all subjects above an age of about twenty. Below this age the numbers decrease with decreasing age and can seldom be identi-fied in infant tissues. The finite number present in adult tissues cannot be shown to increase with increasing age, due to the fact that they are always present in such small numbers as to render any quantitative method based on their extraction ex-ceptionally difficult. The usual method used for their identifica-tion consists of a visual appraisal of histological sections by polar-ized light. If thin sections are cut, the microtome blade tends to pull the rigid, tough fibers out of the tissue rather than to cut through them. They can however be seen clearly in thick sections embedded between the collagen bundles. The greatest number of anisotropic fibers were found in the dermis of cases of scleroderma, and it was from such material that the fibers ex-tracted for chemical identification mentioned above were ob-tained.

The only other occasion in which cellulose has been demon-strated in the animal kingdom is in the silkworm (Shimizu, 1955; Buonocore, 1958) and in the test of the tunicates (Mark and v. Susich, 1929). Hall and Saxl 1961 showed that the pro-tein core associated with the cellulose is identical in each case and suggested on the basis of this, in view of the possible evolutionary relationship between the vertebrates and the tuni-cates, that the appearance of cellulose-containing fibers in aged tissues in mammals might indicate a return to a primitive genetic state due to somatic mutations occurring throughout life.

If it is accepted that at least part of the material which has been designated pseudoelastin can be derived from collagen, then it is conceivable that under conditions of reversion to a more primitive genetic state the mucopolysaccharide normally as-sociated with this form of protein might be replaced by the neutral polysaccharide developed under these conditions.

CONCLUSIONS

In attempting to explain the effects of aging, especially

as they affect tissues with such pronounced physical properties as the connective tissues, one must be prepared to find reasons for changes in physical properties which either render the tissues more or less extensible. Where tissues become more extensible, the natural conclusion to be drawn is that they suffer partial degradation, of a degree which is insufficient to cause complete disruption but adequate for the easier movement of one molecular chain past another. Increased tensile strength, on the other hand, may be associated with the formation of attachments between molecular chains such as will prevent their easy passage past one another. Different connective tissues demonstrate different changes with age, but in the main all the effects observed can be ascribed to either or both of these two phenomena.

The formation of new cross-links taking place simultaneously with the fission of the main chains themselves results in the transformation of rigid rods which are only slightly extensible but which have only slight resistance to dissolution either by chemical solvents or following attack by specific enzymes, to more extensible but less easily soluble structures.

Much early work on the metabolic turnover of connective tissue proteins (Neuberger *et al.*, 1951; Slack, 1957) lead to the assumption being made that the half-life of a structural fiber protein might be similar in length to the half-life of the organism itself. Much of this work was carried out on the fully differentiated limbs or organs of adult animals, when many of the processes which may be ascribed to the early stages of aging had actually taken place. It appears quite likely that during the development of a tissue, either in the interuterine state or at any stage during growth before the tissue has assumed its final form, an appreciable degree of remodelling takes place. This necessitates the removal of certain tissues and the laying down of new. Where this type of remodelling takes place in adult life, as in wound healing or in the resorption of the post partum uterus, the tissue proteins are removed under the action of proteolytic enzymes derived from lysosomal particles in the surrounding cellular tissue (Woessner, 1965). The tissues which can be removed in this way would appear to mainly freshly layed down tissues and the exact chronological sequence which results in the formation of mature aged tissue cannot as yet be determined. The lysosomal enzymes may be reduced in activity, through atrophy of the cellular portions of the tissue, or through the presence of circulating inhibitors, and thus permit cross-linking to proceed unchecked. Or conversely, cross-linking may occur through changes in the environment of the fibres, and this may prevent the lysosomal enzymes from continuing the digestion of proteins as they are able to during youth. Of these two hypotheses, the second would appear to be the more likely, since, as mentioned above, main chain degradation is known to occur even in aged structural proteins, the presence of the cross-links alone preventing solution.

It would appear therefore that the body attempts to carry on its normal metabolic processes of digestion and remodelling, but is increasingly prevented from doing so by the formation of cross-linkages as the chronological age of the organism proceeds. Some of these, such as the linkages which first form intra- and then inter-molecular linkages in the tropocollagen and the desmosine linkages in elastin, appear to be formed during normal physiological activity. Whether other more resistant linkages, such as those produced experimentally by Milch and his colleagues, take over at a later stage has yet to be proved. It does, however, appear that the hypotheses of Bjorksten and Verzar regarding the essential nature of cross-linking in the aging process are of considerable importance at least as far as the structural proteins of the connective tissue are concerned.

In the three preceding chapters, some aspects of the alterations with age of protein synthesis and metabolism were discussed. In the next chapter,we will abruptly change the current theme and discuss the alterations with age of lipids.

REFERENCES

ALTGELT, K.; HODGE, A. J., and SCHMITT, F. O.: *Proc. Nat. Acad. Sci. U.S.A.* 47:1914, 1961.

ASTBURY, W. T.: *J. Int. Soc. Leather Trades, Chem.* 24:69, 1940.

AYER, J. P.; HASS, G. M., and PHILPOTT, D. E.: *Arch. Path. (Chicago)*, 65:519, 1958.

BAKERMAN, S.: *Nature (London)*, 196:375, 1962.

BAKERMAN, S.: *Biochim. Biophys. Acta*, 90:621, 1964.

BAKERMAN, S.: *Nature (London)*, 206:634, 1965.

BAKERMAN, S., and HARTMAN, B. K.: *Biochemistry (Wash.)*, 5:3488, 1966.

BAKERMAN, S., and HERSH, R. T.: *Nature (London)*, 201:190, 1964.
BALO, J., and BANGA, I.: *Biochem. J.*, 46:384, 1950.
BALO, J., and BANGA, I.: *Abst. 3rd Congress Biochem.*, 14:3, 120, 1955.
BANFIELD, W. G.: *Anat. Rec.*, 114:157, 1952.
BANFIELD, W. G., and BRINDLEY, D. C.: *J. Invest. Derm.*, 41:9, 1963.
BANGA, I.: *Nature (London)*, 172:1099, 1953.
BANGA, I.: In *Colloque sur la biochimie du tissu conjonctif*. Boulanger et al., Eds. Paris, Mason, 1963, p. 133.
BANGA, I., and BALO, J.: *Biochem. J.*, 74:388, 1960.
BANGA, I.; BALO, J., and SZABO, D. J.: *Geront.*, 11:242, 1956.
BANGA, I.; LOEVEN, W. A., and ROMHANYI, cy.: *Acta Morph. Acad. Sci. Hung.*, 13:385, 1965.
BANGA, I., and SCHULER, D.: *Acta Physiol. Acad. Sci. Hung.*, 4:13, 1953.
BEAR, R. S.: *Advances in Protein Chemistry*, Anson, M., and Edsall, J., Eds. New York, Academic, 1952, vol. 7, p. 69.
BERTOLIN, A.: *Chir. Pat. Sper.*, 6:1337, 1958.
BJORKSTEN, J.: *The Chemist*, 36:437, 1959.
BJORKSTEN, J.: In *Advances in Protein Chemistry*. Anson, M., and Edsall, J., Eds. New York, Academic, 1951, vol. 6.
BOEDTKER, H., and DOTY, P.: *J. Am. Chem. Soc.*, 78:4268, 1956.
BOWEN, T. J.: *Biochem. J.*, 55:766, 1953.
BUONOCORE, C.: *Amm. Sper. Agraria*, 12:681, 1958.
BURTON, A. C.: *Physiol. Rev.*, 34:619, 1954.
BURTON, D.; HALL, D. A.; KEECH, M. K.; REED, R.; SAXL, H.; TUNBRIDGE, R. E., and WOOD, M. J.: *Nature (London)* 176:966, 1955.
COWAN, P. M.; McGAVIN, J., and NORTH, A. C. T.: *Nature (London)*, 176:1062, 1955.
CIFERRI, A., and RAJAGH, L. V. J.: *Geront.* 19:220, 1964.
CZERKAWSKI, J. W.: *Nature (London)*, 194:869, 1962.
EJIRI, I.: *Japan J. Derm. Urol.* 41:8, 64, 95, 1937.
EJIRI, I.: *J. Derm. Urol.* 41:8, 64, 95, 1937.
FABER, M., and MØLLER-HOU, G.: *Acta Path. Microbiol. Scand.*, 31:377, 1952.
FINDLAY, V. H.: *Brit. J. Derm.* 66:16 1954.
FITTON-JACKSON, S.: *Proc. Roy. Soc. [Biol.]*, 144:566, 1956.
BRANZBLAU, C.; SEIFTER, S., and GALLOP, P. M.: *Biopolymers*, 2:195, 1964.
FULLMER, H. M., and LILLIE, R. D.: *J. Histochem. Cytochem.*, 5:11, 1957.
GALLOP, P. M.: *Biophys. J.*, 4:79, 1964.
GRASSMAN, W.; HANNIG, K.; ENDRES, H., and REIDEL, A.: In *Connective Tissue*. Tunbridge, R. E., Ed. London, Blackwell, 1957.
GALLOP, P. M.; SEIFTER, S., and MEILMAN, E.: *Nature (London)*, 183:1659, 1959.
GRASSMAN, W.; ENDRES, H., and STEBER, A.: *Z. Naturforsch.*, 96:513, 1954.
GROSS, J.; HIGHBERGER, J. H., and SCHMITT, F. O.: *Proc. Nat. Acad. Sci. U.S.A.*, 40:679, 1954.

GUSTAVSON, K. H.: *The Chemistry and Reactivity of Collagen.* New York, Academic, 1956.

HAKAMORI, S.: In *Biochemistry and Medicine of Mucopolysaccharides.* Egami, F., and Oshima, Y., Eds. Tokyo, Res. Assoc. of Mucopolysaccharines, 1962.

HALL, D. A.: *Nature (London)* 168:513, 1951.

HALL, D. A.: *Biochem. J.,* 59:459, 1955.

HALL, D. A.: *Experientia, Suppl.* 4:19, 1956.

HALL, D. A.: *Gerontologia (Basel),* 1:347, 1957.

HALL, D. A.: In *Connective Tissue.* Tunbridge, R. E., Ed. London, Blackwell, 1957.

HALL, D. A.: *Int. Rev. Cytol.* 8:212, 1959.

HALL, D. A.: *Elastolysis and Ageing.* Springfield, Thomas, 1964.

HALL, D. A.: In *Structure and Function of Connective and Skeletal Tissues.* Fitton-Jackson, S.; Harkness, R. D.; Partridge, S. M., and Tristram, G. R., Eds. London, Butterworths, 1966.

HALL, D. A., In press.

HALL, D. A., and CZERKAWSKI, J. W.: *Biochem. J.,* 80:121, 1961a.

HALL, D. A., and CZERKAWSKI, J. W.: *Biochem. J.,* 73:356, 1959.

HALL, D. A., and CZERKAWSKI, J. W.: *Biochem. J.,* 80:128, 1961b.

HALL, D. A., and GARDINER, J. E.: *Biochem. J.,* 59:465, 1955.

HALL, D. A.; HAPPEY, F.; LLOYD, P. F., and SAXL, H.: *Proc. Roy. Soc. [Biol.],* 151:497, 1960.

HALL, D. A.; KEECH, M. K.; REED, R.; SAXL, H.; TUNBRIDGE, R. E., and WOOD, M. J.: *J. Geront.* 19:338, 1955.

HALL, D. A.; LLOYD, P. F.; SAXL, H., and HAPPEY, F.: *Nature (London),* 181:479, 1958.

HALL, D. A.; REED, R., and TUNBRIDGE, R. E.: *Nature (London),* 170:264, 1952.

HALL, D. A., and SAXL, H.: *Nature (London),* 187:547, 1960.

HALL, D. A., and SAXL, H., *Proc. Roy. Soc. [Biol.],* 202:161, 1961.

HALL, D. A.; TUNBRIDGE, R. E., and WOOD, G. C.: *Nature (London),* 172:1099, 1953.

HALLOCK, P., and BENSON, I. C.: *J. Clin. Invest.* 16:595, 1937.

HANNING, K.: *Fed. Proc.* 91:1, 1960.

HAPPEY, F.; MACRAE, T. P., and NAYLOR, A.: In *Nature and Structure of Collagen.* Randall, J. T., Ed. London, Butterworth, 1953.

HARKNESS, M. L. R.; HARKNESS, R. D., and McDONALD, D. A.: *Proc. Roy. Soc. [Biol],* 146:541, 1957.

HART, C.: *Zbl. Allg. Path.* 19:1, 1908.

HARTMAN, B. K., and BAKERMAN, S.: *Biochemistry (Wash.),* 5:222, 1966.

HASS, G. M.: *Arch. Pathol.* 35:29, 1943.

HEIKKINEN, E., and KULONEN, E.: *Experientia,* 20:310, 1964.

HOSPELHORN, V. D., and FITZPATRICK, M. J.: *Biochim. Biophys. Res. Commun.* 6:191, 1961.

KARKELA, A., and KULONEN, E.: *Acta Chem. Scand.*, 13:814, 1959.
KEECH, M. K.: *Yale J. Biol. Med.*, 26:295, 1954.
KEECH, M. K.: *Ann. Rheum. Dis.*, 17:23, 1958.
KEECH, M. K.: *J. Path. Bact.*, 81:505, 1961.
KEECH, M. K., and REED, R.: *Ann. Rheum. Dis.*, 16:35, 198, 1957.
KESSLER, A.: ROSEN, H., and LEVENSON, S. M.: *Nature (London)*, 184: 1640, 1959.
KIRK, J. E., and DYRBYE, M.: *J. Geront.*, 12:23, 1957.
KISSMEYER, A., and WITH, C.: *Brit. J. Derm.*, 34:175, 1922.
KONNO, K., and ALTMANN, K. I.: *Nature (London)*, 181:994, 1958.
KRAFKA, J., JR.: *Arch. Path. (Chicago)*, 23:1, 1937.
KRAMER, D. M., and MILLER, H.: *Arch. Path. (Chicago)*, 55:70, 1953.
KULONEN, E.; VIRTANEN, U. K., and SALMENPERÄ, A.: *Acta Chem. Scand.* 16:1579, 1962.
LABELLA, F. S.: *Arch. Biochem.*, 93:72, 1961.
LABELLA, F. S.: *J. Geront.* 17:8, 1962.
LABELLA, F. S., and LINDSAY, W. G.: *J. Geront.*, 18:111, 1963.
LANSING, A. I.: Ciba Foundation Symposium on Ageing, No. 1, 1954.
LANSING, A. I.; ALEX, M., and ROSENTHAL, T. B.: *Geront.* 5:112, 1950.
LANSING, A. I.; BLUMENTHAL, H. T., and GRAY, S. H.: *J. Geront.*, 3:87, 1948.
LANSING, A. I.; COOPER, Z. K., and ROSENTHAL, T. B.: *Anat. Rec.* 115:340, 1953.
LANSING, A. I.; ROBERTS, E.; RAMASARMA; ROSENTHAL, T. B., and ALEX, M.: *Proc. Soc. Exp. Biol. Med.*, 76:714, 1951.
LOEVEN, W. A.: *Acta Physiol. Pharmacol. Neerl.*, 9:473, 1960.
LOEWI, G.; GLYNN, L. E., and DORLING, J.: *J. Path. Bact.* 80:1, 1960.
LOOMEIJER, F. J.: *J. Atheroscler. Res.*, 1:62, 1961.
MARK, H., and v. SUSICH, G.: *Z. Phys. Chem.*, 4:431, 1929.
MEYER, K.; HOFFMAN, P., and LINKER, A.: In *Connective Tissue.* Tunbridge, R. E., Ed. Oxford, Blacwell, 1957, p. 26.
MILCH, R. A.: *Gerontologia (Basel)*, 7:129, 1963.
MILCH, R. A.; JUDE, J. R., and LUGOVOY, J. K.: *J. Clin. Invest.*, 27:446, 19 . .
MILCH, R. A., and MURRAY, R. A.: *Proc. Soc. Exp. Biol. Med.*, 111:551, 1962.
MILCH, R. A.; MURRAY, R. H., and KENMORE, P. I.: *Proc. Soc. Exp. Biol. Med.*, 111:554, 1962.
MILLER, E. J.; MARTIN, G. R., and PIEZ, K. A.: *Biochem. Biophys. Res. Commun.*, 17:248, 1964.
MOON, H. D., and RINCHART, J. F.: *Circulation*, 6:481, 1952.
MUIR, H.: *Int. Rev. Connect. Tissue Res.*, 2:101, 1964.
MYERS, V. C., and LANG, W. W.: *J. Geront.* 1:141, 1945.
NAGEOTTE, J.: *C. R. Soc. Biol. (Paris)*, 96:828, 1927.
NÄNTÖ, V.; MAATELA, J., and KULONEN, E.: *Acta Chem. Scand.*, 17:1904, 1963.

NEMETH-CROKA, M.: In *International Conference on Gerontology.* Balazs, A., Ed. Budapest, Akademiai Kiado, 1965.

NISHIHARA, T., and DOTY, P.: *Proc. Nat. Acad. Sci. U.S.A.,* 44:411, 1958.

OREKHOVITCH, V. N., and SHPIKITER, V. O.: *Biokimiia,* 20:438, 1955.

OREKHOVITCH, V. N., and SHPIKITER, V. O.: In *Connective Tissue.* Tunbridge, R. E., Ed. Oxford, Blackwell, 1957.

PARTRIDGE, S. M.; DAVIS, H. F., and ADAIR, G. S.: *Biochem. J.,* 61:11, 1955.

PARTRIDGE, S. M.; ELSDEN, D. F., and THOMAS, S.: *Nature (London), 197:* 1297, 1963.

PETRUSKA, J. A., and HODGE, A. J.: *Proc. Nat. Acad. Sci. U.S.A.,* 51:210, 1961.

PIEZ, K. A.: *J. Biol. Chem.,* 239:PC4315, 1964.

PIEZ, K. A.; MILLER, E. J., and MARTIN, G. R.: In *Advances in Biology of Skin, Vol. VI—Aging.* Montagna, W., *et al.,* Eds. 1965.

PIEZ, K. A.; WEISS, E., and LEWIS, M. S.: *J. Biol. Chem.,* 235:1987, 1960.

PUETT, D.; CIFERRI, A., and RAJAGH, L. V.: *Biopolymers,* 3:439, 1965.

RAJAGH, L. V.; PUETT, D., and CIFERRI, A.: *Biopolymers,* 3:421, 1965.

RIDGE, M. D.: Ph.D., Thesis, Leeds University, 1965.

RIDGE, M. D., and WRIGHT, V.: *British J. Derm.* 77:12, 639, 1965.

RIDGE, M. D., and WRIGHT, V.: *Gerontologia, (Basel),* 12:174, 1966.

ROJKIND, M.; BLUMENFELD, O. O., and GALLOP, P. M.: *J. Biol. Chem.* 241: 1530, 1966.

SCARCELLI, V.: *Nature (London),* 191:710, 1961.

SCHMITT, F. O.; HALL, C. E., and JAKUS, M. A.: *J. Cell Comp. Physiol.* 20: 11, 1942.

SCHMITT, F. O., and HODGE, A. J.: *Proc. Nat. Acad. Sci. U.S.A.,* 46:186, 1960.

SCHROEDER, W. A.; HONEN, L., and GREEN, F. C.: *Proc. Nat. Acad. Sci. U.S.A.,* 39:23, 1953.

SEIFTER, S., and GALLOP, P. M.: The structure proteins. In *The Proteins.*

SEIFTER, S.; GALLOP, P. M., and FRANZBLAU, C.: *Trans. N. Y. Acad. Sci.* 23:540, 1961.

SHOCK, N. W.: *A Classified Bibliography of Gerontology and Geriatrics.* Stanford, Stanford.

SLATER, R. S.: Ph.D. Thesis, Leeds University, 1966.

SMITH, J. G., JR.: *Arch. Derm. (Chicago),* 88:832, 1963.

SMITH, J. G., JR.; DAVIDSON, E. A., and CLARK, R. D.: *Nature (London),* 195:716, 1962.

SMITH, J. G., JR.; DAVIDSON, E. A., and HILL, R. L.: *Nature (London),* 197:1108, 1963.

SMITH, J. G., JR., and LANSING, A. I.: *J. Geront.* 14:496, 1959.

SOBEL, H., and MARMORSTEN, J.: *J. Geront.,* 11:2, 1956.

STEIN, W. H., and MILLER, G., JR.: *Biol. Chem.,* 125:599, 1938.

SAXL, H.: *Gerontologia (Basel),* 1:142, 1957.

SAXTON, J. A., JR.: *Arch. Path. (Chicago),* 34:262, 1942.

SCHULTZ-HAUDT, S. D., and EEG-LARSEN, N.: *Biochim. Biophys. Acta, 51:* 560, 1961.

SHIMIZU, M.: *C.R. Soc. Biol., 149:*853, 1955.

THOMAS, S.; ELSDEN, D. F., and PARTRIDGE, S. M.: *Nature (London), 200:* 651, 1963.

TOLNAY, P., and BAGDY, D.: *Abst. 5th Congress Biochem.,* p. 127.

TUNBRIDGE, R. E.; ASTBURY, W. T.; TATTERSALL, R. N.; REED, R.; EAVES, G., and HALL, D. A.: *Rev. Med. Liege, 5:*671, 1950.

TUNBRIDGE, R. E.; TATTERSALL, R. N.; HALL, D. A.; ASTBURY, W. T., and REED, R.: *Clin. Sci., 11:*315, 1952.

UNNA, P. G.: *Histopathology of the Diseases of the Skin,* trans. by Walker, N. New York, Macmillan, 1896.

VERZAR, F.: *Helv. Physiol. Acta, 13 C:*64, 1955.

VERZAR, F.: *Lectures on Experimental Gerontology.* Springfield, Thomas, 1963.

VERZAR, F., and MEYER, A.: *Gerontologia (Basel), 3:*184, 1959.

VERZAR, F., and MEYER, A.: *Gerontologia (Basel), 5:*163, 1961.

VIES, A., and ANESEY, J.: *J. Biol. Chem., 240:*3899, 1965.

WIGGERS, C. J.: *Amer. J. Physiol., 123:*644, 1938.

WILENS, S. L.: *Amer. J. Path. 13:*811, 1937.

WITH, T. K.: *Acta Med. Scand. 128:*25, 1947.

WOESSNER, J. F., JR.: *Int. Rev. Connect. Tissue Res., 3:*201, 1965.

WOOD, G. C.: *Biochim. Biophys. Acta, 15:*311, 1954.

WOOD, G. C.: *Biochem. J., 69:*539, 1958.

WOOD, G. C.: *Biochem. J., 75:*598, 1960.

WOOD, G. C., and KEECH, M. K.: *Biochem. J., 75:*588, 1960.

WYCKOFF, R. W. G., and COREY, R. B.: *Proc. Soc. Exp. Biol. Med., 34:*285, 1936.

YU, S. Y., and BLUMENTHAL, H. T.: *Fed. Proc. 19:*19, 1960.

Chapter 5

LIPIDS AND PIGMENTS

PERCY J. RUSSELL

INTRODUCTION

IN THE PRECEDING CHAPTERS, we have discussed the protein changes with age; it has been shown that there are both quantitative and qualitative changes in these components. In this chapter, we will discuss lipids; these are related to age-associated disease processes and are important in obesity and in atherosclerosis. Obesity and atherosclerosis are related to the metabolism and the mechanisms which determine the fate and character of the lipoidal material with time.

Obesity is accompanied with a statistically shorter span of life. There is a gradual accumulation of fat in the males up to the sixth decade and then a decline, while the female accumulates fat continuously (Payne, 1949). There is, then, a tendency towards obesity with age. Obesity is most simply and conveniently defined as a body weight which is 10 per cent above the normal body weight for a given height, age, and sex. The "normal weights" have been established from large amounts of data gathered by various health organizations and insurance companies. It is recognized that the body weight parameter is a convenient index of obesity, though certainly not an exact one (Brozek and Keys, 1951).

Although the casual relationships are not known, obesity appears to aggravate, to exaggerate, or to predispose the individual to a variety of disease states. Diabetes as a cause of death, for example, is four times greater in the obese than in the individual of normal weight. Cardiovascular renal disease is 149 percent times the expected value for those of normal weight; cirrhosis is 200 percent times the normal value in the obese;

and mortality from appendicitis and gallbladder disease are likewise higher in the obese individual. Obesity then, if not a direct result of the aging process, is a problem to be reckoned with by the aged.

In the aging organ there is much difficulty in relating the changes directly to the aging process. One of the major contributors to secondary effects is atherosclerosis. The diminished vascular flow to various organs in atherosclerosis cannot have anything but deleterious effect on those organs. Whether or not atherosclerosis is a natural consequence of age in humans is of little consequence. It is, in fact, a major affliction of the aged, natural or otherwise, and the causative factors contributing to the condition are intimately bound up in fat metabolism. For the purposes of the immediate discussion, a description of the factors thought to contribute to or aggrevate the atherosclerotic condition shall first be described.

ATHEROSCLEROSIS

Definition of Terms

There are three types of arterial disease—atherosclerosis, diffuse hyperplastic sclerosis, and medical or Mönckeberg's sclerosis; these may be all considered under the general term arteriosclerosis. Atherosclerosis is a disease which affects the intima of the aorta and its main branches. It shows focal thickenings or plaques consisting of fibrous and fatty material which may encroach upon the lumen of the blood vessel, reducing the blood supply and resulting in ischemia or death of the part. Diffuse hyperplastic sclerosis occurs in the smaller arteries in hypertension. Medial or Mönckeberg's sclerosis affects the muscular arteries, especially those of the extremities. The discussion in this chapter will revolve around atherosclerosis, since it is the most important arterial disease, pathologically and clinically.

Factors Contributing to Atherosclerosis

There appear to be several aspects of the disease related to its cause, prevention, and cure. It is generally felt that atherosclerosis is not a natural, inescapable consequence of the aging human. Atherosclerosis is absent in some aged individuals; and the condition is not only absent in many animals, but also difficult to induce experimentally (Gresham and Jennings, 1962; Page and Brown, 1952; Roseman *et al.*, 1953; Steiner and Domanski, 1943; Steiner and Kendall, 1946). The disease has been viewed as a derangement of lipid metabolism (Bronte-Stewart, 1961) and the relationship between cholesterol and atherosclerosis was noted as early as 1913 (Antischkow, 1913). The disease is often considered as preventable and reversible. In this connection, the consideration is that atherogenic alteration may be brought about by nutrition. The development of athero-sclerosis is, by this view, considered in part a result of the lifespan diet patterns.

The metabolic concept of atherosclerosis derives from three main lines of evidence. The clinical-pathological evidence shows that foam cell cushions are made up of cholesterol and lipid in the intima of arteries. It has also been observed that hyper-cholesterolemia frequently, though not necessarily, preceded atherosclerosis. Epidemiological evidence indicated that athero-sclerosis may vary in entire human populations (Alexander, 1949; Benjamin, 1946; Donnison, 1929; Oppenheim, 1925; Steiner, 1946). The experimental evidence comes from animal studies, where experimentally induced atherosclerosis in animals resulted from high cholesterol, high lipid, dietary regimens (Cali and Adinolfi, 1955; Cohn, 1964; Dauber and Katz, 1942; Page and Brown, 1952; Roseman *et al.*, 1953; Steiner and Domanski, 1943; Steiner and Kendall, 1946).

In addition to the dietary factors that are considered as contributing factors to atherosclerosis, mechanical or physical factors appear to be involved. Those regions of the body and those blood vessels which are most subject to physical pressures also appear to be most subject to atherosclerosis. Atherosclerosis was found to be more pronounced in the legs than the arms (Helvelke, 1956), more pronounced in the right hand than the left (Helvelke, 1956), and appeared in those areas of the blood vessel walls subjected to the greatest blood pressures (Gruner *et al.*, 1953; Gubner and Ungerleider, 1949).

The difficulty with assessing the contribution of the various factors which influence the course of the atherosclerotic condition is that it is difficult to differentiate between hereditary and the environmental factors. The common denominator of all of the factors is that they all require a long period of time to reveal influence. The natural aging of the collagen and the changes which accompany the loss of elasticity and the change in the physical properties of the arterial walls surely contribute to the atherosclerotic condition. In this respect, and to the degree that it is a contributing cause, the natural aging process is a causative factor. Similarly, the influence of the diet over the lifetime of the individual is also a factor in promoting or preventing atherosclerosis. The predisposition for the cell walls to age along certain lines, indeed, the structure of the walls before and during the aging process, must be under some genetic direction. The dietary latitude allowed for an individual to promote or prevent the atherosclerotic condition should be viewed against the physical and metabolic background of that individual, which again is ultimately related in some degree to hereditary factors. The argument then is not whether natural aging or diet or heredity are the causative agents, but how much each contributes. Individual variations being marked in many parameters and in many instances, it would not be surprising if there were a considerable degree of variation of the contributions of various causative factors in various individuals.

To say that aging or diet or heredity are separately or together the causative factors in atherosclerosis implies separate or cooperative mechanisms. Common to all theories concerned with the development of atherosclerosis is some alteration in the metabolism or fate of fat and cholesterol. None of the lipotropic agents appear to have any pronounced effect on the cause or cure or course of atherosclerosis. Atherosclerotic lesions have been characterized by Sf 20-100 and Sf 100-400 lipoproteins which increase with the degree of atherosclerosis (Hunter *et al.*, 1963), and a close relationship between the disease and the Sf 12-400 lipoproteins in the plasma has been noted (Gofman *et al.*, 1954a; 1954b). The β-lipoprotein fraction increases and the α-lipoprotein fraction decreases in atherosclerosis (Barr, 1953). This is the same general type of change which occurs in the aging process.

The level of cholesterol in any individual, whether high or

low, appears to be reasonably constant (Morrison *et al.*, 1949; Steiner and Domanski, 1943). In point of fact, many older persons with coronary or peripheral atherosclerosis have normal or low blood levels of cholesterol (Gertler *et al.*, 1950; Kountz *et al.*, 1945; Morrison *et al.*, 1948). Attention should be drawn to the fact that most of the blood cholesterol is synthesized *de novo* (Gutman, 1953). Special diets which lowered the blood cholesterol remained so in spite of a cholesterol supplement to these diets (Keys, 1953; Keys *et al.*, 1950); but when fat which was free of cholesterol was added to such a diet, the serum cholesterol concentration increased in proportion to the amount of fat added (Keys *et al.*, 1950). A comparison of the poor in Italy, Spain, and Portugal, who lived on an essentially fat deficient diet, with the inhabitants of two cities in the United States, showed that after thirty years of age the cholesterol content of serum is dependent upon the total fat in the diet and not the cholesterol content. The incidence of degenerative diseases of the heart in various countries also would appear to be directly related to the total caloric contribution of fats in the diet according to some views (Keys *et al.*, 1952).

Development of Atherosclerosis

There are various views of the course of atheromateous degeneration. In one (Lansing *et al.*, 1950), the changes in the elastic tissues is one primary contributing cause. By this view, fibrosis of the intima is preceded by calcification of the elastic tissue of the arterial media without cholesterol deposition. The changes in the media are followed by the atheromatous degeneration of the arterial walls. In the other view (Duguid, 1946, 1948), the formation of mural thrombi initiates the development of the atheromatous thickening of the artery. The fibrin which is deposited in the internal surface of the artery becomes a focal point for the atheromatous degeneration of the arterial wall. Neither view excludes the other.

Moreton (1947, 1948) has proposed a theory of atherosclerosis which is a consequence of the normal physiological process of the digestion and absorption of fatty meals during the lifetime. During alimentary lipemia, small particles of fat pass through the arterial intima without retention or deposition. The larger particles, however, are arrested by the phagocytic function of the endothelial cells and the barrier action of the internal elastic membrane in the intima. At this point, some of the lipid is deposited, but the triglycerides and fat are rapidly reabsorbed from the deposited mixed lipid. The cumulative effect of the relatively insoluble material in the fat particles retained in the elastic membrane results in the atherosclerotic infiltration and the transformation of the intima and other parts of the arterial wall. The hyperlipemic basis for Moreton's theory has some support. Alimentary hyperlipemia has been observed to be more pronounced and to last longer in aged individuals (Becker, 1949), longer in individuals with atherosclerosis (Bauer and McGavack, 1962), and longer in individuals with coronary disease (Antognetti and Scopinaro, 1954) than in normal individuals. Dogs injected with various macromolecular substances such as methyl cellulose, pectin, gum acacia and polyvinyl alcohol revealed a deposition of these macromolecular substances in the endothelial cells of the intima, which were transformed into foam cells. Later the entire vascular wall underwent changes with the formation of nests of degeneration (Hueper, 1941, 1945). Hueper (1942, 1945) postulates that any macromolecular substance can produce this macromolecular atheromatosis. The percentage of large lipid particles in the serum of atherosclerotics has been observed to be about twice that observed in normal individuals (Zinn and Griffith, 1950).

Summary

The development of atherosclerosis has been examined from various points of view. It is generally considered that atherosclerosis is not a natural consequence of old age, although this opinion is not shared by all (Gubner and Ungerleider, 1949; Lober, 1953; Wells, 1933). It appears that the various theories of the development of atherosclerosis presented are not in the least contradictory. On the contrary, the various views appear to be specific aspects of the disease which complement one another. Heredity, which may predispose the individual to certain dietary and physical limits, the effects of the diet over a lifetime, the change in physical character of the arterial walls with age—all of these factors play a role in the development of the disease. Each of these factors has some influence on the fate and the metabolism of lipids. Like the three blind men and their description of the proverbial elephant, each view appears right, though different, within the limits of the area investigated.

EFFECTS OF DIETARY LIPIDS

The effect of the diet in relationship to atherosclerosis has already been mentioned. The lifespan dietary habits of an individual then could have profound effects on the disposition of lipid material in later life. We will therefore examine some of the effects of dietary lipids. Adaptive hyperlipogenesis in rats trained to consume an entire day's ration in two hours resulted in an increase in the formation of lipid and a change in the enzyme profile of the liver cells and the adipocytes. The dehydrogenases (Tepperman and Tepperman, 1964), glucokinase and fatty acid synthetase (Hubbard *et al.*, 1961), and malic enzyme (Lodja and Fabray, 1959) were all observed to increase under this condition. These observations indicate that in the face of a specific dietary environment, animals will respond by an alteration of their metabolic patterns. Unfortunately, an assessment of the ultimate effect of such changes with time and age are presently difficult to measure. High carbohydrate diets have been reported to increase the triglycerides in plasma, to produce a relative block in lipolysis, and to increase the transfer of free fatty acids to triglycerides when compared to isocaloric normal diets (Waterhouse *et al.* 1963). The composition of the erythrocyte membrane has been shown to depend on the diet (Kummerow, 1964). An increase in linoleic acid in the diet resulted in an increase in the linoleic content of the membrane of the red blood cells. Red blood cells with the increased content of linoleic acid were less susceptible to hemolysis (Kummerow, 1964).

The effect of altered quantities and kinds of fat on cell membranes generally are unknowns in any estimate of the effect of fats in the diet. Unsaturated fats, such as safflower oil, in the diet have been suggested as a means of lowering serum cholesterol, which some believe is the ultimate cause of atherosclerosis (Cohn, 1964). In rats, it was shown that safflower oil did lower serum cholesterol, but did so by altering the blood-liver partition. Safflower oil addition to the diet caused an accumulation of cholesterol in the liver primarily, but increases in cholesterol by lung, kidney, heart, testes, muscle and spleen tissues were also observed (Bloomfield, 1964). The possibility also exists that large amounts of unsaturated fats may have some deleterious effects. The unsaturated fats in triglycerides are readily oxidized *in vitro* (Kummerow, 1964) and the preoxidation products of unsaturated fat are considered as generally harmful to cellular membranes (Tappel, 1962).

The observations cited above indicate some of the effects the dietary lipids may have in an individual. If one is to consider the time factor in relation to the changes observed, the effect of the diet over a lifetime could be great indeed. It would appear that there can be no really perfect diet since perfect suitability must be measured against highly individual needs and constant change of requirements. Highly saturated fats lead to increased serum cholesterol, highly unsaturated fats appear to transfer cholesterol to other tissues and may lead to increased lipid peroxidation products. Generally, each kind of dietary fat has its own benefit in moderation and its own harm in excess.

Digestion and Absorption

The digestion of fat appears to depend on emulsification and hydrolysis by pancreatic lipase. A description of these processes has been given by Frazer (Frazer, 1946, 1961; Turner *et al.*, 1960; Verzar and McDougall, 1936; Verzar and Freyberg, 1956). The extent of hydrolysis of fat still appears to be a moot question. One of the reasons for some of the confusion would appear to be the use of the per cent of fat hydrolyzed as a measure of the extent of hydrolysis. Such a parameter presupposes that the limiting factor will at all times be the fat. Once the hydrolytic enzymes approach saturation with fat, per cent hydrolysis then begins to lose meaning. It has in fact been observed that when little fat is ingested there is almost 100 per cent hydrolysis, and with the increasing ingestion of fat comes a decreasing per cent of fat hydroylzed.

The extent of hydrolysis is of interest here insofar as the products of hydrolysis affect emulsification. Emulsification in the small intestinal lumen depends on three components: fatty acids, lower glycerides, and bile salts. A fine emulsification is required for the entrance of fat into the intestinal villi. Hydrolysis of the fat is also required and patients with faulty pancreatic lipase show an inability to make effectively fine emulsions. The fate of the phospholipids during the digestive processes is still largely unknown. Pinocytosis of particulate fat has been observed and fat particles accumulate in the cell, then pass through into the intercellular spaces to the coria of the villi. The fat particles usually leave the intestinal cell and pass selectively into the central lacteal rather than into the blood, but blood flow is so large compared to the lymph that the majority of the fat particles pass into the portal circulation.

The normal response to a fatty meal then is a hyperlipemia which reaches a maximum in about two hours after ingestion and lasts totally about six hours in a normal adult. In the aged, the prolongation of alimentary hyperlipemia previously mentioned has been observed to last as long as twenty-four hours (Becker *et al.*, 1949), which would then constitute a permanent state of hyperlipemia for one fatty meal a day. Fat in the blood during alimentary hyperlipemia may be divided into three forms: visible particulate fat, invisible particulate fat (chylomicra), and unesterified fatty acids, usually bound to albumin. In the aged and atherosclerotics, the visible particulate fat form in increased (Antognetti and Scopinaro, 1954; Barritt, 1956; Zinn and Griffith, 1950). In alimentary hyperlipemia, the principal increase in fat is in the chylomicron fraction, which means a great increase in the neutral fat with a smaller increase in phospholipids.

Chylomicra

Since the chylomicra are an important and major form of lipid presented to the body, it is of interest to consider some of the properties of these particles. Greater than 90 per cent of the chylomicra are composed of triglycerides, the remainders are cholesterol, phospholipid, and a small amount of protein (Anfinsen *et al.*, 1952). Of pertinent interest, are the observations that the physical properties and the shape of synthetic lecithin micelles were greatly influenced by the fatty acid composition. In addition, phospholipase A hydrolyzed various mixed synthetic lecithin micelles at greatly differing rates. The rates of hydrolysis by phospholipase A were attributed to the micellar properties (Bird *et al.*, 1965). A correlation of the micellar properties of synthetic lecithins with the hydroylsis rates indicated that the more spheroid the micelle the less the micelle is subject to hydrolysis by phospholipase A (Attwood *et al.*, 1965). In other words, the asymmetrical micelles are more readily attacked. A summary of some of this data is given in Table XV. The most asymmetric of the synthetic micelles, the γ'-oleyl-β-butyryl-L-α-lecithin, had physical properties which were similar to mixed lecithin-lysolecithin sols. The possibility exists that the rates of removal of chylomicra from the blood may reside partially in the differences in the physical properties of the chylomicra. For example, the prolonged alimentary hyperlipemia of the aged and atherosclerotics, previously mentioned, may be the reflection of differences from the normal fatty acid composition of the triglycerides and the phospholipids of chylomicra.

TABLE XV

RELATIONSHIP BETWEEN THE SHAPE OF SYNTHETIC PHOSPHO LIPID MICELLES AND HYDROLYSIS BY PHOSPHOLIPASE*

Fatty acid composition of L-γ-lecithin	Micellular weight	Axil ratio for prolate ellipsoids	% hydrolysis by phospholipase A in 1 hr
Di-butyryl-	10^4	spheroidal	5
Di-oleyl-	3×10^6	spheroidal	37
α'-butyryl-β-oleyl-	2×10^6	8	62
α'-oleyl-β-butyryl-	3×10^6	70	100 in 5 min

*Attwood *et al;* 1965.

The mechanism of removal of chylomicra from the blood and into the tissues is often viewed against the observations of Hahn (Hahn, 1943) that in dogs heparin cleared the turbidity of blood serum due to fatty meals. It has been reported that the administration of heparin relieves the postprandial lipemia in normal and atherosclerotic persons (Block *et al.*, 1961; Gilbert and Nalefski, 1949; Graham *et al.*, 1951 Gruner *et al.*, 1953), and that the clearing effect of heparin was less pronounced in the atherosclerotic person as compared to the normal person (Block *et al.*, 1951). The effects of heparin, an antiprothrombin polysaccharide, are credited to the activation of a lipoprotein lipase (Jeffries, 1954; Weld, 1944) which brings about marked changes in the serum lipoprotein fractions (Gofman *et al.*, 1954a; Lever *et al.*, 1953; Nikkila, 1952). It has been suggested that a derangement in the clearing mechanism which involves heparin may be responsible for the accumulation of cholesterol and macromolecular lipoproteins in the plasma and thus contribute to the atherosclerotic and hyperlipemic states (Friedman *et al.*, 1955). Not all agree on the role of heparin. Some investigators consider that the role of intravascular hydrolysis is a minor path in the removal of lipid from the blood (Olivecrona, 1962; Bragdon and Gordon, 1958), and the removal of intact chylomicra has been demonstrated (Borgstrom *et al.*, 1957; Austin *et al.*, 1961). The order of importance of various tissues in the removal of chylomicra appears to be liver first, followed by adipose tissue and carcus (Olivecrona, 1962). This view does not explain the effect of heparin, although the importance of intravascular lipolysis could be related to changes in the physical properties of the chylomicra so that removal by other mechanisms is facilitated (Borgstrom *et al.*, 1961). The effect that composition has on the susceptibility of various synthetic phospholipid micelles to enzymatic attack has already been mentioned. It has also been observed that the chylomicra of choline deficient animals were resistant to D-lecithinase and were more slowly cleared by heparin (Bronte-Stewart, 1961). Along these lines, it has also been suggested that the properties of the chylomicra change with age (Sobel *et al.*, 1963) in dogs. It seems evident that there is more than a single mechanism involved in the removal of chylomicra from the blood, one dependent on and the other independent of hydroylsis. An assessment of the importance of any proposed mechanism may well be a function of the experimental conditions. The removal of chylomicra from the blood appears to be a complex process with parts of the fat particles being removed at different rates. It was observed that components comprising about 5 per cent of the composition of the chylomicra were removed at a much slower rate than the other 95 per cent (French and Morris, 1957). The slowly metabolized fractions of the chylomicra have been considered as the lipoprotein fraction (George *et al.*, 1961) and the phospholipids (Barnett *et al.*, 1963). The lipoprotein fraction is divided as the α-lipoproteins and the β-lipoproteins. These fractions have been partially characterized (Avigan *et al.*, 1956). The α-lipoproteins are 35 per cent lipid, have a single polypeptide chain and have the dimensions of 300 by 50 Å. The β-lipoprotein fraction is 75 per cent lipid, also has a single polypeptide chain and is larger and more spherical dimensions, 185 by 185 Å. The lipoproteins are highly permeable to water and the associated free cholesterol and phospholipids exchange readily with the environs. By comparison, the neutral fat and esterified cholesterol are slow to exchange and suggests that the protein is stabilized in a neutral fat-esterified cholesterol matrix (Avigan *et al.*, 1956). The lipoproteins are synthesized by the liver at all times and in the intestinal wall during digestion (Byers and Friedman, 1960; Havel and Goldfien, 1961). Lipoproteins are thought to be required for the release of triglycerides (Vaughn, 1962).

Fatty Acids, Fats, and Cholesterol

The synthesis and the transformations of fatty acids in the body are extremely complex. There are apparently families of unsaturated fatty acids which derive from the family heads of oleic, linoleic, and linolenic acids. Each family head may undergo a series of chain lengthenings and dehydrogenations to become more unsaturated. The oleic acid family of compounds which derive from palmitic acid may be formed endogenously from acetyl-CoA. Linoleic and linolenic, the polyunsaturates, must be derived from the diet and are therefore classified as essential. It has been shown that the various families of unsaturated fatty acid may inhibit one another's formation. Linoleic and linolenic are mutually and competively inhibitory in the chain lengthening and the dehydrogenation steps (Holman, 1964), and oleic acid is antagonistic to linoleic metabolism (Mead, 1961, 1963). The significance of these polyunsaturated acid in terms of their precise nutritional need or their role in the general metabolism of fatty acids and fat at present is obscure.

The synthesis of the triglycerides proceeds through the D-α, β-diglyceride plus acetyl-CoA, the initial precursor being phosphatidic acid (Kennedy, 1957). The synthesis of the phospholipids is very complex and very diverse. The center relationships of some of the various precursors to the triglycerides and phospholipids is given in Figure 10.

INTERRELATIONSHIP OF PHOSPHOLIPID AND NEUTRAL FAT SYNTHESIS

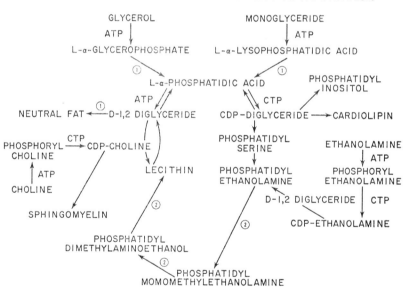

① ACTIVATED FATTY ACIDS, RCOCoA   ② METHYLATION VIA ADENOSYL METHIONINE

FIGURE 10. Interrelationship of phospholipid and neutral fat synthesis.

The synthesis of cholesterol in mammals proceeds from acetyl-CoA. The quantities of cholesterol formed is under feedback control, whereby the final product, cholesterol, inhibits further synthesis of itself by inhibiting reactions leading to cholesterol formation in the liver (Gould and Taylor, 1950). The step involved in this feedback inhibition is the reduction of β-hydroxy-β-methylglutaryl CoA to mevalonate (Siperstein, 1960) as indicated in Figure 11, which outlines the pathway for the synthesis of cholesterol.

SYNTHESIS OF CHOLESTEROL AND THE RELATIONSHIP TO FAT METABOLISM

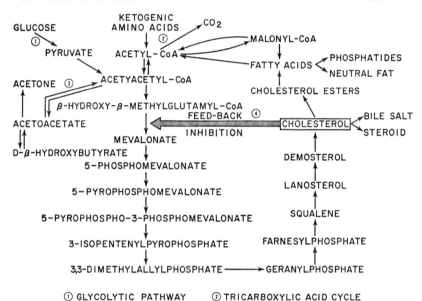

① GLYCOLYTIC PATHWAY   ② TRICARBOXYLIC ACID CYCLE
③ EXTRAHEPATIC TISSUE   ④ BILE SALTS, SQUALENE OR ANY
STEROL CONVERTIBLE TO OR ARISING FROM CHOLESTEROL

FIGURE 11. Synthesis of cholesterol and the relationship to fat metabolism.

Summary

The effect of fat in the diet on the aging individual, which in this presentation has included general aspects of digestion, absorption, and synthesis, still appears obscure. There are no definitive studies which attempt to correlate the "normal" metabolic pathways for fat, fatty acids, cholesterol, and chylomicrons with a given age, which in turn could serve for comparison at other ages. Indeed, normal for one age may not be normal for another. Dietary affects are conflicting, and the differentiation between environmental (dietary) and genetic effects are never clearly defined. Of the factors which may alter the metabolism of fat, the changes in the properties of the chylomicra appear interesting since this is the major form of fat as initially presented to the body for further utilization or storage. Even so, the initiating causes for any change observed in the aged may be easily lost in the slow, progressive, accumulative affects which defy detection at any point in time. Too little reasearch is, in fact, directed specifically toward ascertaining this kind of information. Especially lacking is the basic research which is more likely to reveal primary and initiating causes.

PIGMENTS

General Characteristics and Origin

The accretion of neutral fat occurs inter- and intracellularly with some sexual differences in man. In the aging cell, fatty and pigment degenerations are common (Keys *et al.*, 1950). One of the first signs of age in tissue culture is the appearance of fatty granules or vacuoles in the protoplasm, which later completely fills the protoplasm and cytolysis develops (Failla, 1960). Electron microscopic observations also indicate that phospholipid constituents of cartilage cells undergo modification with increased tissue age. These changes occur at the same time as changes in the physical state of the collagen takes place (Barnett *et al.*, 1963). Age pigment formation appears to be the natural result of an accumulation of lipid peroxidation products.

Muhlmann (1914) was the first to ascribe importance to the accumulation of pigment granules in aged cells. He considered the pigments as degenerative waste products which replaced active cytoplasm. The pigment which accumulates in a variety of aging tissues (Hamperl, 1934), and in the heart muscle and nerve especially, is called the senility pigment or the ceroid pigment or the lipofuscin pigment. Age pigment has also been reported in stillborns (Andrews *et al.*, 1962). The pigment occurs within the cells as lipofuscin granules which may be isolated by differential centrifugation (Heidenreich and Siebert, 1955). The average pigment composition is 60 per cent protein, 25 per cent lipid and 15 per cent carbohydrate (Hendley *et al.*, 1963). The brown-colored age pigment is acid-fast, sudanophilic and fluoresces green-yellow when activated by long wave-length ultraviolet light (Mildvan and Strehler, 1960). No enzymatic activity has been associated with the pigment itself (Bourne, 1960), though the granules with which the pigments are associated do possess a variety of enzymatic activities (Hirsch and Ahrens, 1958; Bjorkerud, 1962; Strehler *et al.*, 1962). The origin of the pigment has not been definitely established. The suggested sites of origin have been, at one time or another, the mitochondria (Hess, 1955), the Golgi apparatus (Bondareff, 1957; Gatenby, 1953), and the lysosomes (Essner and Novikoff, 1960; Strehler, 1962).

An enzymatic profile of the lipofuscin granules appears to rule out mitochondria as a site of origin since none of the oxidase activities and components associated with mitochondria were found in these granules (Hendley *et al.*, 1963; Strehler, 1962). Phosphatase activity (Culkin and Kuntz, 1952) and cathepsin activity (Strehler *et al.*, 1962) are the most characteristic enzymatic activities associated with the lipofuscin granules. The RNase activity of the granules is low compared to the DNase activity (Strehler *et al.*, 1962). In general, the enzymatic profile seems most like that of the lysosomes than any of the other subcellular particles. Strehler *et al.*, (1962) considers that the lipofuscin pigments are an accumulation of the auto-oxidation products of lipids of the lysosomes. They further suggest that the lysosomes do not turn over as do the other parts of the cell since the lysosomal enzymes are, for the most part, lytic in nature and as such are harmful to the cellular organization. The lipofuscin, then, acts as an envelop for potentially lytic enzymes. Lipofuscin has the property of being stable to the lytic enzymes of the lysosomes.

Lipid Peroxidation and Pigments

There are several lines of evidence to indicate that the lipofuscin pigment is a product of lipid peroxidation. Histochemical studies (Hendley *et al.*, 1963; Siebert *et al.*, 1962) indicate that the character of the lipofuscin pigment is what would be expected of a lipoprotein derived by a peroxidation process. A direct measurement of peroxidation products in the pigments as thiobarbituric acid reactants (Pease, 1960) supports this view. Tappel (1965) has shown that a model system of protein and lipid under conditions of lipid peroxidation results in products similar to the lipofuscin pigment. Presently, this seems to be the best simple model for testing a phenomenon which may be basic to the aging process. It has shown that mitochondrial lysis by ferrous ions, ascorbate, and glutathione may initiate the peroxidation of lipids (Hunter *et al.*, 1963). These findings would appear to oppose the general role of antioxidants *in vivo* discussed later. Under the condition of vitamin E deficiency, it has been shown that lipid peroxides may form as a result of electron transport activity (Corwin, 1962).

Pigment Formation and Theories of Aging

Isolated lysosomes undergo lipid peroxidation at one-third the rate of isolated mitochondria and one-tenth the rate of microsomes (Tappel, 1965). The difference in the rates of lipid peroxide formation correlates well with the lower lipid content of the lysosomes. Lipid peroxidation damage is similar in some respects to radiation damage, but much less severe (Desai and Tappel, 1963). The damage in both instances is due to the formation of lipid-free radicals which can react with protein and cause a cross-linking reaction (Tappel, 1965). The similarity of the age pigment to the oxidation products of lipids-plus-protein has been pointed out (Strehler *et al.*, 1962). If the accumulation of age pigment is viewed in the light of the investigations above, some support is rendered to the view that the aging process is fundamentally a chemical one in which cross-linking reactions are basic to the process (Bjorksten, 1958).

In this connection, the study of the aging process by means of radiation-accelerated aging would seem to be more than reasonable. There appears to be little difference between normal senescence and radiation-accelerated aging with respect to the correlation between the degree of histopathology and the degree of atherosclerosis (Casarett, 1960). Part of the parenchymal senescence is attributed to a reduced blood supply (Casarett, 1960). The somatic mutation theory, which implies changes in the chemistry of the organism as a result of genetic alterations

(Curtis, 1958; Failla, 1960), and the cross-link theory of aging (Bjorksten, 1958) are both basic in attempting to arrive at the initiating causes of the aging process. There does not appear to be any conflict between the two theories, principally because of the general, nonspecific nature of the somatic mutation theory.

The Role of Antioxidants

Pigments due to vitamin E deficiency and senility appear to be similar (Payne, 1949). Ultramicroscopic analysis of the structure of the age pigment in the human and rat ganglion and the pigment in ganglion of young rats subjected to vitamin E deficiency all appear similar (Sulkin and Sulkin, 1962). There exists several lines of evidence that free radical products of lipid peroxidation are the basic damaging cause in aging, as indicated in irradiation-accelerated aging and in vitamin E or antioxidant deficient states of nutrition (Andrews *et al.*, 1962; Hardman, 1962; Ord and Stocken, 1961; Sinex, 1961). It has been suggested that vitamin E, vitamin C, TPNH, and glutathione act synergistically for an antioxygenic effect *in vivo* (Uri, 1960). This view is to be contrasted with the lytic effects of antioxidants on mitochondria *in vitro* and subsequent stimulation of peroxidation (Hunter *et al.*, 1963). The unsaturated fats in triglycerides are steadily oxidized *in vitro* in the absence of fat-soluble antioxidants (Kummerow, 1964). Vitamin E is especially easy to oxidize in the presence of unsaturated fat, and the distribution and retention of the vitamin appears to be tissue dependent. Brain, for example, retained ^{14}C-dl-tocopherol acetate longer than liver in rats on a vitamin E free diet for eight days (Weber and Wiss, 1963). The feeding of high amounts of unsaturated fats to elderly men appeared to deplete them of vitamin E, but it must be emphasized that this does not imply a deficiency state. A supplement of vitamin E to the elderly lowered the susceptibility of their erythrocytes to hemolysis by hydrogen peroxide (Dayton *et al.*, 1965). It has been shown that lipid peroxidation was concurrent with hemolysis (Tsen and Collier, 1960), and a change in the permeability of the membranes by lipid peroxidation products has been suggested (Chappel and Grenville, 1960). The efficiency with which mitochondria converted oxidation energy to chemical energy was shown to be lower than normal in vitamin E deficient rabbits (Zalkin and Tappel, 1960). The antioxidants would appear to have an important role in membrane stabilization and may possibly assist as a deterrent to the accumulation of age pigment and peroxidations generally.

Summary

It is difficult to detail any concrete process whereby pigment formation may or may not occur. The roles of the various subcellular particles in pigment formation are yet very unclear. Much of the material presented has been related more by inference than by direct demonstration. Again, much of the fault lies in the paucity of information available that derives from basic research specifically directed toward the problem of the aging process. Other aspects of the general problem of lipids and the aging process were not discussed because there does not appear to be any direct thread linking the observations with the more general aspects of metabolism. Among things unmentioned are the changes in the plasmalogen content of the cells with age. Almost absent in the newborn, the plasmalogen content increases up to sexual maturity and then declines (Albert and LeBlond, 1949). There is no explanation for the changes of this class of lipid compounds with age. Of particular interest is the observation that with mitochondria from aged rats, the substrate β-hydroxybutyrate showed both a lowered oxidation rate and a lowered rate of inorganic phosphate esterification (Weinbach and Garbus, 1959). The other substrates showed no change associated with age. The observation concerning β-hydroxybutyrate is of particular interest because it has been shown that the enzyme β-hydroxybutyrate dehydrogenase requires a phospholipid containing unsaturated fatty acids for activity (Fleisher *et al.*, 1962). In general, the metabolism of the lipids is not well understood at any age. The enzymes involved in their synthesis and degradation have not been well characterized because the substrates are water-insoluble for the most part and the enzymes appear to be unusually unstable by ordinary standards. To compound the matter, the amount of research at the basic level which seeks answers to the aging process is

142   *Aging Life Processes*

small indeed. Perhaps, accelerated aging processes will spur general interest in this direction, and newer methods along with braver men will combine to shed light upon the problems of lipids, pigments, and aging.

REFERENCES

55555

ALEXANDER, F.: *New Eng. J. Med., 240*:1035, 1949.

ALBERT, S., and LeBLOND, C. J.: *J. Anat., 83*:183, 1949.

ANDREWS, F.; PIPER, P.; NORTHRUP, R.; TRENK, B., and BJORKSTEN, J.: *J. Amer. Geriat. Soc. 10*:649, 1962.

ANFINSEN, C. B.; BOYLE, E., and BROWN, R. K.: *Science, 115*:583, 1952.

ANTISCHKOW, N.: *Beitr. Path. Anat., 56*:379, 1913.

ANTOGNETTI, L., and SCOPINARO, D.: *Arch. Margliano Pat. Clin., 9*:1, 1954.

ATTWOOD, D.; SAUNDERS, L.; GAMMACK, D. R.; DE HASS, G. H., and VANDEENEN, L. L. M., *Biochim. Biophys. Acta, 102*:301, 1965.

AVIGAN, J.; REDFIELD, R. R., and STEINBERG, D.: *Biochem. Biophys. Acta, 20*:557, 1956.

BARNETT, C. H.; COCHRANE, W., and PALFREY, A. J.: *Ann. Rheum. Dis. 22*:389, 1963.

BARR, D. P.: *Circulation, 8*:641, 1953.

BARRITT, D. W.: *Brit. Med. J., 2*:640, 1956.

BAUER, H. G., and McGAVACK, T. H.: *Proc. 6th Int. Congr. Geront., 57*:67, 1962.

BECKER, G. H.; MEYER, J., and NECHELES, H.: *Science, 110*:529, 1949.

BENJAMIN, E. L.: *U. S. Naval Med. Bull., 46*:495, 1946.

BIRD, Ph. R.; DE HAAS, G. H.; HEEMSKERK, C. T. Th., and VAN DEENEN, L. L. M.: *Biochim. Biophys. Acta, 98*:566, 1965.

BJORKERUD, S.: *Proc. 6th Int. Congr. Geront., 57*:32, 1962.

BJORKSTEN, J.: *J. Amer. Geriat. Soc., 6*:740, 1958.

BLOCK, W. J.; BARKER, N. W., and MASON, F. D.: *Circulation, 4*:674, 1951.

BLOOMFIELD, D. K.: *J. Clin. Med., 64*:613, 1964.

BONDAREFF, W. J.: *Geront., 12*:364, 1957.

BORGSTROM, B.; TRYDING, N., and WESTOO: *Acta Physiol. Scand., 40*:241, 1957.

BORGSTROM, B.; WLODAWER, P., and NAITO, C.: *Collogues Intern. Center. Nat. Recherche,* Paris, 1961, p. 125.

BOURNE, G. H.: In *Biology of Aging.* Strehler, B. L., Ed. New York, Stechert, 1960, p. 133.

BRAGDON, J. H., and GORDON, R. S.: *J. Clin. Invest., 37*:574, 1958.

BRONTE-STEWART, B.: *Fed. Proc. 20*:127, 1961.

BROZEK, J., and KEYS, A.: *Brit. J. Nutr., 5*:194, 1951.

BYERS, S., and FRIEDMANN, M.: *Amer. J. Physiol., 198*:629, 1960.

CALI, A., and ADINOLFI, M.: *G. Geront., 3*:464, 1955.

CASARETT, G. W.: In *Biology of Aging*. Strehler, B. L., Ed. New York, Stechert, 1960, p. 147.

CHAPPEL, J. B., and GRENVILLE, G. C.: *Biochim. Biophys. Acta*, *38*:483, 1960.

COHN, C.: *Fed. Proc.*, *23*:76, 1964.

CORWIN, L. M.: *Arch. Biochem.*, *97*:51, 1962.

CURTIS, H. J.: *Radiat. Res.*, *9*:104, 1958.

DAUBER, D. V., and KATZ, L. N.: *Arch. Path. (Chicago)*, *34*:937, 1942.

DAYTON, S.; HASHIMOTO, S.; ROSENBLUM, D., and PEARCE, M. L.: *J. Lab. Clin. Med.*, *65*:739, 1935.

DESAI, I. D., and TAPPEL, A. L.: *J. Lipid Res.*, *4*:204, 1963.

DONNISON, C. P.: *Lancet*, *1*:6, 1929.

DUGUID, J. B.: *J. Path. Bact.* *58*:207, 1946.

DUGUID, J. B.: *J. Path. Bact.*, *60*:57, 1948.

DUSTIN, J. P.; FREDRICKSON, D. S.; LAUDAT, P., and ONO, K.: *Fed. Proc.*, *20*:270, 1961.

ESSNER, N., and NOVIKOFF, A.: *J. Ultrastruct. Res.*, *3*:374, 1960.

FAILLA, G.: In *The Biology of Aging*. Strehler, B. L., Ed. New York, Stechert, 1960, p. 170.

FISHER, A.: *Biology of Tissue Cells*. New York, Cambridge P., 1946.

FLEISCHER, S.; BIERLEY, G.; KLUOWEN, H., and SLAUTTERBACK, D. B.: *J. Biol. Chem.*, 237:3264, 1962.

FRAZER, A. C.: *Physiol. Rev.*, *26*:103, 1946.

FRAZER, A. C.: *Fed. Proc.* 20 (Supp. 7):146, 1961.

FRENCH, J. E., and MORRIS, B.: *J. Physiol.*, *138*:326, 1957.

FRIEDMAN, M.; ROSENMAN, R., and BYERS, S. O.: *J. Geront.*, *10*:60, 1955.

GATENBY, J. B.: *J. Roy. Micr. Soc.*, *73*:61, 1953.

GEORGE, E. P.; FARKAS, G. S., and SOLLICH, B. S.: *J. Lab. Clin. Med.*, 57: 167, 1961.

GERTLER, M. M.; GARN, S. M., and LERMAN, J.: *Circulation*, *2*:205, 1950.

GILBERT, N. C., and NALEFSKI, L. A.: *J. Lab. Clin. Med.*, *34*:797, 1949.

GOFMAN, J. W.; DeLALLA, O.; GLAZIER, F.; FREEMAN, N. K.; LINDGREN, F. T.; NICHOLS, A. V.; STRISOWER, B., and TAMPLIN, A. R.: *Plasma*, 2:413, 1954a.

GOFMAN, J. W.; GLAZIER, F.; TAMPLIN, A.; STRISTOWER, B., and DeLALLA, O.: *Physiol. Rev.*, *34*:589, 1954b.

GOULD, G. R., and TAYLOR, C. B.: *Fed. Proc.*, *9*:179, 1950.

GRAHAM, D. M.; LYON, T. P.; GOFMAN, J. W.; JONES, H. B.; YANKLEY, A.; SIMONTON, J., and WHITE, S.: *Circulation*, *4*:666, 1951.

GRESHAM, G. A., and JENNINGS, A. R.: *An Introduction to Comparative Pathology*. New York, Academic, 1962, p. 332.

GRUNER, A.; HILDEN, K., and HILDEN, T.: *Scand. J. Clin. Lab. Invest.*, 5: 241, 1953.

GUBNER, R., and UNGERLEIDER, H. E.: *Amer. J. Med.*, *6*:60, 1949.

GUTMAN, A. B.: *Amer. J. Med., 14*:1, 1953.
HAHN, P.: *Science, 98*:19, 1943.
HAMPERL, H.: *Virchow Arch. Path. Anat., 292*:1, 1934.
HARDMAN, D.: *Radiat. Res., 16*:753, 1962.
HAVEL, R. J., and GOLDFIEN, A.: *J. Lipid Res., 2*:389, 1961.
HEIDENREICH, O., and SIEBERT, G.: *Virchow Arch. Path. Anat., 327*:112, 1955.
HELVELKE, G.: *Angiology, 7*:39, 1956.
HENDLEY, D. D.; MILDVAN, A. S.; REPORTER, M. C., and STREHLER, B. L.: *J. Geront., 18*:250, 1963.
HESS, A.: *Anat. Rec., 123*:299, 1955.
HIRSCH, J., and AHRENS, E. H.: *J. Biol. Chem., 233*:311, 1958.
HOLMAN, RALPH T.: *Fed. Proc., 23*:1062, 1964.
HUBBARD, D. O.; McCAMAN, R. E.; SMITH, M. R., and GIBON, D. M.: *Biochem. Biophys. Res. Commun., 5*:339, 1961.
HUEPER, W. C.: *Arch. Path. (Chicago), 31*:11, 1941.
HUEPER, W. C.: *Arch. Path. (Chicago), 33*:267, 1942.
HUEPER, W. C.: *Arch. Path. (Chicago), 39*:121, 1945.
HUNTER, F. E.; GEBICKI, J. M.; HOFFSTEN, P. E.; WEINSTEIN, J., and SCOTT, A.: *J. Biol. Chem. 238*:828, 1963.
JACOBI, H. P.; NG, Y. C.; WAN, A. T.; STAGEMAN, P. J., and TREMAINE, M. M.: *Proc. 6th Int. Congr. Geront., 57*:5, 1963.
JEFFRIES, G. H.: *Quart. J. Exp. Physiol., 39*:261, 1954.
KENNEDY, E. P.: *Ann. Rev. Biochem., 26*:119, 1957.
KEYS, A.: *J. Mount Sinai Hosp. N. Y. 20*:118, 1953.
KEYS, A.; FIDANZA, F.; SCARDI, V., and BERGAMI, G.: *Lancet, 2*:209, 1952.
KEYS, A.; MICKELSEN, O.; MILLER, E. V. O., and CHAPMAN, C. B.: *Science, 112*:79, 1950.
KORENCHEVSKY, V.: *Physiological and Pathological Aging.* New York, Hafner, 1961.
KOUNTZ, W. B.; SONNEBERG, A.; HOFSTATTER, L., and WOLFF, G.: *Biol. Sympos., 11*:79, 1945.
KUMMEROW, F. A.: *Fed. Proc., 23*:1053, 1964.
LANSING, A.; ALEX, M., and ROSENTHAL, T. B.: *J. Geront., 5*:314, 1950.
LEVER, W. F.; SMITH, P. A. J., and HURLEY, N. A.: *Science, 118*:653, 1953.
LODJA, Z., and FABRY, P.: *Acta Histochem. (Jena), 8*:289, 1959.
LOBER, P. H., *Arch. Path., (Chicago), 55*:357, 1953.
MEAD, J. F.: *Fed. Proc., (Chicago), 20*:952, 1961.
MEAD, J. F.: *Ann. Rev. Biochem., 32*:241, 1963.
MILDVAN, A. S., and STREHLER, B. L.: *Fed. Proc., 19*:231, 1960.
MORETON, J. R.: *Science, 106*:190, 1947.
MORETON, J. R.: *Science, 107*:371, 1948.
MORRISON, L. M.; GONZALES, W. T., and HALL, L.: *J. Lab. Clin. Med., 34*:1473, 1949.

MORRISON, L. M.; HALL, L., and CHANEY, A. R.: *Amer. J. Med. Sci., 216*: 32, 1948.

MUHLMANN, M.: *Virchow Arch. Path. Anat., 215*:1, 1914.

NIKKILA, E. A.: *Scand. J. Clin. Lab. Invest., 4*:369, 1952.

OLIVECRONA, T.: *Acta Physiol. Scand., 55*:170, 1962.

OLIVECRONA, T.; GEORGE, E. P., and BORGSTROM, B.: *Fed. Proc., 20*:92, 1961.

OPPENHEIM, F.: *Chin. Med. J. (Peking),* 39:1067, 1925.

ORD, M. G., and STOCKEN, L. A.: In *Mechanisms in Radiation Biology.* Errera, M., and Forssberg, A., Ed. New York, Academic, 1961, p. 259.

PAGE, I. H., and BROWN, H. B.: *Circulation, 6*:681, 1952.

PAYNE, F.: *J. Geront., 4*:193, 1949.

PEASE, A. G. E.: *Histochemistry Theoretical and Applied,* 2nd ed. Boston, Little, 1960.

ROSEMAN, R. H.; BYERS, S. O., and FRIEDMAN, M.: *Amer. J. Physiol., 175*: 307, 1953.

SIEBERT, G.; DIEZEL, P. B.; JOHR, K.; KRUG, E.; SCHMITT, A.; GRUEN-BERGER, E., and BOTTKE, I.: *Histochemie,* 3:17, 1962.

SINEX, F. M.: *Science,* 134:1402, 1961.

SIPERSTEIN, M. D.: *Amer. J. Clin. Nutr., 8*:645, 1960.

SIRI, W.: In *Biological Aspects of Aging.* Shock, N. W., Ed. New York, Columbia, 1962, p. 58.

SOBEL, H.; PARSA, K., and MASSERMAN, R.: *J. Geront., 18*:340, 1963.

STEINER, A., and DOMANSKI, B.: *Arch. Intern. Med.* (Chicago), *71*:397, 1943.

STEINER, A., and KENDALL, F. E.: *Arch. Path. (Chicago), 42*:433, 1946.

STEINER, P. E.: *Arch. Path. (Chicago), 42*:359, 1946.

STREHLER, B. L.: *Time, Cells and Aging.* New York, Academic, 1962.

STREHLER, B. L.; HENDLEY, D., and MALKOFF, D.: *Proc. 6th Int. Congr. Geront.,* 57:31, 1962.

SULKIN, N. M., and KUNTZ, A.: *J. Geront., 7*:533, 1952.

SULKIN, N. M., and SULKIN, D.: *6th Int. Congr. Geront.,* 57:30, 1962.

TAPPEL, A. L.: In *Lipids and Their Oxidation.* Schultz, H. W., Ed., Westport, Conn., Avi Pub., 1962, p. 367.

TAPPEL, A. L.: *Fed. Proc., 24*:73, 1965.

TEPPERMAN, H. M., and TEPPERMAN, J.: *Fed. Proc., 23*:73, 1964.

TSEN, C. C., and COLLIER, H. B.: *Canad. J. Biochem. Physiol., 38*:957, 1960.

TURNER, D. A.; COX, E. V.; BALINT, J. A.; PRIRRIE, R.; FLETCHER, R. F.; HUANG, E., and CEVALLOS, W. H.: *Fed. Proc., 19*:876, 1960.

URI, N.: In *Autooxidation and Antioxidants.* Lindberg, W. O., Ed. New York, Interscience, 1960, vol. I, p. 133.

VAUGHN, M.: *J. Lipid Res., 2*:293, 1962.

VERZAR, F., and McDOUGALL, E. J.: *Absorption from Intestine.* London, Longmans, 1936.

VERZAR, F., and FREYBERG, V.: *J. Geront. 11*:53, 1956.

WATERHOUSE, C.; KEMPERMAN, J. H., and STORMONT, J. M.: *J. Lab. Clin. Med., 63*:605, 1963.

WEBER, F., and WISS, O.: *Helv. Physiol. Pharmacol. Acta, 21*:131, 1963.

WELD, C. B., *Canad. Med. Assoc. J., 51*:577, 1944.

WEINBACH, E. C., and GARBUS, J.: *J. Biol. Chem., 234*:412, 1959.

WELLS, H. G.: In *Arteriosclerosis*. Gowdry, E. V., Ed. New York, MacMillan, 1933.

ZALKIN, H., and TAPPEL, A. L.: *Arch. Biochem., 88*:113, 1960.

ZINN, W. J., and GRIFFITH, G. C.: *Amer. J. Med. Sci., 220*:597, 1950.

Chapter 6

THEORIES

JOHAN BJORKSTEN

There are many theories as to the cause of aging. This is so because investigators, as in other scientific fields, have tended to base their hypotheses on the interpretation of data obtained in their own areas of investigation and interests. That age changes occur in many different molecular systems can be seen from the information given in the preceding chapters. The changes are described in both qualitative and quantitative terms. One of the main difficulties is the problem of assigning these changes as to cause or effect. As an example, the level of estrogens in females changes with age, but the primary reason is the alterations in the cells that cause these changes.

There are definite advantages as well as disadvantages in the fact that no one theory has been generally accepted by the scientific community as the basis of aging. One advantage is that no one theory on aging has hardened into scientific dogma to the exclusion of other theories prior to absolute confirmation. A disadvantage is that there will be time and effort and money spent on attempts to substantiate theories that are not useful in describing aging. In this chapter, a survey of the different theories of aging, with arguments for and against these theories is given. The theory that appears to have the most scientific basis is emphasized.

The theories on aging may be divided into three groups:

I. The very *general* theories, which, regardless of possible philosophic merit, do not offer much aid to those planning experiments or seeking therapies.

II. The *intermediate* theories, which have a firm experimental basis and relate to one or more areas of the aging syndrome, but which rest on other primary chemical causes.

III. The *basic* theories which relate to experimentally verifiable causes.

We shall discuss these in order.

I. GENERAL THEORIES

The general theories are that aging is due to the following:

1. Depletion of irreplaceable matter due to the rate of living (Pearl, 1920).

2. A statistical normal distribution on the basis of undefined variables (Pütter, 1921).

3. Vitality is depleted and mortality is inversely proportional to the vitality (Brody, 1923).

4. Converging of physiological variables to cause aging (Sacher, 1956; Tamplin, 1959).

5. The limiting value of undefined variables (Yockey, 1958).

6. Accumulation of stresses and consequent stress damage (Selye, 1959).

7. Unfavorable ratio between the work output demands and the rate at which a subsystem can function. The vitality of a subsystem is defined as the maximum rate at which energy can be expended to restore its original condition (Strehler and Mildvan, 1960).

8. That aging is an adaptive effect to increase the survival value of the species by eliminating older individuals. This concept was originated by Weismann (1891) who stressed the utility of death from the standpoint of the group. Medvedev (1964) takes the more specific view that the death of the old is useful particularly because it will limit the mutational changes which would occur if old individuals would continue to live and to reproduce, and which would reach a level evolutionarily lethal to the species.

Whatever merit these and similar theories might have from a philosophical standpoint, they do not come sufficiently close to the underlying chemistry even to begin to explain how aging is caused. Neither do they provide useful suggestions on how aging might be braked or reversed.

II. INTERMEDIATE THEORIES

9. *Progressive Cell Death*

The fact of progressive decrease in the number of many cells with aging has been clearly established (Ellis, 1920; Gardner, 1940; Rockstein, 1950). This theory, succinctly formulated by Heilbrunn (1943), as gained impetus with Hayflick's (1965) impressively documented statement that normal diploid somatic cells invariably die after 50 ± 10 cell divisions and that only certain mutated cells continue to divide indifinitely. Puck *et al.* (1966) express a different opinion and the matter is still unresolved. This theory would have to be supplemented with some additional explanation of what causes these cell deaths.

10. *Cybernetic Theory*

The slowing down of transmission rate of neutral impulses results in a lack of coordination which finally disorganizes the living system beyond repair (Still, 1956). The fact of a progressive increase in transmission time as expressed in nervous and endocrine reaction times has been apparent in most studies of these physiologic changes with age (Still, 1956). It is bound to have an influence on the progress of aging symptoms. Still has convincingly shown that it is possible for a multicelled organism to die (be disorganized) even though all its vital cells may still be alive. This cybernetic theory in itself does not carry an explanation as to how aging causes the increased transmission time (Still, 1958), although it would seem to necessarily involve chemical changes in the stable chemical parts of non-dividing nerve cells.

11. *Hormonal Imbalance*

This theory was first advanced by Brown-Séquard (1889) and brought to particular prominence by the work of Steinach (1920) and Voronoff (1920 and 1929). However, it is fully established that hormones exert a powerful controlling and governing influence which extends to the aging syndrome. Any imbalance in the initial well-functioning hormonal system is bound to affect the functioning of the entire organism. It has been established beyond any question that administration of hormones or stimulation or replacement of endocrine glands can alleviate even advanced aging symptoms. But what caused the hormone-producing glands themselves to decline in their activity to "age?"

12. *Enzyme Deterioration*

The theory that enzyme deterioration is a major factor in aging has grown out of the work of many researchers, each of whom contributed some proven facts on the decline in enzyme content and/or activity with age (Meyer *et al.,* 1940; Bourne, 1957; Kirk, 1959; Mandel, 1961; Bertolini, 1962; Ghiringhelli, 1963; bibliography, Bjorksten, 1966; Zorzoli, Chapter 3).

It is thoroughly established that the content of most, though not all, enzymes of cells and tissues decreases with progressing age. This can certainly be an intermediate cause of many of the changes which occur in aging and definitely is a factor in some of them. But here again, the questions arise: What has caused the enzyme deterioration? Why are the few enzymes which increase with age particularly among those concerned with protein and DNA metabolism? (Bjorksten, 1966).

13. *Autoimmunity Reactions*

Walford (1962) pointed out the development of auto-immunity with aging and consequent age-dependent pathology. As age progresses, very large molecules will emerge or be changed so that they will no longer be recognized by the body's immunological defenses, but will be attacked.

This concept, based on a large number of observations by many authors, has been summarized in depth by Blumenthal (1964).

This is undoubtedly an important mechanism in the aging syndrome. It is not limited to dependence on somatic mutations, for certainly many cross-linked, and probably even some mono-reacted, large molecules, will result in immunologic disharmony and intolerance. Walford (1964) points out that the auto-immunity theory is wholly compatible with the cross linkage concept discussed below.

14. *Somatic Mutations*

The theory of somatic mutations (Danielli 1956; Failla, 1957, 1958) states that mutations of somatic cells cause formation of inferior cells by spontaneous changes in nucleic acid templates.

It has been observed that mutated cells form in old individuals. For example, senile pigmented areas in the skin may be one example. However, there has not been advanced any evidence that this mechanism affects aging as a whole or affects longevity in any statistically observable way.

Genetic changes are due to changes in nucleic acids which are derivatives adenosine, cytosine, guanine and thymine. This is true for the highest as well as the lowest organisms. Therefore, if mutations were the principal cause of aging, the life expectancy should be more nearly the same for all organisms in view of the similarity in the chemical mechanics of heredity (Bjorksten, 1962, p. 126).

On the other hand, if mutations were limiting the length of life, one would expect that diploid organisms would live longer than haploids, since they have a double set of chromosomes and thus a reserve set for the event that one chromosome should be damaged. However, such is not the case (Clark and Rubin, 1961; Clark and Rockstein, 1963; Clark, 1964).

A pertinent experiment was reported by P. Alexander and D. I. Connell (1962) who fed to 11- to 14-week-old rats at three weekly intervals doses of two cross-linking mutagenic substances (Myleran® and chlorambucil) and of one non-crosslinking mutagenic agent (ethyl methane sulfonate).

If aging were due to somatic mutations, it could be expected that all three of these would cause a similar degree of life shortening. Alexander and Connell (1962) found, however, that only the cross-linkers induced such life shortening similar to aging without specific general symptoms, while the non-crosslinking ethyl methane sulfonate, though equally mutagenic, and used in higher concentration did not cause any comparable life shortening. J. P. Welch (1967, p. 16) also considers this finding "profoundly damaging to the simple hypothesis that somatic mutations are responsible for aging."

At the present time, a preponderance of evidence summarized by Welch favors the conclusion that somatic muta·tions play only a minor role in the aging process.

Some authors (*e.g.*, Curtis, 1963) use the word *mutation* to denote changes in DNA molecules, even in nonreplicating cells. This brings the subject out of genetics and into chemistry, in which context it is discussed below.

15. *Continuous Radiation Damage as a Cause of Aging, or the Free Radical Theory*

The effect on longevity of free radial scavengers found in Harman's studies is of a low order of magnitude, particularly in work with rats other than special low longevity races. Since the effect of radiation and free radicals is principally to create crosslinkages, they will be further discussed below in that context. Since the radiation to which a person is exposed in the normal course of a lifetime from cosmic radiation, potassium isotopes, and other sources is about 200 r (about 3600 r is required on slow radiation to cause symptoms of senility in mammals), it is not seen how radiation could play any major part in the normal aging process.

16. *Toxins Formed in the Digestive Tract*

This theory (Metchnikoff, 1903) deserves attention as an early approach to a problem, the importance of which is not yet fully recognized, and no doubt may well account to some extent for the development of the overall aging syndrome. It is not known what is the relative importance of toxins formed in the digestive tract nor how effective are the defense mechanisms.

17. *Reticulocytic Effects*

Bogomolets (1946) observed, in postmortems of centenarians, that the connective tissue was in a remarkable state of preservation. A mistake may have been made in ascribing the result of longevity to a single, easily observed tissue, rich in readily examinable and extracted collagen, without corresponding study of the condition of the other less rapidly observed proteins and the nucleic acids. Since all of these contain the same reactive groups, it stands to reason that all proteins and nucleic acids will be similarly affected by the same overall influences of the chemical ambient. If this is such that collagen rapidly ages throughout the body, and not only in localized areas, it is reasonable to assume that the same will hold true of every other amino-type polymer in the body including all proteins and nucleic acids. Therefore it is faulty reasoning to accept the condition of collagen as a proof that this is where therapy must be applied.

However, some of the experimental work of Bogomolets and his co-workers is in many respects very interesting. In particular, Medvedeva's (1939) data point to a resolubilization of insoluble protein from several organs as a result of treatment with antireticulotoxic serum. This may indicate that the experimental suggestions of Bogomolets' work have been exhausted.

III. THEORIES—INCLUDING THE INITIATING STEPS IN THE AGING PROCESS

18. *The "Clinker" Theory*

Prior to the advancement of this theory by Mühlmann (1900), Eisig (1887) had noted the accumulation of colored particles and ascribed these in part to storage of what might have been termed "clinkers" of metabolism, although he did not connect them with aging.

Alpatov and Nastiukova (1948) have suggested that accumulation of physiologically inactive optical isomers may play a part in the aging syndrome, and Blagovestchenski (1950) in similar context has pointed to accumulation of cyclic compounds.

It is not apparent that combustion or normal metabolism would leave nonremovable inert residues in all types of aging organisms or tissues in quantity sufficient to account for aging.

19. *The Protein Hysteresis Theory*

This theory is based on the observation of coagulation of protein materials, and Ruzicka (1924) ascribed this to effects of fluctuation of pH with age.

The hysteresis theory has also been embraced by Bancroft *et al.* (1934, a,b, 1935) and by Nagornyi (1940). Ruzicka's assumption that the hysteresis observed is due to pH effects has not been confirmed.

20. *Thermal Denaturation Theory*

Sinex (1957, 1960) proposed that irreplaceable molecules are rendered nonfunctional by thermal denaturation. The theory of absolute reaction rates is used to predict the rate at which denaturation may be expected. According to that theory, denaturation, or inactivation, first requires an activating step which involves a considerable increase in both heat content and entropy. This activation step is considered to be a rate-limiting reaction and is followed by spontaneous denaturation of the molecule which is now in the activated state. Sinex contends that the changes found in collagen during senescence resemble those produced *in vitro* by heat, and that these changes may occur *in vivo* at 38°C.

This theory is based on the assumption that thermal molecular motion may cause microconcentrations of fast molecules capable of causing denaturation of irreplaceable large molecules. However, as a matter of practical observation, such inactivation by merely standing around is extremely slow in comparison with observed reactions with cross-linking agents demonstrably present in living organisms. This applies to proteins and particularly to DNA. Watson (1968) indicates that DNA is "very, very, stable."

Thermally denatured large molecules do not present steric hindrances for enzyme action; in the case of proteins, the process should, therefore, be reversible and would not appear a good explanation for something as irreversible as aging.

The susceptibility of denatured proteins to the action of hydrolases was brought out already by Anson and Mirsky (1934), and the literature of the following years is replete with papers reporting instances where denaturation of proteins resulted in enhanced protein digestibility, but none showing the reverse. This has been reviewed, for example, by Putnam, F. W. (1953) and by Green, N. M., and Neurath, H. (1954).

21. *Calcification—Caliciphylaxis Theory*

The assumption that uncontrolled deposits or reactions of calcium cause a large number of the symptoms of aging and senility is the basis for this theory (Selye, 1959, 1962).

In its support, Selye has shown that rats, rendered calcified by high fat diet, can regain their youthful appearance by mobilizing calcium with vitamin D and causing its selective precipitation with ferric chloride. This is applied so as to cause deposition in the skin which can be shed, thus removing the calcium.

However, the results obtained by Selye have not been proved beyond certain specific conditions. For general applicability it will be necessary to show that macromolecules, i.e. collagen, other proteins, and nucleic acids of the young, artificially calcified animals, change their properties, i.e. shrinkage temperature, molecular weight, swellability, solubility in anhydrous hydrogen fluoride, and enzymatic hydrolysability. In addition, it will be necessary to show that natural calcification of senile animals can also be reversed. In any event, Selye's results are valuable and interesting. As related to the broader aspects of aging, this theory will stand or fall on what can be accomplished experimentally with senile organisms.

22. *The Cross-linkage Theory*

Large molecules necessary for life processes are progressively immobilized in all cells and tissues by cross-linkage. This can be due to reaction directly between the large molecules, though more commonly by contact with small cross-linker molecules; that is, molecules capable of reacting with two different large molecules so as to effect a cross-link between these, thereby reducing their mobility and forming aggregates which have entirely different diffusion, permeability, solvation properties, etc., compared with the original component molecules. Cell death and, less frequently, mutation can be caused particularly by cross-linkage of DNA. While damage to DNA often can be repaired in the cell, a nonbreakable crosslinkage between the two helices makes it impossible for one of these to act as template in repairing the other, for example by the mechanism postulated by Howard-Flanders and Boyce (1966). Such damage is therefore fatal.

The cross-linkage agents have been shown to be present abundantly in the normal human body and their random contact with large molecules results in "hits" of cross-linkage (Bjorksten, 1941, 1942, 1951, 1962 and 1968; Bjorksten and Champion, 1942; Milch, 1965.)

Special cases of cross-linkage have been stressed. For example, Theory 15 (Continuous Radiation or Free Radical Effects) is a special case of the cross-linkage theory, for cross-linkage is the principal chemical effect of ionizing radiation which is mediated through free radicals. The other main effect of radiation is chain fission, but this is less likely to cause lasting effects such as aging, because fragments of molecules formed by fission are usually small enough to be excretable.

The concept of cross-linkages being an important factor in aging was introduced by Bjorksten (1941, p. 750). The agents are normally present in organisms in such abundance that to give the theory a plausible form it was necessary to explain not why we age, but rather why aging does not proceed to a conclusion in a matter of months rather than decades. This consideration led to two answers.

The first defense mechanism against aging by cross-linking of large molecules was described as follows:

> In the living organism this tanning (= cross-linking) is counteracted by the continued state of flux of protein molecules, which are continually split and resynthesized. In this interplay of synthetic and splitting reactions, the protein molecules are broken down before tanning has gone very far and resynthetized in a nontanned state. (Bjorksten, 1942.)

This mechanism is accentuated in rapidly dividing cells, which therefore age much more slowly than substantially nondividing cells.

The other defense mechanism is more specific to blood vessels, heart and breathing muscles, and intestinal organs subject to peristalsis. The effect of pulsation in the arterial system mitigates the effect of cross-linkages by their orientation (Bjorksten and Champion, 1942).

Theoretical development of the cross-linking theory has been carried further by Carpenter (1965, 1966, 1968). Working with two extremely simplified mathematical systems on the basis of diffusion of molecules, Carpenter deduces that the number of types of complex molecules accumulated should be less in young than in old organisms; that the more cells that are adjacent to the original cell, the more rapidly the complex molecules tend to accumulate so that fat animals will tend to accumulate molecules and thus age more rapidly than thin animals of the same species; and that elimination of the more complex molecules accumulated in an organism should tend to increase the diffusion rates of less complex molecules. The calculations of Carpenter and Loynd (1968) indicate that lipofuscin in the human myocardium has an age pigment precursor.

The human organism is pervaded by numerous cross-linking agents such as formaldehyde; acetaldehyde; glyoxal; glycolaldehyde; glyceraldehyde; pyruvaldehyde; croton aldehyde (Milch, 1965); malic, citric, succinic, and fumaric acids; quinones; orthoquinones (from catechol and adrenalin) (Ball and Chen, 1933; Green and Richter, 1937); many metallic cross-linkers such as, silicon, copper, aluminum, and manganese (Zinsser, 1957; Bjorksten, 1958, 1962 and 1964); and oxidizing fats (Gustavson, 1962). Unsaturated fats on oxidation form a broad range of aldehydes, peroxides, and free radicals which are important cross-linkers, particularly in view of the proximity of fats to enzymes and structural proteins in membranes. The occurrence of cross-linkage is unavoidable with all of these cross-linking agents available in the body in ample quantities. It is kept somewhat in check only by the rapid turnover which in dividing cells breaks down mildly cross-linked and still hydrolyzable molecules and resynthetizes them, thus restoring them to the non-crosslinked state. (Bjorksten, 1942, p. 2; 1958, pp. 741 and 742).

Cross-linking has been proven for DNA and for collagen (von Hahn and Verzar, 1963; von Hahn, 1963) and has been indicated by a 99 per cent probability (Student's test) for rat liver proteins (Bjorksten *et al.*, 1960).

Many workers have shown that collagen is cross-linked. These include Verzar (1956, 1964), Bakerman (1964), and Veis and collaborators who found that collagen is increasingly polymerized during maturation and involving formaldehyde and acetaldehyde (Veis and Drake, 1963; Veis and Borcover, 1964). Milch (1963 and 1965) and Milch *et al.* (1963) elabroated on this and performed important *in vivo* experiments. The *in vivo* transition in human skin of the extractable collagen to the insoluble form is due to the formation of intermolecular cross-links and follows an exponential course with age, according to Bakerman (1962). Lysine-derived cross-links form important structural components in aging elastin since Partridge and co-workers (1963, 1964) and Thomas *et al.* (1963) have shown that condensation of 4 lysine residues forms a cyclic quaternary crosslink, desmosine, and an isomer, isodesmosine, as shown below:

Desmosine
_____

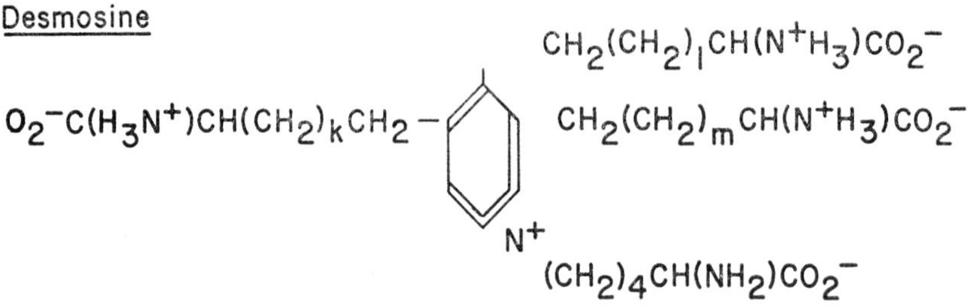

$$O_2^-C(H_3N^+)CH(CH_2)_kCH_2-$$

$$CH_2(CH_2)_lCH(N^+H_3)CO_2^-$$

$$CH_2(CH_2)_mCH(N^+H_3)CO_2^-$$

$$N^+$$

$$(CH_2)_4CH(NH_2)CO_2^-$$

Isodesmosine
_____

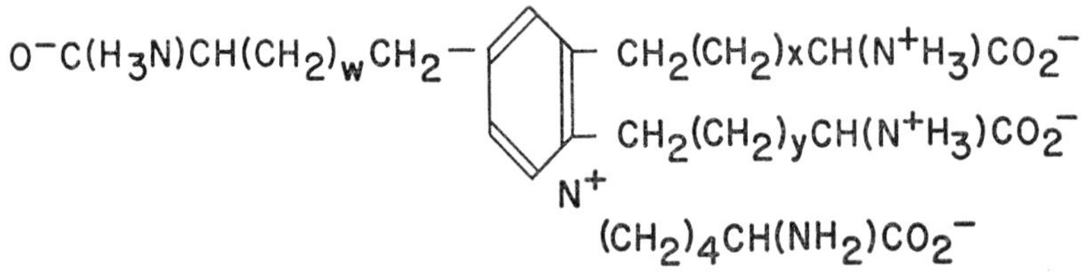

$$O^-C(H_3N)CH(CH_2)_wCH_2-$$

$$CH_2(CH_2)_xCH(N^+H_3)CO_2^-$$

$$CH_2(CH_2)_yCH(N^+H_3)CO_2^-$$

$$N^+$$

$$(CH_2)_4CH(NH_2)CO_2^-$$

(from Thomas *et al.,* 1963)

The importance of tyrosine as a starting point of cross-linkage formation in collagen is stressed by LaBella and Lindsay (1963) and LaBella and Paul (1965), who noted a decrease in tyrosine concentration with age in collagen. At the same time, an agewise increase in the content of a fluorescent component is seen in both collagen and elastin. The spectrum of this fluorescent accumulation resembles that of certain newly synthesized, substituted benzoquinones, hence allowing speculation that oxidation of constituent tyrosine residues to reactive quinoid structures occurs, and that these are capable of binding covalently to adjacent functional groups. LaBella and Paul (1965, p. 58) estimate that only a portion of the quinone cross-linkers can have originated in this manner and that the balance is deposited from body fluids.

Quinoid compounds are also implicated by isolation from aged heart muscles under circumstances which show that they were bound so firmly that only violent hydrolytic conditions with concentrated acids could free them.

Ogino and co-workers have isolated 5-hydroxyanthranilic acid from the urine of patients with senile cataracts.

5-hydroxyanthranilic acid

Quinoniminecarboxylic acid, an oxide of the above, produces cataracts when injected intraperitoneally into vitamin C deficient guinea pigs (Uyama *et al.,* 1953; Ogino and Ichihara, 1957). In the lens of animals they have shown that the power of forming Vitamin C decreases with age (Ogino, 1952). From the urine of animals with experimental cataracts (such as naphthalene, dinitrophenol and galactose cataracts and those formed from abnormal tyrosine metabolism) quinone derivatives can also be isolated, and these substances in turn can produce cataracts in Vitamin C deficient animals (Uyama and Ogino, 1956).

Since all other proteins and nucleic acids contain the same reactive groups on which the cross-linking agents act, and since the cross-linking agents are obviously there and active, there is no reasonable doubt that the same mechanism is functioning to gradually cross-link all of these large molecules as well as it has been found to apply to DNA, collagen, and rat liver proteins.

The cross-linkage theory is further supported by the finding of an accumulation of nitrogenous insoluble material in many organisms and tissues as, for example, lipofuscin (Medvedeva, 1939; Heidenreich and Siebert, 1955; Strehler *et al.*, 1959); Bjorkerud, 1964; Bjorksten *et al.*, 1962).

With numerous cross-linking agents simultaneously available, the insoluble material formed on aging could be a conglomeration where any cross-linking agent available has reacted with any two large molecules which come within its path.

The composition of the resultant cross-linked conglomerations will vary with organism, organ, nutrition, etc. For example, the work of Zinsser, *et al.* (1957) has produced x-ray spectrographic evidence of cross-linkages with metal oxide spacings in human aorta. This is supported by the large increase in the content of polyvalent metals with aging in arteries and other circulatory organs (Zinsser *et al.*, 1962). On the other hand, rat tail tendons contain practically no metal oxides. It would seem that these never get through the walls of the capillaries. Lower aldehyde molecules, on the other hand, migrate easily through proteinaceous material and effect cross-linkage (Bjorksten, 1941, 1942) or are formed *in situ* by oxidation of unsaturated fats (Bjorksten and Collbring, 1964; Andrews *et al.*, 1965.)

The types of cross-linking agents listed above could thus be coacting in a disordered "as available" fashion to produce the phenomenon we know as aging or senility and to trigger concomitant pathology by any or all of the *intermediate* processes (9-17) above.

The considerable shortening of life expectancy by overfeeding indicates that the intermediates of the Krebs cycle and/or the nitrogen cycle play a significant part in the total amount of cross-linking.

With low caloric intake, the oxidation process proceeds readily to the innocuous end products $H_2O + CO_2$. With overfeeding, however, processing time is slowed down at intermediate points in the metabolism so that accumulation of intermediate products occur. Since many of these are powerful cross-linking agents, acceleration of the aging process by overfeeding is expectable.

THE POSSIBILITY TO RETARD OR REVERSE AGING

The value of theories lies in the experiments they suggest for further penetration and in the practical application to which they lead. We shall discuss the theories in this light.

The general theories (1-8 above), yield nothing in this regard. Analyzed semantically, their statements cancel out, so that the remainder is something practically obvious such as "the lower the physiological condition, the more progressed is the aging," or "the less the resistance to traumata, the shorter is the average longevity." On such generalities no rational experimental program or therapy can be built.

The *intermediate* theories are more fruitful:

9. *Progressive Cell Death*

This theory gives us a point to watch and a criterion for the progress of age which Rockstein (1950) has used in the study of the aging of insects. It suggests the importance of determining unequivocally the causes of this cell death. This is the level where the prevention must be applied, for it does not seem plausible that dead nerve or muscle cells could be revived or replaced.

10. *Cybernetic Theory*

This suggests the need for a thorough study of the central mechanism accounting for the deterioration of the speed of transmission and for therapies involving methods to bring back the speed of reaction. This theory is fully compatible with theories 11, 12, 13, 15, and 22. The pertinent pharmacology, even at the present state of evolution, may be able to design experiments to prove the extent to which this mechanism may be responsible for the aging syndrome.

11. *Hormonal Imbalance*

This theory has led to the gland transplantation therapies of Steinach (1920) and Voronoff (1920), as well as to the present successful work based on anabolic sterol products. The correction of thyroid and other imbalances also belongs in this group, and Niehans' cellular therapy might be viewed as a special case of it (Niehans, 1954). All in all, the success of these approaches in practical therapy, though limited, leaves no doubt as to the merits of the concept and the reality of its assumptions.

At the same time, we must not lose sight of the fact that none of these therapies makes possible any really drastic extension of life beyond the present major limits; so that while most useful, this theory covers a part only of the total events connected with aging and senescence. As already pointed out, it does not go back to ultimate causes, for it does not explain the causes of the hormonal imbalance involved.

12. *Enzyme Deterioration*

This theory suggests the use of enzymes, or proenzymes to replace the deficiencies which develop with aging. This has been done successfully with digestive enzymes, but becomes much more difficult when intracellular enzymes are involved. It was long believed that enzymes administered externally, orally, or even intravenously would not be sufficiently stable or selectively applicable to reach their destination in active state. However, more recent work has shown that at least some (Smyth *et al.*, 1961) proteases orally administered can penetrate in an active state (Martin, 1964; Cirelli, 1964; Innerfield, 1966). Application in precursor state may also be possible. This has not been sufficiently explored.

It is possible that some or most of the success of treatments with embryonal extracts (Niehans, 1954) may be due to enzyme activator or precursor effects, as well as to hormone effects and proliferation of embryonic cells. Compensation for the deterioration of enzymes may also be possible by the induction (or adaption) of greater quantities or concentrations of an enzyme by substrate administration. The substrates could be administered by incorporation into the regular diet.

Enzyme induction has been long known to occur in microorganisms. In connection with conditions for the study of enzyme formation, H. von Euler and collaborators found that the saccharase content of yeast increased several hundred per cent if the organisms were treated with a strong sugar solution containing electrolytes and a nitrogen source (Euler and Kullberg, 1911). Euler and Johansson (1912 a,b) concluded on the basis of their work that an increase in saccharase under these nutritional conditions is not dependent on adaption because it also could be caused by glucose which is not a substrate for saccharase; and that it is not due to a general increase in vitality since the total fermentive effect does not increase, but has unknown causes. In later work, Euler and Svanberg (1919 a,b) and Svanberg (1920) were able to increase the invertase content twelve fold, and Willstätter (1925), by stimulation with very small concentrations of sucrose, was able to attain still greater increases in saccharase content.

However, enzyme induction has also been demonstrated in rats and humans. Knox and Mehler (1951) first adapted tryptophane pyrrolase by administering an excess of tryptophane, and after five hours the liver activity of that enzyme had increased up to ten fold. The same group showed adaption of a tyrosine transaminase (tyrosine-α-ketoglutarate) in rat liver (Lin and Knox, 1957). The reverse process (repression) is also possible in rats as shown by Franz *et al.*, (1954). They demonstrated a decreased liver synthesis of cholesterol after administration of 1 per cent cholesterol in diets.

Glucose-6-phosphate dehydrogenase activity in the rat liver was shown to be markedly affected by changes in diet by Chang *et al.* (1964). Later work on the same enzyme by Chang and Adams (1965) showed the enzyme was suceptible to carbohydrate changes. The highest level of enzyme occurred in livers when sucrose was fed, and the lowest level when the carbohydrate source was starch.

Irwin and Richardson (1966) reported a study with human females and found significantly higher levels of lactate dehydrogenase and alkaline phosphatase on sugar diets compared to starch diets.

While the concentration of most enzymes in the body decreases with aging, the cathepsins are an outstanding exception. (Barrows, 1960; Barrows *et al*, 1962; Barrows and Roeder, 1962).

Could this be because of an evolutionary advantage for those individuals who maintain a maximal percentage of endocellular proteases? This would be consistent with the view that a rapid turnover of protein counteracts cross-linkages (Bjorksten, 1942). If so, any nutritional or other steps that increase the activity or the range of substrates acted upon by endocelluar proteases could be expected to have a beneficial effect.

13. *Autoimmunity Reactions*

If this is a major mechanism in aging, favorable therapeutic results should be obtainable with substances suppressing immunological sensitivity. Work with such substances is currently under way.

14. *Somatic Mutations*

Once a mutation has occurred, it is probable that only surgery or destructive radiation can remove the resultant mutated tissue. Prevention of mutations presupposes knowledge of their cause.

It would seem that little can be done about effects of cosmic or other ambient radiation (the use of antiradiation chemicals has not been spectacularly successful in extending life where strains with normal longevity were used) or about the thermal motion of molecules at normal temperatures. These remarks also apply to Theory 15 which follows:

15. *Continuous Radiation Damage as a Cause of Aging*

The administration of amino sulfhydryl compounds, serotonin, and other radiation protective substances have not shown any impressive efficacy in prolonging life of mice strains which normally reach senility (Harman, 1957).

16. *Toxins Formed in the Digestive Tract*

This theory has suggested certain dietary practices and the popularity of yoghurt may in part stem from this theory. Some useful results may have ensued, but certainly not on any major scale.

17. *Reticulocytic Effects*

Some favorable results have been reported as achieved by the use of a cytotoxic antimesenchymatous serum (Medvedeva, 1939) in increasing the concentration in liver tissues of soluble globulins and reducing the concentration of insoluble globulins; this work has not been heard much of lately.

The initiating step in the aging process is naturally the point where prevention is most readily applied.

18. *The "Clinker" Theory*

This theory has been discussed and does not appear to play a sufficiently large part in the overall picture to provide a basis for major prevention.

19. *The Protein Hysteresis Theory*

Attempts have been made, particularly by Bancroft and his pupils, to extend life by administering rhodanates to enhance the swelling of protein gels in the organisms. The experimental work did not appear wholly unpromising Bancroft *et al.*, 1934 b, 1935) but was interrupted by Bancroft's death and was not resumed in view of unrelated clinical hazards associated with the habitual use of rhodanates. Some of the results now obtained with dimethyl sulfoxide may be ascribed to swelling or hydration phenomena in proteins and may indicate the need for correlation with Bancroft's work.

20. *Thermal Denaturation Theory*

It is difficult to see how this theory readily could be adapted to countermeasures against aging because thermal molecular motion effects can hardly be modified without disturbing body temperatures, and thermally destroyed large molecules have not been repaired. Their removal occurs naturally, as thermal denaturation is no obstacle to enzyme action.

It is well known that heat sensitivity of cells is reduced, for example, by high carbohydrate concentrations, e.g. the conversion of starch to glucose in plants kept close to freezing temperatures. However, the concentrations needed for this effect seem too high for practical application in aging therapy.

21. *Calcification—Calciphylaxis Theory*

The application of this theory hinges on whether removal of calcium from naturally aged individuals will succeed with senile individuals in the manner it has succeeded with artificially sclerosed young animals. If it does, an important step has been made in the treatment of arteriosclerosis regardless of whether or not this treatment strikes at the basis of the aging process itself.

22. *The Cross-linkage Theory*

The cross-linkage theory centers on the initiating stage of the aging syndrome. Therefore, it provides logical points of attacks for prevention and possibly reversal.

If we accept the evidence that this theory covers a principal path of the aging process, as well as the cause of progressive reduction with age of the level of hormones and of many enzymes, of somatic mutations, progressive cell death, and of the slowing down of transmission speeds of nerve impulses, then the first question is "Could we reduce the level of cross-linkage greatly by a selective diet?" The answer to this is "No." The cross-linking agents are so many and varied, so much a part of essential life processes that they cannot be avoided. Direct cross-linkage between mutually reactive groups or side chains of the large molecules may also occur, particularly if a cross-linkage already has fixed the large molecules in question in the proximity of each other.

What can be done is to keep the overall caloric intake sufficiently low to avoid accumulation of cross-linking intermediates in the bottlenecks of the metabolic pathways. If food intake is moderate, the biological fuel is oxidized to carbon dioxide and water, both clearly innocuous. If it is supplied too rapidly to be metabolized at once at any one of the many steps in the pathway, there will be accumulation of intermediates. Many of these, as previously pointed out, are powerful cross-linking agents. That restriction of food prolongs life was shown by

Northrop's classical work with Drosophila (1917) and confirmed by McCay with rodents (1934), Rudzinska with Tokophrya (1951, 1961, 1962), and by others, and by the general clinical experience with man.

If the effect of overfeeding is due to a back-up of deleterious metabolites at metabolic bottlenecks, then it is expectable that many small meals will be preferable to a few large ones, as this would minimize the occurrence of peak loads which could not be immediately processed. It has been shown that intermittent fasting periods are beneficial regardless of the stage of development. (Carlson, A. J., and Hoelzel, F., 1946; Holeckova, E., and Chvapil, M., 1965).

An adequate level of Vitamin E or a supply of other equivalent antioxidants (Machlin *et al.*, 1959, 1962; Machlin, 1963) will reduce the uncontrolled oxidation which generates aldehydes and peroxides from unsaturated fatty acids, but its benefits are limited to those cross-linkers which result from uncontrolled oxidative processes.

In view of the proximity between oxidizable lipids and enzymes or structural proteins in membranes, the reaction between these is favored and results in formation of cross-linkages. Therefore, one of the most important things that can be done with present information is to minimize the lipid oxidation by use of tocopherols or equivalent antioxidants. However, even along this path, it seems doubtful that life extension beyond about 50 per cent of the present could be attained in higher animals. The effect of oxidizing fats in insolubilizing proteins has long been known. Andrews *et al.* (1965) have shown that fats oxidizing in the presence of proteins cross-link these and that this is blocked by sodium bifulfite, which indicates that aldehydes are the principal oxidation products which effect the cross-linkage.

Also, a reasonable surplus of the structural components of protein and/or nucleic acids would provide a floating supply of easily eliminated reactive groups which can scavenge floating cross-linker molecules from the systems and thus somewhat mitigate the progressive cross-linkage.

Polyvalent metals have been seen as influencing aging. The

basis for this is largely that all of the polyvalent metals accumulate on aging, particularly in the aorta, but also in other organs, in close contact with circulation. A similar buildup does not seem to occur in tendons.

Perhaps the least increase is in calcium and iron (omitting sclerosis effects), which is expectable as living organisms have had to develop effective means for handling these essential elements. Aging effects have been associatd with buildup of copper, a known pro-oxidant (Harman, 1965). The property of cadmium to accumulate in soft, nonosseous tissue (Cotzias *et al.*, 1961) renders it a prime suspect. This is augmented by its property to form insoluble sulfhydryl compounds. The known cumulative effects of lead coupled with the increasing content of lead in city air has given rise to much concern. Yet even more dramatic accumulation occurs of aluminum and probably of silicon (Zinsser and Light, 1965).

Tyler (1953 and 1965) has shown that the lifespan of sea urchin spermatozoa is multiplied several times if polyvalent trace elements are removed from the ambience by chelating agents. The work of Zinsser (1957) and co-workers indicates the significance of this aspect as related to humans. It may be an important facet of the cross-linking mechanism in the circulatory system. Tendons do not show any similar increase in ash and the cross-linking mechanism there is essentially on an organic basis. Periodic removal of metallic cross-linking agents by the administration of ethylene diamine tetra acetic acid, EDTA, amino sulfhydryl compounds, or other applicable chelating agents might have some beneficial effect. The use of zinc salts in geriatric medicine could involve the displacement of cadmium. Such therapies, however, will be powerless against methylene bridges, for example, or against quinone cross-linkages, which are exceptionally stable, a finding carefully quantitated by Ciferri and Rajagh (1964) and Puett *et al.* (1965).

The really dramatic results might be attained only in reversal of aging effects, not in prevention. If means could be provided for breaking down highly cross-linked aggregates in the cells, this would free the space so that the normal anabolic processes could take care of replacement.

In the case of collagen, it has been shown by Schaub (1964)

that post partum in the uterus of rats, even very cross-linked collagen, not normally digestible, will be resorbed. If such a result is possible for one protein, it should be possible for others as well by more or less analogous means.

Lathyrism is the collagen "disease" caused by ingestion of a number of substances such as beta amino propionitrile and isoniacin hydrazide (Levene and Gross, 1959; Bickley, 1964). However, this mechanism so far is limited to new collagen and does not mobilize old and cross-linked collagen as originally hoped by many (Levene, 1966).

The best possibility for a basic attack may be the use of enzymes from soil bacteria. If there were no soil bacteria capable of breaking down even highly cross-linked proteins, then there would be in existence vastly more fossil protein than is now in evidence. It should be possible to isolate the enzymes from such soil bacteria, and with luck and persistence, we might find among them a therapeutic agent capable of breaking the linkages involved or overcoming the steric hindrances they pose against breaking the carbon chains directly (Bjorksten, 1951).

It would not matter if the enzymes obtained broke down all other proteins as well, so long as they *also* would attack the critical cross-linked molecules. An attack on the backbone of the molecule would for this purpose be just as good as an attack on the cross-linkage. The normal anabolic processes would take care of the replacement of normal molecules removed, so long as the dosages were kept within controllable limits.

Recent work has shown that proteolytic enzymes, even given orally, can actually reach the cell plasma in tissues such as liver and kidney (Smyth *et al.*, 1961). The effectiveness of treatment with such enzymes has been shown in both clinical experience and cases of experimentally induced hematomas (Cirelli, 1964; Martin, 1964).

It has also been reported that in wound healing, old cross-linked molecules of collagen can be broken down. The enzymes here involved and the stimulations which cause formation of such enzymes may also provide valuable clues. Pelc (1964) has shown that at least a partial renewal and mending of DNA does occur even in nondividing cells.

Obviously the search for agents to remobilize the highly

cross-linked molecules will not be easy. Products must be screened carefully for toxicity and side effects. The chances for success might be compared to those for making practically applicable antibiotics from microorganisms fifty years ago.

THE FUTURE

The following chart (Fig. 12) depicts the life expectancy of a white male in the United States at age sixty from 1789 till 1963. It is evident that work on controlling aging itself for the male has not yet begun to rise from the platform it has occupied for nearly two centuries (recent years have shown some improvement in life expectancy for the female). In the meanwhile, infant mortality and infectious diseases have been controlled so that work on these as on other specific diseases has reached a point of diminishing return. Nonetheless, the major portion of funds for medical research still continues to be spent on projects of this nature or on palliative or descriptive studies which have no chance of solving the basic problems.

McCay (1942) has pointed out that when the age problem

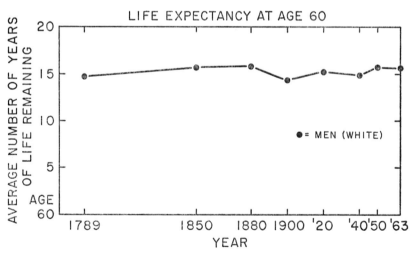

FIGURE 12. Life expectancy of a white male in the United States at age 60 from 1789 until 1963. (From *Vital Statistics of the United States, 1963*, Vol. II, section 5, Life Table 5-5.)

itself has been solved, the age dependent diseases headed by cancer and circulatory diseases will automatically fall in line. The full benefit of all other medical research will only be realized when the process of aging can be braked.

REFERENCES

ALEXANDER, P., and CONNELL, D. I.: The failure of the potent mutagenic chemical, ethyl methane sulphonate, to shorten the life-span of mice. *Unesco Symposium on Cellular Basis and Aetiology of Late Somatic Effects of Ionizing Radiations.* New York, Academic, 1962, p. 277.

ALPATOV, V. V., and NASTYUKOVA, O. K.: Age variations in animals in their reaction to the optical isomers of acriquine. *Dokl. Akad. Nauk S.S.S.R.,* 59:1365, 1948.

ANDREWS, F.; BJORKSTEN, J.; TRENK, F. B.; HENICK, A. S., and KOCH, R. B.: The reaction of an autoxidized lipid with proteins. *J. Amer. Oil Chem. Soc.,* 42 (No. 9):779, 1965.

ANSON, M. L., and MIRSKY, A. E.: The equilibria between native and denatured hemoglobin in salicylate solutions and the theoretical consequences of the equilibrium between native and denatured protein. *J. Gen. Physiol.,* 17:407, 1934.

BAKERMAN, S.: Quantitative extraction of acid-soluble human skin collagen with age. *Nature (London), 196* (No. 4852):375, 1962.

BAKERMAN, S.: Distribution of the alpha and beta components in human-skin collagen with age. *Biochim. Biophys. Acta, 90*:621, 1964.

BALL, E. G., and CHEN, T. T.: Studies on oxidation-reduction. XX-epinephrine and related compounds. *J. Biol. Chem., 102*:691, 1933.

BANCROFT, W. D.; FARNHAM, E. C., and RUTZLER, J. E., JR.: Preliminary tests with sodium rhodanate on rabbits and chickens. *Science, 80*:549, 1934 a.

BANCROFT, W. D.; FARNHAM, E. C., and RUTZLER, J. E. JR.: One aspect of the longevity problem. *Science, 81*:152, 1935.

BANCROFT, W. D., and RUTZLER, J. E., JR.: Reversible coagulation on living tissue. XII. *Proc. Nat. Acad. Sci. U.S.A., 20*:501, 1934 b.

BARROW, C. H., JR.: Age and cellular metabolism of tissues. *Amer. Inst. Biol. Sci. Publ., 6*:116, 1960.

BARROW, C. H., JR., and ROEDER, L. M.: Age differences in the concentrations of various enzymes in tissues of the rat. In *Biological Aspects of Aging.* Shock, N. W., Ed. New York, Columbia, 1962, p. 290.

BARROWS, C. H., JR.; ROEDER, L. M., and FALZONE, J. A.: Effects of age on the activities of enzymes and the concentrations of nucleic acids in the tissues of wild rats. *J. Geront., 17*:144, 1962.

BERTOLINI, A. M.: Modifications of cellular enzymatic systems during aging. *Gerontologia (Basel), 6*:175, 1962.

BICKLEY, H.: Experimental lathyrism: Apparent antithesis of aging in connective tissue. *J. Amer. Geriat. Soc.*, *12*:717, 1964.

BJORKERUD, S.: Isolated lipoprotein granules—A survey of a new field. In *Advances in Gerontological Research*, Strehler, B. L., Ed. New York, Academic, 1964, vol. 1, p. 257.

BJORKSTEN, J.: Recent developments in protein chemistry. *Chem. Industr.*, *48*:746, 1941.

BJORKSTEN, J.: Chemistry of duplication. *Chem. Indust.*, *50*:69, 1942.

BJORKSTEN, J.: Cross-linkages in protein chemistry. In *Advances in Protein Chemistry*. Anson, M., and Edsall, J., Eds. New York, Academic, 1951, vol. 6, p. 343.

BJORKSTEN, J.: A common molecular basis for the aging syndrome. *J. Amer. Geriat. Soc.*, *6*:740, 1958.

BJORKSTEN, J.: Aging: Present status of our chemical knowledge. *J. Amer. Geriat. Soc.*, *10*:125, 1962.

BJORKSTEN, J.: Chemical causes of the aging process. *Proc. of the Scientific Section of the Toilet Goods Assoc.*, *41*:32, 1964.

BJORKSTEN, J.: Enzymes in aging. In *Enzymes in Mental Health*. Neuberg Soc. Third Symposium on Progress in Biochemistry and Therapeutics. New York, 1966, pp. 84-94.

BJORKSTEN, J.: The crosslinkage theory of aging. *J. Amer. Geriat. Soc.*, 23, April 1968.

BJORKSTEN, J.; ANDREWS, F.; BAILEY, JULIA, and TRENK, B.: Fundamentals of aging: Immobilization of proteins in whole-body irradiated white rats. *J. Amer. Geriat. Soc.*, *8*:37, 1960.

BJORKSTEN, J.; ANDREWS, F., and PRAHL, H. F.: Anhydrous hydrogen fluoride as a tool in studying cross-linkages in proteinaceous substances accumulating with age. *Finsk. Kemists. Medd.*, *71*:39, 1962.

BJORKSTEN, J., and CHAMPION, W. J.: Mechanical influences on tanning. *J. Amer. Chem. Soc.*, *64*:868 1942.

BJORKSTEN, J., and COLLBRING, T.: *Proc. of the Scientific Section of the Toilet Goods Assoc.*, *42*:1, 1964.

BLAGOVESTCHENSKI, A. V.: *On Some Biochemical Fundamentals of Evolutive Processes in Plants*. Moscow, Akad. Nauk. S.S.S.R., 1950, p. 139.

BLUMENTHAL, H. T., and BERNS, ALINE W.: Autoimmunity and aging. In *Advances in Gerontological Research*. Strehler, B. L., Ed. New York, Academic, 1964, vol. 1, p. 289.

BOGOMOLETS, A. A.: *The Prolongation of Life*. New York, Duell, Sloan and Pearce, 1946, pp. 81, 85, 86.

BOURNE, G. H.: Histochemical evidence of increased activity of hydrolytic enzymes in the cells of old animals. *Nature (London)*, *179*:472, 1957.

BRODY, S.: The kinetics of senescence. *J. Gen. Physiol.*, *6*:245, 1923.

BROWN-SÉQUARD, CH. E.: *C. R. Soc. Biol.*, *41*:415, 1889.

CARLSON, A. J., and HOELZEL, F.: Apparent prolongation of life span of rats by intermittent fasting. *J. Nutr.*, *31*:363, 1946.

CARPENTER, DONALD G.: Diffusion theory of aging. *J. Geront.*, *20*:191, 1965.

CARPENTER, DONALD G.: Diffusion theory of aging, rectangular parallelipiped Model. *Proc. 7th Int. Cong. Geront.*, Vienna, June 26 to July 2, 1966, p. 39.

CARPENTER, DONALD G.: Biological aging as a diffusion phenomenon. 1968, In press.

CARPENTER, DONALD G., and LOYND, J. A.: An integrated theory of aging. 1968, In press.

CHANG, M. L., and ADAMS, MILDRED: Influence of heredity and of dietary carbohydrate on some of the carbohydrate-metabolizing enzymes in the tissues of the young rat. *Abstr. from Federation of Amer. Soc. for Exper. Biol.*, April 1965.

CHANG, M. L., SCHUSTER, E., and SNODGRASS: Influence of heredity and diet on enzyme activity in rats. *Abstr. 6th Int. Congr. Biochem.*, New York, 1964.

CIFERRI, A., and RAJAGH, L. V.: The aging of connective tissue. *J. Geront.*, *19* (No. 2):220, 1964.

CIRELLI, M. G.: Clinical experience with bromelains in proteolytic enzyme therapy of inflammation and edema. *Med. Times*, 1964.

CLARK, A. M.: Genetic factors associated with aging. *Advances in Gerontological Research*. Strehler, B. L., Ed. New York, Academic, 1964, vol. 1, p. 233.

CLARK, A. M., and ROCKSTEIN, M.: Aging in insects. In *The Physiology of Insects*. Rockstein, M., Ed. New York and London, Academic, 1964, vol. 1, chap. 6.

CLARK, A. M., and RUBIN, M. A.: The modification of X-irradiation of the life span of haploids and diploids of the wasp, *Habrobracon sp. Radiat. Res.*, *15*:244, 1961.

COTZIAS, G. C.; BORG, D. C., and SELLECK, B.: Virtual absence of turnover imcadmium metabolism: Cd^{109} studies in the mouse. *Amer. J. Physiol.*, *201*:927, 1961.

CURTIS, HOWARD J.: Biological mechanisms underlying the aging process. *Science*, *141*:686, 1963.

DANIELLI, J. F.:On the ageing of cells in tissues. "Experimentelle Altersforschung," Verzar, F., Ed., *Experientia Suppl iv*: 55, 1956.

EISIG, H.: Monographie der Capitelliden, Fauna et Flora des *Golfes von Neapel*. 1887, vol. 16.

ELLIS, R. S.: Norms of some structural changes in human cerebellum from birth to old age. *J. Comp. Neurol.*, *32*:1, 1920.

EULER, H., and JOHANSSON, D.: Über die Bildung von Invertase in Hefe. *Hoppe Seyler Z. Physiol. Chem.*, *76*:388-395, 1912 a.

EULER, H., and JOHANSSON, D.: Untersuchung über die chemische Zusammensetzung und Bildung der Enzyme - Über die Anpassung einer Hefe an Galaktose. *Hoppe Seyler Z. Physiol. Chem.* *78*:246-265, 1912 b.

EULER, H., and KULLBERG, S.: Über den Temperaturkoeffizienten der Zersetzung von Invertase. *Hoppe Seyler Z. Physiol. Chem.* 71:134-142, 1911.

EULER, H., and SVANBERG, O.: Sacharasegehalt and Sacharasebildung in der Hefe. *Hoppe Seyler Z. Physiol. Chem.* 106:201-248, 1919 a.

EULER, H., and SVANBERG, O.: Versuche zur Darstellung aktiver Sacharasepräparate. *Hoppe Seyler Z. Physiol. Chem.*, 207:294-296, 1919 b.

FAILLA, G,: Considerations bearing on permissible accummulated radiation doses for occupational exposure. The aging process and cancerogenesis. *Radiology, 69*:23, 1957.

FAILLA, G.: The aging process and cancerogenesis. *Ann. N. Y. Acad. Sci.*, 71:1124, 1958.

FRANTZ, IVAN D., JR.; SCHNEIDER, HENNY, and HINKELMAN, BEVERLY T.: Suppression of hepatic cholesterol synthesis in the rat by cholesterol feeding. *J. Biol. Chem.*, 206:465, 1954.

GARDNER, E.: Decrease in human neurons with age. *Anat. Rec.*, 77:529, 1940.

GHIRINGHELLI, E. M., and GERZELI, G.: Histochemical activities of glandular cells in old rats. *G. Geront.*, 11:1097, 1963.

GREEN, D. E., and RICHTER, D.: Adrenaline and Adenochrome. *Biochem. J.*, 31:595, 1937.

GREEN, N. M., and NEURATH, HANS: Proteolytic enzymes. In *Proteins: Chemistry, Biological Activity, and Methods.* Neurath, H., and Bailey, K., Eds. New York, Academic, 1954, vol. IIB, Chapt. 25, pp. 1172-1173.

GUSTAVSON, K. H.: The crosslinking of proteins by tanning. *Research, 15*: 261, 1962.

VON HAHN, H. P., and VERZAR, F.: Age-dependent thermal denaturation of DNA from bovine thymus. *Gerontologia, (Basel), 7*:105, 1963.

VON HAHN, H. P.: Age-dependent thermal denaturation and viscosity of crude and purified desoxyribonucleic acid prepared from bovine thymus. *Gerontologia (Basel), 8*:123, 1963.

HARMAN, D.: Aging: A theory based on free radical and radiation chemistry. *J. Geront.*, 11:298, 1956.

HARMAN, D.: Prolongation of the normal life span by radiation protection chemicals. *J. Geront., 12*:257, 1957.

HARMAN, D.: The free radical theory of aging: the effect of age on serum mercaptan levels. *J. Geront., 15* (No. 1):38, 1960.

HARMAN, D.: The free radical theory of aging: Effect of age on serum copper levels. *J. Geront. 20* (No. 2):151, 1965.

HAYFLICK, L.: The limited *in vitro* lifetime of human diploid cell strains. *Exp. Cell Res.*, 37:614, 1965.

HEIDENREICH, O., und SIEBERG, G.: Untersuchungen an isoliertem unverändertem Lipofuscin aus Herzmuskulatur. *Virchow Arch. Path. Anat.*, 327:112, 1955.

HEILBRUNN, L. V.: *Outline of General Physiology,* 2nd ed. Philadelphia, Saunders, 1943, p. 623.

HOLECKOVA, E., and CHVAPIL, M.: The effect of intermittent feeding and fasting and of domestication on biological age in the rat. *Gerontologia (Basel), 11:*96, 1965.

HOWARD-FLANDERS, P., and BOYCE, R. P.: DNA repair and genetic recombination: Studies on mutants of *E. coli* defective in these processes. *Radiation Res. Supp., 6:*156, 1966.

INNERFIELD, T.: Quantitative aspects of oral enzyme therapy. *Trans. N. Y. Acad. Sci.,* 412, Jan. 1966.

IRWIN, M. ISABEL, and RICHARDSON, FLORENCE M.: The effect of source of carbohydrate on the levels of glucose, certain enzymes, and nitrogenous components in the blood serum of young women. *Abstracts of Amer. Assoc. Cereal Chemists Ann. Meeting,* New York, April 1966.

KIRK, J. E.: Enzyme activities of human arterial tissue. *Ann. N. Y. Acad. Sci., 72:*1006, 1959.

KNOX, W. E., and MEHLER, A. H.: The adaptive increase of the tryptophane peroxidase-oxidase system of liver. *Science, 113:*237, 1951.

LABELLA, F. S., and LINDSAY, W. G.: The structure of human elastin as influenced by age. *J. Geront.,* 18:111, 1963.

LABELLA, F. S., and PAUL, GERALD: Structure of collagen from human tendon as influenced by age and sex. *J. Geront., 20:*54, 1965.

LEVENE, C. I.: Experimental osteolathyrism. In *International Academy of Pathology Monograph on Connective Tissue.* Wagner, B., Ed. New York, 1966.

LEVENE, C. I., and GROSS, J.: Alterations in the state of molecular aggregation of collagen induced in chick embryos by beta-amino propoinitrile (Lathyrus factor). *J. Exp. Med., 110:*771, 1959.

LIN, E. C. C., and KNOX, W. E.: Adaptation of the rat liver tyrosine-α-keto-glutarate transaminase. *Biochim. Biophys. Acta,* 26:85, 1957.

MACHLIN, L. J.; GORDON, R. S., and MEISKY, K. H.: The effect of antioxidants in vitamin E deficiency symptoms and production of liver "peroxide" in the chicken. *J. Nutrition,* 67:333, 1959.

MACHLIN, L. J.; GORDON, R. S.; MARR, J. E., and POPE, C. W.: Effect of antioxidants and unsaturated fatty acids on reproduction in the hen. *J. Nutrition,* 76:284, 1962.

MACHLIN, L. J.: The biological consequences of feeding polyunsaturated fatty acids to antioxidant deficient animals. *J. Amer. Oil Chem. Soc., 40:*386, 1963.

MANDEL, P.: Metabolism of bovine arterial wall and its changes in young animals. *Metab. Parietis Vasorum, Papres Intern. Cong. Angiol. 5th.* Prague, 1961.

MARTIN, G. J.: Proteolytic enzymes and inflammation. Current Status Excerpta Medica International Congress Series No. 82. *Proceedings of* an *International Symposium on Non-Steroidal Anti-Inflammatory Drugs.* Milan, Sept. 1964, p. 90.

McCay, C. M., and Crowell, M. F.: Prolongation of life span. *Sci. Monthly,* 39:405, 1934.

McCay, C. M.: In *Problems of Aging.* 2nd ed. Cowdry, E. V., Ed. Baltimore, Williams and Wilkins, 1942, p. 720.

Medvedev, Zh. A.: The nucleic acids in development and aging. In *Advances in Gerontological Research.* Strehler, B. L., Ed. New York, Academic, 1964, p. 181.

Medvedeva, N. B.: The variations in nitrogen compounds and proteins in the tissues of the aged and the action of cytotoxic antireticular serum on these variations. *J. Med. Ukr.,* 9:325, 1939.

Metchnikoff, I. I.: *The Nature of Man* (English translation). New York, Putnam, 1903.

Meyer, J.; Spier, E., and Neuwelt, F.: Studies in old age. IV. The clinical significance of salivary, gastric and pancreatic secretions in the aged. *Arch Intern. Med. (Chicago),* 65:171, 1940.

Milch, R. A.: Possible role of aldehyde metabolites in the aging processes of connective tissue. *Southern Med. J.,* 58:153, 1965.

Milch, R. A.: Studies of collagen tissue aging: Interaction of certain intermediary metabolites with collagen. *Gerontologia (Basel),* 7:129, 1963.

Milch, R. A.; Jude, J. R., and Knaack, J.: Effects of collagen reactive aldehyde metabolites on the structure of the canine aortic wall and their possible role in atherogenesis. *Surgery, 54* (No. 1):104, 1963.

Mühlmann, M.: Über die Veränderungen der Nervenzellen in verschiedenem Alter. *Verh. Deutsch. Path., Ges.* 3:148, 1900.

Nagornyi, A. V.: *Aging and Prolongation of the normal life span.* Moscow, Sov. Nauka, 1950.

Nagornyi, A. V.: The problem of old age and longevity. Kharkov State University, 1940. Cited from S. Oeriu: *Proteins in development and senescence. In Advances in Gerontological Research.* Strehler, B. L., Ed., New York, Academic, 1964, p. 30.

Niehans, P.: *Die Zellular therapie.* München and Berlin, Urban and Schwarzenberg, 1954.

Northrop, John H.: The effect of prolongation of the period of growth on the total duration of life. *J. Biol. Chem.,* 32:123, 1917.

Ogino, S., and Ichihara, T.: Biochemical studies on cataract. V. Biochemical genesis of senile cataract. *Amer. J. Ophthal.,* 43:754, 1957.

Ogino, S.: Vitamin C and crystalline lens. II. *Acta Soc. Ophthal. Jap., 56:* 1342, 1952.

Partridge, S. M.: The chemical nature of elastin expose. *Ann. Biochim. Exp. Med.,* 24:133, 1963.

Partridge, S. M.; Elsden, D. F.; Thomas, J.; Dorfman, Albert; Tesler,

ALVIN, and PEI-LEE, Ho.: Biosynthesis of the desmosine and isodes-mosine cross bridges in elastin. *Biochem. J.*, *93*:30c, 1964.

PEARL, R.: *The Rate of Living.* New York, Knopf, 1920.

PELC, S. R.: Labeling of DNA and cell division in so-called nondividing tissues. *J. Cell Biol.*, *22*:21, 1964.

PUCK, T. T.; WALDREN, C. A.. and TJIO, J. H.: Some data bearing on the long term growth of mammalian cells *in vitro.* Contribution No. 277, Univ. Colorado Medical Center, Denver, Colorado.

PUETT, D.; CIFERRI, A., and RAJAGH, L. V.: Interaction between proteins and salt solutions. II. Elasticity of collagen tendons. *Biopolymers, 3*:439, 1965.

PUTNAM, F. W.: Protein denaturation. In *Proteins Chemistry, Biological Activity, and Methods.* Neurath, H., and Bailey, K., Eds. New York, Academic, 1953, vol. IB, Chapt. 9, pp. 825-826.

PÜTTER, A.: Lebensdauer und Alternsfaktor Z. *Allg. Physiol.*, *19*:9(1921.

ROCKSTEIN, M.: The relation of cholinesterase activity to change in cell number with age in the brain of the adult worker honeybee. *J. Cell. Comp. Physiol.*, *35*:11, 1950.

RUDZINSKA, M. A.: The influence on the amount of food on the reproduction rate and longevity of a suctorian *(Tokophrya infusionum). Science, 113*:10, 1951.

RUDZINSKA, M. A.: The use of a protozoan for studies on aging. *J. Gerontol.*, *16*:213, 1961.

RUDZINSKA, M. A.: The use of a protozoan for studies on aging. II. The macronucleus in young and old organisms of *Tokophrya Infusionum*: Light and electron microscope observations. *J. Geronto.*, *16*:326, 1961.

RUDZINSKA, M. A.: The use of a protozoan for studies on aging. III. Similarities between young overfed and old normally fed *Tokophrya infusionum*: A light and electron microscope study. *Gerontologia 6*:206, 1962.

RUZICKA, V.: Beitruge zum Städium der Protoplasmahysteresis und der hysteretischen Vorgänge (zur Kausalität des Alterns). I. Die Proto-plasmahysteresis als Entropieerscheinung. *Arch. mikr. Anat., 101*:459, 1924.

SACHER, G.: On the statistical nature of mortality with especial reference to chronic radiation. *Radiology, 67*:250, 1956.

SCHAUB, M. C.: Abbau von Kollagen durch einen Faktor im Uterus. *Helv. Physiol. Pharmacol. Acta, 22*:C38, 1964.

SELYE, H.: In *Aging - Symposia at Chicago meeting of the American Association for the Advancement of Science.* Shock, N. W., Ed., 1959, p. 261.

SELYE, H.: *Calciphylaxis.* Chicago, U. of Chicago, 1962.

SINEX, M. F.: Aging and the lability of irreplaceable molecules. *J. Geront., 12*:190, 1957.

SINEX, M. F.: Aging and the lability of irreplaceable molecules, II. The amid groups of collagen. *J. Gerontol.*, *15*:15, 1960.

SMYTH, R. D.; BRENNAN, R. M., and MARTIN, GUSTAV, J.: The systematic absorption of an orally administrated proteolytic enzyme, bromelain. *Amer. J. Pharmacol.*, *133*:294, 1961.

STEINACH, E.: *Verjüngung durch experimentelle Neubelebung der alternden Pubertätsdrüse.* Berlin, Springer, 1920.

STILL, J.: Are organismal aging and aging death necessarily the result of death of vital cells in the organism? (A cybernetic theory of aging.) *Med. Ann. D.C.*, *25*:199, 1956.

STILL, J.: The physiology of aging, a research approach. *J. Washington Acad. Sci.*, *48*:224, 1958.

STREHLER, B. L., and MILDVAN, A. S.: General theory of mortality and aging. *Science, 132*:14, 1960.

STREHLER, B. L.; MARK, D. D.; MILDVAN, A. S., and GEE, M. V.: Rate and magnitude of age pigment accumulation in the human myocardium. *J. Geront.*, *14*:430, 1959.

SVANBERG: *Hoppe Seyler Z. Physiol. Chem.*, *109*:65, 1920.

TAMPLIN, A. R.: Quantitative aspects of the relationship of biological measurements to aging processes. *J. Geront.*, *14*:134, 1959.

TAPPEL, A. L. Studies of the mechanism of vitamin E Action. III. *In vitro* copolymerization of oxidized fats with protein. *Arch. Biochem. Biophys.*, *54*:266, 1955.

THOMAS, J.; ELSDEN, D. F., and PARTRIDGE, S. M.: Partial structure of two major degradation products from the cross-linkages in elastin. *Nature*, (London), *200*:651, 1963.

TYLER, A.: Prolongation of life span of sea-urchin spermatozoa and improvement of the fertilization-reaction, by treatment of spermatozoa and eggs with metal-chelating agents (amino acids, versene, DEDTC, oxine, Cupron). *Biol. Bull.*, *104*: (No. 2), 224, 1953.

TYLER, A.: Longevity of gametes; histocompatibility—gene loss and neoplasia. In *Aging and Levels of Biological Organization.* Bruder, A. M., and Sacher, Eds. Sect. II. Genetics and Environment, 1965, Part II, p. 50.

UYAMA, Y.; OGINO, S., and ICHIHARA, T.: The cataractogenic agent in the urine of senile cataract patients. *Acta Soc. Ophthal. Jap.*, *58*:1100, 1954, and *Amer. J. Ophthal.*, *39*:125, 1953.

UYAMA, Y., and OGINO, S.: The metabolism of crystalline lens. IV. *Med. J. Osaka Univ.*, *6*:813, 1956.

VEIS, ARTHUR, and BORCOVER, D. E.: The mode of incorporation of formaldehyde into ichthyocol. *Fed. Proc.*, *23*: No. 2, 1964.

VEIS, ARTHUR, and DRAKE, MAURICE P.: The introduction of intramolecular covalent cross-linkages into ichthyocol tropocollagen with monofunctional aldehydes. *J. Biol. Chem.*, *238*:2003, 1963.

VERZAR, F.: Aging of the Collagen filer. *Internat. Revue of Connective Tissue Research*, 2:243, 1964.

VERZAR, F.: Biologie des Alterns. *Handbuch der praktischen Geriatrie.*, 1:101, 1965.

WALFORD, R. L.: Further considerations towards an immunologic therory of aging. *Experimental Gerontology*, 1:73, 1964.

VERZAR, F.: *Experientia, Suppl. 4:35, 1956.*

VORONOFF, S.: *Etude des moyens de relever l'energie vitale et de prolonger la vie.* Paris, Grasset, 1920.

VORONOFF, S.: *Testicular Grafting from Ape to Man.* London, Bretano, 1929.

WALFORD, R. L.: Auto-immunity and aging. *J. Geront. 17:281, 1962.*

WATSON, J. D.: The double helix. New York, Atheneum, p. 153.

WELCH, J. P.: Somatic mutations and the aging process. Adv. in Gerontol. Research, 2:1-36, 1967.

WEISMANN, A.: *Essays Upon Heredity and Kindred Biological Problems.* London and New York, Oxford U. P. (Clarendon, 1891.

WILLSTÄTTER, R.; LOWRY, C. D., JR., and SCHNEIDER, K.: Invertinanreichung in der Hefe. *Hoppe Seyler u. Physiol. Chem. 146:158-180,* 1925.

YOCKEY, H.: On the role of information theory in mathematical biology. In *Radiation Biology and Medicine.* Cambridge, Mass., Addison Wesley 1958, p. 250.

ZINSSER, H. H.; BUTT, E. M., and LEONARD, J.: Metal content correlation to aging aorta. *J. Amer. Geria. Soc., 5:20, 1957.*

ZINSSER, H. H.: BJORKSTEN, J.; BRUCK, E. M.; BAKER, R. F.; KAEBURN, L.: KINNEAR, J.; COHEN, A.; ANDREWS, F.; SARFATI, I., and LIGHT, J.: The freezing pool: A unified sequence of the aging process. In *Medical and Chemical Aspects of Aging.* H. T. Blumenthal, Ed. New York, Columbia, 1962, p. 475.

ZINSSER, H. H., and LIGHT, T.: The nature of x-ray diffraction pattern in aged aorta. Abstract to Gerontological Soc., 1965.

ZORZOLI, A.: See Chapter 3.

INDEX

A

Acetaldehyde, 157
Acetyl CoA, 134
Acid desoxyribonuclease, 67, 75
Acid phosphatase, 64, 66, 67, 69, 74, 75
Acid ribonuclease, 75
Aconitase, 58
Actinic elastosis, 105
Active transport, 69
Adenosine, 151
Adenosine triphosphatase, 73
Adrenalin, 157
Albumin, 9, 131, 157, 168
Albuminoid fraction, 109
Aldehydes, 99, 167
Aldolase, 55, 56, 72
Alkaline DNase, 67, 69
Alkaline hydrolysis, 97
Alkaline phosphatase, 64, 66, 163
Alpha amino groups, 113
Alpha-4-dinitrophenylhydrazone, 99
Alpha lipoproteins, 134
Amino acids, 24-29
  analysis of elastin, 100
  brain, 27
  cerebrospinal fluid, 27
  essential, 26
  free amino acids, 28
  metabolism, 25
  nitrogen, 100
  urinary, 25
Amino sugar level, 86
Amino sulphydryl compounds, 164, 168
Anabolic processes, 168, 169
  sterol products, 162
Anabolism, 38
Antibody formation, 9
Anti-oxidants, 140, 141, 167
Anti-radiation chemicals, 164
Aorta, 106, 107

hexosamine content, 89
hexuronic level, 89
polysaccharide, 89
Arginine, 100
Arterial changes, 84
  tissue, 28, 55, 83
Arteries, enzymes, 55-58
Arteriocapillary fibrosis, 14
Arteriosclerosis, 14, 124, 166
  atherosclerosis, 124
  diffuse hyperplastic sclerosis, 124
  Monckeberg's sclerosis, 124
Arthritis, 14
Ascorbate, 139
Aspartic acid, 97, 100
Atheromatous degeneration, 127
Atherosclerosis, 14, 123, 124-129
  coronary, 6, 127
  definition, 124
  peripheral, 127
Autoimmunity reactions, 150, 164

B

Bacteria, 169
B-complex vitamins, 25
Benzoquinones, 159
Beta-amino propionitrile, 169
Beta glucuronidase, 57, 74
Beta hydroxy-dimethylglutaryl CoA, 136
Beta hydroxybutyrate, 141
Beta hydroxybutyrate dehydrogenase, 141
Beta lipoproteins, 134
Bile salts, 131
Biological alterations, 4
  factors in human mortality, 17
  life expectancy, 17
Biology, 4-22
Blood, enzymes, 59-60
Body composition, 8-9
Bones, 12

C

Cadmium, 168
Calcification-calciphylaxis, 155
  theory, 166
Calcium, 166, 168
  cross linkage, 111
  salts, 80, 99
Cancer, 5
Carbohydrate, 114
  catabolism, 99
Carboxyl groups, 97, 98
Cardiovascular renal disease, 123
Cartilage, 89
Catabolism, 23
Catechol, 157
  amines, 58, 59
Cathepsin, 63, 64, 75, 163
  activity, 138
C-dl-tocopherolacetate, 140
Cell, calssification, 9
  death, 149
  division, 5
  progressive, 149, 161
Cellular changes, 9-11
Cellular phase, 86
Cellulose, 114, 115
  fibers, 81
Cerebral vascular accidents, 14
Ceroid pigment, 137
Chelating agents, 168
Chemical composition of body, 8, 9
Chlorambucil, 151
Cholesterol, 86, 125, 126, 127, 130,
      134, 135, 136, 163
  esterified, 134
  hypercholesterolemia, 125
Cholinesterase, 67, 72
Chromosomes, 151
Chronic irradiation, 13
Chronological age, 6
Chylomicron, 131-134, 137
Circulatory system enzymes, 55-58
Cirrhosis, 123
Citric acid, 157
  cycle, 58
"Clinker theory," 153, 165
Clostridial collagenase, 102
Clostridium histolyticum, 94

Collacin, 100
Collagen, 13, 14, 79, 83, 86, 87,
      92-98, 100, 109, 114, 115, 126,
      153, 155, 157, 158, 159, 169
  acidophilic region, 102
  arginine content, 102
  biosynthetic, origin, 103
  cross linkage, 97, 98
  degradation, 94, 101
  elastin ratio in tissue, 90
  estimation, 90
  fiber, 83, 85, 89, 93, 104
    methods for demonstrating
      changes, 93
    physical properties, 99
    staining properties, 98
  heterogeneity, 101
  hydroxyproline, 102
  metabolism, 31
  molecule, 101
  partial hydrolysates, 101
  peptides, 102
  physical properties, 93
  proline, 102
  treated with collagenase, 94
Collagenase, 94, 105, 114
Collagenous components, arterial tis-
    sue, 84
Collastin, 100
Collidines, 113
Connective tissues, 79-122
  fibrous elements, 81
  properties, 81
  tensile properties, 85, 88
Copper, 157, 168
Coronary atherosclerosis, 5
Costal cartilage, 89
Creatine phosphokinase, 58
Creatinine, 9, 25
Cross-linkage, 83, 94, 95, 99, 104,
      107, 116, 117, 156, 157
  agents, 157
  cyclic quarternary, 58
  desmosine, 111
  intermediates, 166
  intermolecular, 158
  reaction, 139
  theory, 140, 155, 160
Crotonaldehyde, 157

Purine-pyrimidine ratio, 40
Pyrophosphatase, 63, 64

Q

Quinoid compounds, 159
Quinone cross linkages, 168
  linkers, 159
Quinone derivatives, 159
Quinones, 157

R

Radiation damage, 139, 152, 164
Redox indicator, 27
Regeneration, 11
Regenerative capacity, 9
Regulatory genes, 40
Renal blood flow, 68
Repression, 163
Reticulin, 81
Reticulocytic effects, 152, 165
Retine, 14
Rheumatoid arthritis, 5
Rhodanates, 165
Ribonucleic acid, 42-79
  content of tissues, 42
  labeled, 44
  metabolism, 42
  pool, 44
  synthesis, 23, 35, 39, 43, 44
Ribose-5-phosphate isomerase, 57

S

Saccharase, 163
Safflower oil, 129, 130
Scleroderma, 115
Sclerosis, 124
Senescence, 27, 54, 63, 67
Senescent
  kidney, 70
  liver, 66, 75
  skeletal muscle, 73
Senile cataracts, 159
  elastosis, 105
Senility, 160
  pigment, 137
Serine, 98
Serotonin, 164
Serum cholesterol, 129

Serum levels, 33
  albumin, 33, 34
  amino acids, 27
  aspartic acid, 27
  globulin, 33
  glutamic acid, 27
  lipid, 6
  nitrogenous compounds, 25
  nonprotein nitrogen, 25
Sickle cell anemia, 5
  trait, 6
Silicon, 157, 168
Skeletal muscle, 73
Skin, 11, 83, 115
  collagen synthesis, 86
  elasticity, 81
  grafts, 12
  hexosamine and hexuronic acid
    level, 89
  load extension curve, 82, 83
Sodium bisulfite, 167
Somatic mutations, 139, 150, 151,
    164, 166
  theory, 140
Speed of transmission, 161
  reaction, 161
Spermatazoa, 168
Spherocytosis, 5
Spinal cord, enzymes, 72
Spleen, 6, 81
Stable cells, 10
Striated muscle, enzymes, 72-74
Substrate, 111
  interaction with enzymes, 110
  isotopically labeled, 28
  monomers, 110
Succinic acid, 157
  dehydrogenase, 58, 61, 69
Succinoxidase, 58, 59, 61, 63, 64, 69
Sucrose, 163
Sulfhydryl groups, 29

T

Telopeptides, 95, 98, 102
Temperature of denaturation, 38, 39
Tendons, 83, 168
  collagen in, 93
Tensile analysis of artery walls, 84

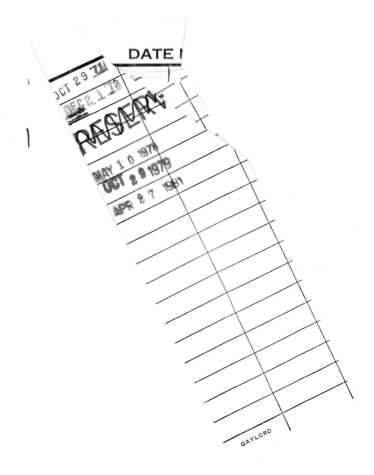